ASIAN STUDIES ASSOCIATION OF AUSTRALIA

Southeast Asia Publications Series

BEING MALAY IN INDONESIA

Histories, Hopes and Citizenship in the Riau Archipelago

GW00506049

BEING MALAY IN INDONESIA

Histories, Hopes and Citizenship in the Riau Archipelago

Nicholas J. Long

Asian Studies Association of Australia

in association with

UNIVERSITY OF HAWAI'I PRESS

HONOLULU

Published in Singapore by:
NUS Press
National University of Singapore
AS3-01-02, 3 Arts Link
Singapore 117569

Published in North America by:
University of Hawai'i Press
2840 Kolowalu Street
Honolulu, HI 96822 USA
www.uhpress.hawaii.edu

Library of Congress Cataloging-in-Publication Data

Long, Nicholas J., author
    Being Malay in Indonesia: histories, hopes and citizenship in the Riau Archipelago / Nicholas J. Long.
        pages cm. – (Asian Studies Association of Australia Southeast Asia publications series)
    Published in Singapore by NUS Press.
    Includes bibliographical references and index.
    ISBN 978-0-8248-3865-2 (pbk.: alk. paper)

    1. Malays (Asian people) – Indonesia – Riau (Province) – Ethnic identity.
2. Riau (Indonesia: Province) – Economic conditions. I. Title. II. Series:
Southeast Asia publications series.

DS632.M27L66 2013
305.899'28059814 — dc23   2012049300

Cover image: Gobang Dance, courtesy of Adi Pranadipa

Printed in Singapore

For my teachers and my friends

Contents

List of Maps   viii

List of Tables   viii

List of Illustrations   ix

Acknowledgements   xi

Chapter 1   Introduction   1

Chapter 2   Provincial Capital   30

Chapter 3   Poisoned Histories   63

Chapter 4   Marketplaces   98

Chapter 5   Neighbourhoods   127

Chapter 6   Hauntings   148

Chapter 7   The Human Resources Crisis   173

Chapter 8   Achieving Malayness   206

Conclusion   242

Glossary   252

Bibliography   256

About the Author   274

Index   275

List of Maps

Map 0.1   The Riau Archipelago   xiii

Map 0.2   Tanjung Pinang   xiv

List of Tables

Table 2.1   Tanjung Pinang's population in 2010 by
self-declared ethnic group   43

Table 2.2   Riau Islands Province's population in 2010 by
self-declared ethnic group   43

Table 8.1   A judging grid for a *pantun* competition   229

List of Illustrations

Figure 2.1   A harbourside billboard welcoming visitors to "The pinnacle of the Malay civilisation, Riau Islands Province"   31

Figure 2.2   Artist's impression of Tanjung Pinang in the 1840s   34

Figure 2.3   Tanjung Pinang's total population, 1983–2010   39

Figure 3.1   Aristocratic graves on Penyengat attract a regular stream of local tourists and pilgrims   66

Figure 3.2   A graffiti mural of Raja Ali Haji. This picture was drawn in September 2011, shortly before the artist left Tanjung Pinang to study in Java. "If anyone ever asks me what I've done for my town," he wrote on his Facebook profile, "I'll say that I painted a picture of Raja Ali Haji, the author of *Gurindam Duabelas*. That's how much I love my homeland."   69

Figure 4.1   The Gelanggang Klenteng in 1956   108

Figure 5.1   Independence Day races in Fadli's neighbourhood   133

Figure 5.2   A neighbourhood *arisan*   135

Figure 6.1   A Chinese family burns offerings to ghosts in a Tanjung Pinang shopping mall   164

Figure 7.1   A billboard advertising the 2006 MTQ (Qur'an recitation contest). The slogan reads: "Kepulauan Riau's first provincial-level MTQ: a means of increasing the quality of human resources that are of good moral character."   181

Figure 7.2   The Riau Islands *pencak silat* team training by the roadside   191

Figure 8.1   An "attractively plump" male beauty contest
               participant, alongside the female compere   214

Figure 8.2   The Batam team   233

Figure 8.3   The Indragiri Hulu team   233

Acknowledgements

It would not have been possible to write this book without the support and assistance of countless people in the Riau Islands. Their willingness to help me has been both humbling and inspiring. I would like to thank everyone who took the time to share their everyday activities, opinions and life stories with me, all of those who assisted with the mundane practicalities of my research, and the families I lived with for being so hospitable and making Tanjung Pinang a second home. Conscious of the risks that many of them have taken in sharing their experiences and views with me so fully, I have developed a range of measures to conceal my interlocutors' true identities in the text, including anonymisation and the use of pseudonyms. In the case of public figures, I have used their real names when referring to material already in the public domain, such as their writings, speeches, or media coverage of their actions, but have taken steps to conceal their real identities at all other times.

My relationship with the Riau Islands began as a graduate student at the University of Cambridge, where I was very fortunate to enjoy the mentorship of Leo Howe as supervisor and Susan Bayly as faculty advisor. Their support and advice over the years have been invaluable. More generally, I am grateful to everyone in the Division of Social Anthropology — my peers, colleagues, students and the admin team — for providing such a wonderful intellectual environment, both whilst I was a student and as a staff member. St Catharine's College and Wolfson College both very generously provided me with fellowships whilst I was completing the manuscript. It has been a privilege to be a member of two such dynamic and supportive institutions. The final stages of editing and production were completed after taking up a lectureship at the London School of Economics and Political Science, and it is hard to imagine a more welcoming department in which to enter. I look forward to many exciting times ahead. Lastly, I would like to thank Michele Ford for her keen interest in my work, many enlightening conversations about life in the Riau Islands, and for facilitating a Visiting

Fellowship at the University of Sydney, which contributed substantially to the quality of the argument.

My work on this book was financially supported by the Economic and Social Research Council of the United Kingdom [grant numbers PTA-031-2004-00183; RES-000-22-4632], a British Academy Postdoctoral Fellowship, and the Evans Fund at the University of Cambridge. In Indonesia, sponsorship for my research was provided by LIPI, RISTEK, UNRI and STISIPOL Raja Haji. I am grateful to all these bodies for their support.

The manuscript was greatly improved by the insightful commentary on earlier drafts that was provided by Robert Hefner, James Laidlaw, Barbara Andaya and two anonymous readers for the ASAA Southeast Asia Publications Series. Howard Dick, the ASAA Southeast Asia Series editor, has also been an invaluable source of advice and encouragement. In addition, I would like to thank Virginia Hooker for her very helpful reading of Chapter 3, Philip Stickler for preparing wonderful maps and Keith Foulcher for his help with translating Suryatati's poems. Adi Pranadipa kindly provided the cover image, which depicts a performance of *gobang* (a "traditional Malay" dance from the Anambas Islands) staged by the Sanggar Budaya Warisan Pulau Penyengat at the Parade Tari Daerah Provinsi Kepri 2011, in Kijang. Credit for the final cover design lies with the staff of NUS Press, who have been a pleasure to work with in all aspects of the production process. I would particularly like to thank Eunice Low for her careful copyediting of the text. However, my greatest thanks are reserved for everyone who, through their interest in my work, their ideas and critiques, their moral support, Skype calls, care packages, and field visits, not only helped me refine my arguments in this book, but ensured that it was a constant pleasure to do so. Though they are too numerous to name individually, I hope none of them will be in any doubt as to how appreciative I am.

Portions of Chapter 6 were previously published within the article "Haunting Malayness: The Multicultural Uncanny in a New Indonesian Province", *Journal of the Royal Anthropological Institute (New Series)* 16, 4 (2010): 874–91. Portions of the material in Chapter 8 were previously published in "How to Win a Beauty Contest in Tanjung Pinang", *Review of Indonesian and Malaysian Affairs* 41, 1 (2007): 91–117. I am very grateful that I am able to reproduce those texts here.

Nicholas J. Long
London, September 2013

Map 0.1 The Riau Archipelago

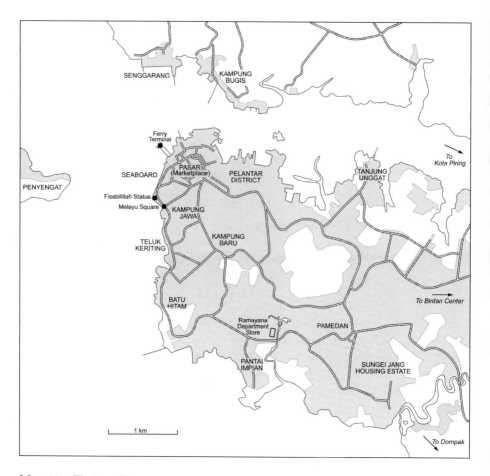

Map 0.2 Tanjung Pinang

1

Introduction

Indonesia's Riau Archipelago is a place of remarkable diversity. A group of over 3,200 islands nestling in the waters of the South China Sea (Map 0.1), only a few kilometres of water separate grimy industrial ports from picturesque tropical islands in which small fishing villages stand on wooden platforms above the tidal zone. Some islands are remote and inaccessible; others enjoy high-speed ferry connections to Singapore and a flow of international visitors, currency and investment. It is a place that was once home to a powerful precolonial sultanate, where Islamic intellectuals wrote treatises on the correct code of conduct for Malays and Muslims, where the first Malay-language dictionary was compiled, and where people who proudly self-identify as Malays live, work and do their very best to preserve Malay culture. The region has also long been home to one of Indonesia's most vibrant Chinese populations, was once both a sanctuary for South Vietnamese refugees and a haven for Eastern Indonesian pirates and mercenaries, and is now trying to reinvent itself as a centre of global manufacturing. Scores of migrants arrive every day hoping to "make it big", while indigenous "sea gypsies" (*orang laut*) struggle to preserve their nomadic seafaring way of life. Life in the Riau Islands is about much more than being Malay. Yet the issue of Malayness is never far away. This book seeks to explain why that should be — and in doing so uncovers the subtle and often surprising ways in which decentralisation policies can unsettle and refashion social and political life.

First Steps

It had never been my intention to write about "Malayness". My first journey to the Riau Islands had left me intrigued by the region's transforming relationship with nearby Singapore. Visiting the town of Tanjung Pinang at the beginning of 2004, I met tour guides and hoteliers who spoke with bitterness of Singapore's incursions into their territory. The city-state had appropriated large swathes of land on the islands of Bintan and Batam, relocating villages to make way for industrial parks, beach resorts and golf courses as part of a trans-national "Growth Triangle" collaboration. Meanwhile, ferries teeming with working-class Singaporean men were arriving at the Riau Islands' harbours, where crowds of prostitutes and motorcycle taxi drivers waited in anticipation of the visitors. Sex and drug tourism sustained a huge part of the islands' economy. While the Indonesians I met recognised this, they did so with bitterness in their voices. "I hate Singaporeans," one taxi driver told me, "I hate what they do to our women." Another told me that Singapore had "colonised" his island.

I was struck by the difference the next time I stepped off the international ferry. It was July 2005, barely 18 months after my first trip to the islands, and I was returning to conduct a pilot field study. I had planned to interview tourists and tour guides, sex workers and their clients. But my prospective respondents were nowhere to be seen. A few taxi drivers remained in the car park, giving their horns a half-hearted honk as they saw me wandering past, suitcase in hand. Without the surging masses that had met me on my first visit, the area seemed desolate indeed. As I was to learn, many things had changed over the past year. A new provincial government had cracked down on open prostitution, confining it to designated "brothel villages" (*lokalisasi*) out of town. Singaporean tourists, meanwhile, had lost their taste for Indonesian adventures: fears of disease, terrorism, and the rise of low-cost airlines had seen the Riau Islands' appeal usurped by destinations in Malaysia, Vietnam and Thailand. Even the much-vaunted industrial parks were beginning to see their factories scale down operations or relocate.

With Singapore's presence seen as less oppressively "colonial" than before, other issues were dominating Riau Islanders' thoughts. As part of a national trend towards decentralisation following the end of President Suharto's authoritarian "New Order" regime, the Riau Archipelago became an autonomous province in 2004, separating from the Eastern Sumatran province of Riau, to which it had been attached since 1957. Tanjung Pinang was designated its capital. While I was living there, just a year after the new province had been created, the likely impact of this change was a matter of intense speculation. Riau Islanders wondered whether provincial autonomy would be able to reverse the economic downturn brought about by Singapore's retreat and allow the region and its population to enjoy the global competitiveness for which they so desperately longed. They worried that the new administration might leave them worse off than under the unified province. Perhaps most of all, they questioned what the implications would be of their province, which contained a vibrantly multiethnic population, having explicitly been created "for Malays".

The issues at the heart of these contemporary concerns are also matters of long-standing interest for scholars of Southeast Asia: the nature of Malay identity; the sociality and politics of plural societies; the consequences of Indonesia's post-authoritarian turn to decentralisation and democracy; and the intersection of local, national, and transnational registers of citizenship and belonging in an archipelago that was once said to epitomise the future of an increasingly globalised and even "borderless" world (Ohmae 1994; Ong 2000). They also touch on more general questions for the social sciences regarding the consequences of decentralisation, the character of life within newly autonomous polities, and how the very incipience of such spaces provides both opportunities and challenges for those hoping to call them their new home. These were issues that confronted me each day that I conducted fieldwork in the Riau Islands. By thinking through those everyday experiences, I seek to develop a conceptual framework for the study of nascent autonomy: one which could profitably be employed in the study of other instances of decentralisation, particularly those conducted in the name of regional or ethnic identity categories, within and beyond Southeast Asia.

My argument is an anthropological one: the puzzles and questions that drive my enquiry were identified through long-term ethnographic fieldwork, as was the evidence on which I base my conclusions. I have worked in the provincial capital of Tanjung Pinang for over 30 months, starting in 2005, the year after the Riau Islands formally became a province. A methodology of participant observation and ethnographic interviewing allowed me to learn about the life stories of a broad spectrum of Riau Islanders, detect moments of nuance and inconsistency in their accounts, and compare how they behaved in the diverse social contexts in which they were enmeshed. It also afforded the opportunity to observe first-hand the deep emotional impacts that categories of "Malayness", "regionality", "citizenship" and "belonging" had on my informants' lives.

The analytic approach that I develop in this book is therefore informed by anthropology's long-standing attention to the contextual deployment of concepts and categories, but also by its more recent "affective turn". This phrase denotes a renewed attention to those embodied states of being that define the textures of everyday life (and may then come to be interpreted as "emotions", "moods" or "feelings") including those that seem to arise seemingly autonomously from the surrounding environment or the body itself: feeling "edgy", "excited", or "wired"; a sense of foreboding or anxiety that cannot be shaken off; a sudden flush of embarrassment, perhaps for no reason in particular; an intense attraction or an instant loathing. Current scholarly interest in these states of being, which are referred to in the literature as "affects" or "affective states", derives from a growing dissatisfaction with the constructivist theoretical approaches that dominated the social sciences during the 1980s and 1990s. These emphasised the role of language and narrative in the "social construction" of what one experienced as "real", but in doing so they ignored "the very fabric our being" and so failed "to account for the fullest resonance of the social world we wish to understand" (Hemmings 2005: 548–9). Political economy approaches, which focus on how the large-scale structures of state and economy transform the field of social action, have also tended to neglect the question of how the social world is experienced at the very smallest scale. Yet, my argument in this book is that if we are to understand the impacts that regional autonomy and political reform have had in Indonesia, we need to examine the ways in which they have changed the conditions of everyday life, and the states of being of which it is composed.

Decentralisation, and the political economic changes with which it has been associated — democratisation, increased fiscal autonomy and a changing relationship with neighbouring Singapore — transformed Riau Islanders' embodied and emotional experiences of the world. It gave experiences of the everyday a distinctive resonance, as did the social processes that it set in motion, most notably a new public preoccupation with "Malayness", as islanders questioned who or what could be classified as "Malay" and interrogated the substantive nature of Malay experience. Above all, it radically affected islanders' capacities to feel "at home" in their neighbourhoods, in their towns or villages, in their province and in the world at large.

For many, being in the new province was an unsettling and uncomfortable experience. Others found it joyful and affirming, although such pleasures frequently proved to be unstable. Documenting and accounting for those new experiences and dispositions is the central task of this book. Yet I also wish to argue that these affective states are not merely products of the broader context in which they emerge; they are also *productive* in themselves — moving some people to action and others to apathy, but in each case changing the character of social relations and giving rise to new articulations of public culture. They change the context in which claims about Malay identity, citizenship and regional autonomy take place and thereby open up new vistas for how those concepts might be studied. In other words, they provide crucial insights into what it means to be Malay in Indonesia.

A New Approach to Regional Autonomy

The decentralisation of governance is an increasingly widespread phenomenon in contemporary nation-states (Bardhan 2002: 185). As sociologist Vedi Hadiz (2010) has argued, the Indonesian case offers a particularly compelling insight into its dynamics, potential and pitfalls. From the mid-1960s, Indonesia had been ruled by the highly centralised, technocratic and authoritarian New Order. Following this regime's demise in May 1998, Indonesia underwent an intense process of "*Reformasi*", a term referring to political and administrative reform but also a common label for the post-Suharto period in general. Reform measures focused primarily on the need for democracy, but as part of the democratisation process, reformers argued that relations between Jakarta and the regions needed to be restructured. The result has been described as "one of the most radical decentralisation programmes attempted anywhere in the world" (Aspinall and Fealy 2003: 3).

In August 1999, under transitional President B.J. Habibie, the Indonesian government passed two laws that established guidelines for decentralisation, widely referred to in Indonesia as "regional autonomy" (*otonomi daerah*). Law No. 25/1999 was concerned with fiscal balance, allowing regions to get a larger share of the revenue generated within their territory. While this heightened the appeal of decentralisation for many resource-rich parts of the nation, it was Law No. 22/1999 that bespoke the more fundamental and far-reaching change. This law gave regional governments much greater authority over local affairs, allowing, for example, regional parliaments to appoint leaders without requiring approval from the Ministry of Internal Affairs. What was meant by "regions" within this legislation was not Indonesia's then 27 provinces but the much smaller political units of regencies (*kabupaten*) and municipalities (*kota*). Such a definition was officially justified as a means of supporting democratisation by bringing government as close as possible to the people. However, it was widely interpreted as a means of safeguarding the integrity of the Republic by circumventing the possibility that provinces, having been granted greater autonomy, might attempt to secede outright (Aspinall and Fealy 2003: 4).

Decentralisation has nevertheless had a variety of ramifications at the provincial level. The hitherto secessionist provinces of Aceh and Papua, for example, received special forms of autonomy intended to to keep them within the Republic. More generally, as George Quinn (2003: 164) observes, the 1999 laws brought into the open centrifugal movements that were directed against local centres rather than against Java or Jakarta. In some cases, this resulted in regencies dividing to produce two new regencies; in others, individual regencies (or conglomerates thereof) lobbied hard to be established as provinces in their own right. Taken together, both trends constituted the phenomenon of *pemekaran* ("blossoming"), the proliferation of administrative units across Indonesia. Before Reformasi, there were 27 provinces and 293 regencies and municipalities. By 2010, those numbers had increased to 33 and 491, respectively, with 50 further autonomous regions in the queue for approval (Apriadi Gunawan 2010). Amongst these newly created political entities was Riau Islands Province. Formally approved in 2002, it came into being as Indonesia's 32nd province on 1 July 2004.[1]

---

[1] Indonesia gained seven new provinces through *pemekaran* but lost the province of East Timor, which in 1999 separated to become an autonomous state. The other newly created provinces were West Irian Jaya (now called West Papua) and North Maluku (both of which were initially approved in 1999), Banten, Bangka Belitung and Gorontalo (approved in 2000), and West Sulawesi (approved in 2004). For a discussion of how the creation of the Riau Islands province compares with these other instances of *pemekaran*, see Kimura (2013).

Pemekaran has led to a growing recognition that the study of contemporary Indonesia needs to pay close attention to questions of localism, regionality and local politics, topics that, in the past, were often subordinated to the analysis of the centralised New Order regime (Hadiz 2010: 12). Yet there is still much work to be done. As Gerry van Klinken (2007b: 150, 161) notes, studies of autonomy have been dominated by "public policy specialists interested in budgets and service delivery [and] political scientists interested in centre-periphery shifts", with the result that everyday lives and social worlds that comprise the "rapidly changing empirical territory of the post-1999 autonomy regime" remain poorly charted.

Researchers seeking to redress this problem have frequently sought to do so by examining the intersections between notions of ethnicity, indigeneity, religion, or "culture" (especially "traditional" customs or *adat*) and Indonesia's regional autonomy programme.[2] Their work has helped us to understand the character of political movements that seek to make claims in the name of cultural and ethnic categories, but rather more attention has been given to the emergence of such movements, and the claims that they make, than to the long-term social consequences of the political transitions that they set in motion. An associated problem has been a tendency within the broader literature on autonomy to assume that communal and/or ethnic identities are relatively stable, thereby providing sharp lines of cleavage for *pemekaran* (e.g. Bünte 2007: 117; Steenbrink 2008). An ethnographic focus on the social, experiential and affective realities that decentralisation engenders can therefore offer insights into a process in which, as Klinken (2007b: 150) emphasises, unintended consequences have been just as significant as intended ones.

Decentralisation in Bad Faith

Riau Islands Province was created because of deep-seated grievances against the previous provincial administration, which stood accused of neglecting the archipelago and its indigenous Malays, using them to extract revenue whilst underinvesting in local services and infrastructure. This pattern was often described by my interlocutors as a

---

[2] Examples include Erb *et al.* (2005), Henley and Davidson (2007), Sakai (2002), Schulte Nordholt and Klinken (2007), and Tyson (2010).

form of "colonialism". Not all instances in which a new Indonesian province or regency has been created were fuelled by such perceptions, but many were (Jones 2010; Quinn 2003).[3] Moreover, as both S.S. Meenakshisundaram (1994: 10) and Ted Gurr (2000) have argued, the worldwide political climate is currently a favourable one for resentment-driven decentralisation movements. They link this to positive coverage of the East European Bloc's experiences of rejecting arrogant, corrupt and inefficient centralised bureaucracies, as well as the efforts of NGOs and international organisations to persuade separatist movements that they should lobby for autonomy within the encompassing state, rather than pursue full secession. The lessons that can be learnt from the Riau Islands thus stand to be of value to a much broader comparative enquiry.

In resentment-driven decentralisation, the nascent province rests its legitimacy on the promise of negating existing conditions, yet has only those self-same conditions at its disposal to effect the transformation. In the Riau Islands, this proved to be a particularly grave paradox, because it was widely considered that one of the most serious consequences of underinvestment in the region had been the underdevelopment of its human capital. Riau Islanders therefore worried that they, and those governing them, might lack the skills to forge a bright future as an autonomous province. As I will reveal through the book, this anxiety informed their ongoing evaluations of the newly-formed province, transformed the relations between members of different ethnic (and sometimes also religious) identity categories, influenced interactions with neighbouring Singapore, and led to the prevalence of a disposition of "bad faith".

In *Being and Nothingness*, Jean-Paul Sartre (2003 [1943]: 90) introduced the notion of "bad faith" as an evanescent cognitive condition in which the subject strives to constitute itself in the mode of what it is not. When he wrote this, he had in mind situations in which subjects attempted to stave off the anguish that attended the painful realisation of their own radical freedom. Thus, in one of his

---

[3] Roth (2007: 127) suggests that *pemekaran* is fuelled by the ambitions of local elites, but even this analysis begs the question of how the rationale behind *pemekaran* is presented to the public, wherein the rhetoric of overcoming neglect and historical injustice often plays a significant role.

most celebrated examples, Sartre identified the bad faith affecting a café waiter as follows:

> What I attempt to realise is a being-in-itself of the café waiter, as if it were not in my power to confer value and urgency upon my duties and the rights of my position, as if it were not my free choice to get up each morning at five o'clock or to remain in bed ... Yet there is no doubt that I *am* in a sense a café waiter — otherwise could I not just as well call myself a diplomat or a reporter? But if I am one, this can not be in the mode of being-in-itself. I am a waiter in the mode of *being what I am not* (Sartre 2003 [1943]: 83).

However, the concept can also be applied more widely to various different contexts of self-fashioning. While Sartre's argument is centred on subjects' efforts to deny, avoid, or suppress a very particular, existentialist, notion of the authentic self, his conceptualisation of bad faith can be used to illuminate ethnographic circumstances in which other traumatic notions of authentic selfhood prevail.[4] In this book, I use it a means of elucidating the complex and constantly changing attitudes that officials and citizens in the Riau Islands have towards the possibility of transforming their province by turning its population into higher quality "human resources", for the endeavours that such policies inspire are widely experienced as a mode of "being what one is not".

At the heart of any moment of bad faith is a duplicity in which "I must know in my capacity as deceiver the truth which is hidden from me as the one deceived ... and this not at two different moments [...] but in the unitary structure of a single project" (Sartre 2003 [1943]: 72). This model of a double, dissonant way of thinking can help to explain some of the impulses and motivations that underpin apparently self-defeating choices on the part of citizens

---

[4] "Authenticity" might not be a universal ethical preoccupation — but when it *is* a concern, this model can be productively applied. The ontological commitments that I retain concern the human being's pervasive capability to recognise apparent dualities and subject them to interpretive scrutiny as "pretense" or "false beliefs" — a position which draws support from advances in cognitive research that have indicated this might be a distinctive (and universal) human characteristic that manifests from a very young age (Flavell 1999; Leslie 1987).

and provincial administrators, as they are simultaneously convinced that they might be able to improve themselves and their province *and* that their failure is inevitable. Moreover, the concept of bad faith involves an inherent dynamism that allows for the possibility of constantly changing dispositions. Bad faith can evanesce towards "good faith", in which one fully believes one's conceit, or Sartrean "cynicism", in which the deception is admitted — although the anguish of facing one's authenticity can prove so painful that the subject quickly falls into bad faith once again.

Tracing and accounting for such fluctuations is crucial for understanding the complex affective and emotional states that characterise Riau Islanders' experiences of living in their newly created province. It also points to the value of developing more dynamic models of political psychology than those that have hitherto predominated in the discipline of anthropology. These latter include Marxist models of "false consciousness" mystified by ideology or hegemony, Foucault-inspired theories of a mind that "internalises" or is "subjectified" by discourse, and those notions of "agency" and "resistance" that present the individual as a sovereign decision-maker. As Katherine Frank (2006) has argued, none of these approaches adequately theorises the psychological base of political action; nor, I would add, the nature of consciousness. In recent decades, increasing numbers of political anthropologists have attempted to rectify this situation by engaging with concepts from the field of psychoanalysis, but such efforts have also shown a tendency to generate analyses that are static in character, emphasising the durability of "psychic attachments" to such entities as the state, the nation, or capitalism (Hage 1996; Navaro-Yashin 2002; Rickert 2007). Although these accounts were engaging with the genuinely pressing question of how to explain instances of stasis in political ideals and values (even in contexts marked by seemingly high levels of political critique), there was a serious problem with the theoretical framework on which they drew. By placing analytic weight on enduring attachments, the framework projected stasis into the future. For example, Yael Navaro-Yashin (2002: 159) even went as far as to suggest that the Turkish citizens she worked with would "remain forever (forseeably) locked into [statism]". A different approach is therefore needed to make sense of political life in contexts within which attitudes and convictions are volatile, or have the potential to become so. A Sartrean model of consciousness proves valuable in precisely that regard.

Of course, the fact that so many Riau Islanders seem to feel that the provincial government's "human development programmes" place them in a mode of "being what they are not" is historically contingent, associated with the moment of becoming a new province and the powerful opportunities for reinvention that this appears to offer. For that very reason, however, an analytical framework of "bad faith" may prove illuminating in the many other regions of the world where decentralisation, regional autonomy, or other instances of dramatic political change are bound up with anxieties about human resource quality and the need to overcome the scarring effects of having been held back.

Yet the concept about which the greatest number of people spoke to me most anxiously for the longest periods of time — the concept that seemed to tyrannise some people's every waking hour — was not "development" (*pembangunan*) or "human resource quality" (*kualitas sumber daya manusia*), but "Malayness" (*kemelayuan*). At first glance, this seems surprising. Malayness was not a new identity foisted onto the region — the Riau Islands have been seen as a "heartland of Malay culture" for hundreds of years (Putten 2011). To understand why the renewed emphasis on Malayness has proven so unsettling, and what the implications of that might be for the study of decentralisation more broadly, we therefore need to take a closer look at what "being Malay" actually entails.

The Uncertainties of Malayness

It was shortly after the end of Ramadan, and the town of Tanjung Pinang was awash with festivities. Townsfolk visited each other's houses, exchanging small gifts and cakes, and gathered in larger numbers at *halal bihalal* ceremonies, in which they could offer each other mutual forgiveness for the sins they had committed during the previous year. Such ceremonies did not only serve a religious purpose. One of the most prominent *halal bihalal* staged in 2006 was arranged by the group *Azam Melayu Satu*, an organisation whose name translates as "With the Intention of One Malayness". This event, which has now become an annual fixture, was intended to foster a sense of social cohesion amongst the people of Tanjung Pinang and featured as its highlight a poetry recital by the town's mayor, Hj. Suryatati Abdul Manan. Suryatati is a noted local poet, and her work, which encompasses her experiences of life as a politician, wife, widow and mother, is widely admired by residents of the town, who appreciate her honesty, sincerity and wit.[5] The poem that she chose to deliver at the *halal bihalal* ceremony spoke directly to a question that preoccupied many who lived in the town: what it meant to be Malay in contemporary Indonesia.

Am I A Malay ...?

How can you spot a Malay?
The key giveaway is their obedience
To everything they've been taught
They respect their parents
So that their lives will be blessed.
They speak politely, in words gentle to the ear.
They greet people with terms like
'Pak Long', 'Pak Ngah' and 'Pak Busu'.
Those are Malays' favourite ways of addressing people.
There are other names too, like
'Pak Cik', 'Mak Cik', 'Ma', 'Bapak', 'Tok', 'Nek' and
   'Oneng-oneng',
'Atan', 'Awang', 'Amat', 'Dolah', 'Timah', 'Salmah' and 'Bedah':
These are all typical Malay names.

It's such a shame ...
These nicknames have been swept away by globalisation,
Replaced with words like 'Uncle', 'Aunty', 'Mami' and 'Papi'.
Timah has become 'Tince', Salmah is now 'Sherly',
Dolah is 'Delon' and Atan is 'Antoni'.
When Malays are in the city, they feel embarrassed
To use the language their mothers taught them.
They all want to be thought of as townsfolk,
No-one's just a villager any more.

However ... when it's time for the regional elections
They all fall over each other to show off their local roots,
Coming out with things like
'That fellow Dolah is the son of Pak Busu, who was born on a
   Sunday'.
Actually, it's not hard to tell if someone's a Malay.

---

[5] For a literary analysis of Suryatati's work, see Riau Wati (2009).

You don't need to test his urine or his DNA.
All you need to do is ask this simple question:

'Hey, where are you going?'
'Nothing,' he replies.
'What are you up to?'
Again the reply is 'Nothing'.
It's already certain that this is a genuine Malay.
Whatever he's doing, the answer is always 'Nothing'.
When in fact, he may be off to the office of the mayor or the
    regent,
A folder tucked under his arm.
He's out to bid for a project, because
If he doesn't get the contract, there'll be no money coming in.

He is very engaged and fiery when talking about politics,
But unfortunately he only does this in coffee shops.
In front of official bodies he lacks the courage to speak out,
But catch him on his own again and he'll vent his spleen right
    at you.

But this is an old story.
Malays today are different.
They are aware of their rights and responsibilities
And they understand the world is changing.
They speak up for reform
And want to be masters of their own domain.
Upholding tradition is their catch-cry.
They reject anything that threatens their dignity,
And they're suspicious of sweet talk and flattery
From those who claim to be Malay.
Come, you Malay sons and daughters,
Don't be seduced any more
By false promises.
Let us join together to develop our country.
Malays will never disappear from this earth.

— Suryatati A Manan 2007: 53–4

The audience concurred that this was an excellent poem. It
combined humour as it parodied the stereotype of the lazy Malay,
wandering around, doing "nothing", with an inspirational rallying
call for Malays to stand up for their rights against the vagaries
of globalisation and "pretend Malays". Yet there is also something

unsatisfying about the poem. As it slips and slides between notions of "then" and "now", the hallmarks of "a genuine Malay" become all the more unclear. Despite the triumphant tone of the final stanza, the question in the poem's title, "Am I A Malay...?" remains as open as ever.

There was a pointed irony to the fact that Suryatati should broach this question at all. At the time of the recital, she was embroiled in a high-profile legal case against Hendry Frankim, a prominent local politician and member of the Regional Representative Council (Dewan Perwakilan Daerah, DPD), one of Indonesia's two national parliamentary chambers. The issue at stake was none other than whether she was Malay. The controversy had emerged when the newspaper *Komunitas* ran a front-page article on the mayor's proposal to open a new foodcourt in the central thoroughfare of Tanjung Pinang's marketplace. Concerned about the disruption this might cause to local residents and shopkeepers, Frankim was quoted expressing his disapproval of the scheme. A Chinese Indonesian himself, he was alleged to have commented that "Chinese people are usually clever. Our mayor is of Chinese descent, but stupid!" (*Komunitas* 2005).

Frankim's remarks caused an uproar. The problem was not so much the rudeness of labelling the mayor "stupid" but rather the insinuation that she was not "a genuine Malay" (*orang asli Melayu*). A defamation case was launched. Suryatati asserted that she herself had forgiven Frankim, but was pursuing the prosecution at the behest of various community leaders (*tokoh masyarakat*) who had been outraged by his claim. Come the hearing in July 2007, the courtroom was overflowing. The judge turned to Suryatati and asked her whether she was Chinese. "As far as I know," she replied, "my parents were Malay." The onlookers burst into spontaneous applause, and Frankim was sentenced to three months' imprisonment.[6]

Amongst the public, however, opinion prevailed that Suryatati did indeed have Chinese roots. "She must have Chinese ancestry," reasoned one Minangkabau shopkeeper, "just look at her slanting eyes!" Another man, who asked to remain completely anonymous,

---

[6] Major developments in the case were documented by the local media (*Batam Pos* 2007; *Posmetro Batam* 2007a, 2007b). Frankim later went on to seek immunity from the jail sentence on the basis of his membership in the Regional Representative Council (*Suara Karya* 2007).

claimed to have met the mayor's birth parents. "Her parents are Chinese, but she was adopted by Malays," this friend explained. "She still visits her biological parents a lot and has good, close relationships with them. But she denies her ancestry for political purposes. She wants to claim she is genetically descended from her adoptive family." A group of customers in a Chinese restaurant refused to discuss the matter, but in doing so made it very apparent what their thoughts on it were. "We cannot discuss that", one of them told me. "If we spoke truthfully, it would be very dangerous for us if someone overheard."

What makes this legal case — and the air of secrecy and subterfuge surrounding Suryatati's "real" ethnicity — particularly intriguing is the assumption that having Chinese ancestry would disqualify Suryatati from being a "genuine" Malay. This stands sharply at odds with the attitudes towards adoption reported in previous studies of Malay kinship, both in the Riau Islands (Wee 1985: 517–9) and elsewhere. Anthropologists have repeatedly argued that unwanted Chinese children are willingly adopted by Malays, and thereafter considered to have "entered Malayness" (*masuk Melayu*). Malay identity, in this understanding, stems from a process of enculturation into Malay customs (*adat*), language and Islam. Descent and biogenetics, and their physiognomic traces, were explicitly noted as absent concerns amongst commoner — if not aristocratic — Malays, painting a picture of Malay society's "remarkable absorptive capacity" (Djamour 1959: 93; Nagata 1979: 46).

According to this logic, there would be no inconsistency between Suryatati having Chinese ancestry and also being Malay. Indeed Suryatati intimated as much in a second poem entitled "Am I A Malay?" (2007). Remaining evasive over whether she actually had been adopted, the poem draws on the Malayness of her upbringing and values — and her devotion to her Malay parents — to disparage those who would suggest she was anything other than Malay:

Not once in their lives
Did my mother and father
Ever mention
That I was an adopted child
[...]

They educated me in the ways of the Malays,
And made the Malay village unquestionably my home

All my relatives were genuine Malays,
They were fluent in the Malay tongue,
And always dressed in Malay clothes.
Malay songs consoled their spirits,
Malay cuisine was their choice of food,
Malay customs were their pride.
[...]

Sadly, my mother and father
Were not here to witness, were unable to hear,
That startling legal testimony
Claiming I was of C H I N E S E descent!

For their part, mother and father
Never doubted who I was.
My spirit, soul and feelings are still Malay,
And my mother and my father are still my parents
Even though there are those who wonder,
AM I A MALAY?

— Suryatati A Manan 2007: 51–2

Yet for all Suryatati's emphasis on the cultural and spiritual dimensions of Malayness, the legal proceedings that surrounded Frankim's remarks showed that ancestry and biological descent carried very real political significance. So in what does Malayness inhere? Biology? Or the multiple tropes of Malayness suggested in Suryatati's poems: language, courtesy, custom, having been born in the region, diffidence, pride in fighting for one's rights, and vigilance against impostors? These questions cannot be answered straightforwardly, but that very fact makes two things evident. First, it is very difficult to classify someone as "Malay" and to be sure what this classification signifies. Second, the negotiation of this categorical minefield is perilous. One false step, as Hendry Frankim found out, can lead to ruin and loss of liberty. The stakes might not be clear, but they can be high.

Rethinking Malayness

Suryatati was not the first person to have trouble pinning down the category of "Malayness". Scholars working in contexts across Southeast Asia have experienced difficulties as well. Indeed, in their introduction to a volume devoted to investigating the category, Timothy

Barnard and Hendrik Maier (2004: ix–x) go so far as to describe it as "one of the most challenging and confusing terms in the world of Southeast Asia" and suggest that its precise meanings "have never been established, and never will be". Instead they, and the contributors to their volume, turn their attention to tracing the multiple trajectories that the notion of "Malayness" has taken in different settings and different periods. This gives a sense of the category's startling range whilst subverting and questioning the attempts, characteristic of (ethno)nationalist politics in Southeast Asia, to bound or delineate it — an analytic strategy which has been developed further in two insightful recent monographs by Joel Kahn (2006) and Anthony Milner (2008).

Such an approach holds great promise for reassessing the complexities of being Malay in the Riau Islands. The question of Malay identity in this region of Indonesia has already been broached by scholars, perhaps most notably Vivienne Wee, whose detailed doctoral research on the topic has been seminal to ethnographic work ever since. Wee travelled to the Riau Islands to study what she terms "undiluted *ur*[proto]-Malayness", prompted by the perception that many of the "Malays" she knew in Singapore were "actually" Javanese migrants (1985: 2–3). What this formulation fails to recognise is that any supposedly originary "*ur*-Malayness" visible in the Riau Islands is perceptible only because of a set of historically contingent criteria for deciding what makes a Malay undiluted. Indeed, the model of gradated "hierarchies of being" that she eventually documented represents only one ideology of Malayness that exists in the region, one principally adhered to by descendants of the precolonial aristocracy. There are many others. Cynthia Chou (2003) has revealed the salience of Malay identity to seafaring populations of *orang laut*, whilst Minako Sakai (2004) reports the emergence of Indonesia-wide networks seeking to reclaim Minangkabau identity as a form of being Malay. Historians of the region have illuminated the changing role that "Malayness" played in the operation of the Riau-Lingga sultanate (Matheson 1979, 1986; Putten 2004). Yet while each of these studies gives insight into the lives of specific populations, their circumscribed focus gives little purchase on the obvious question that they raise when read collectively: how do ideas about Malayness interact *with each other*, and with broader trends in public and political culture?

Such an enquiry affords new perspectives on the remarkable flexibility of Malayness. Though early scholars such as Judith Djamour (1959) had recognised the mercurial and incorporative character of Malay identity, it was Judith Nagata who first began to ask outright "What is a Malay?" This question formed the title of one her most influential essays (Nagata 1974), in which she advanced the idea that ethnicity could be situationally selected. Muslim individuals whom she had met in the Malaysian city of Georgetown might, she noted, present themselves as "Malay" in some circumstances, whilst defining themselves as "Indian", "Arab", or "Indonesian" in others. She thus argued that ethnicity should not be seen as "a fixed anchorage to which the individual is unambiguously bound" and that individuals could exploit advantages inherent in marginal or dual ethnic status to their own benefit (1974: 332–3).

This argument made an important contribution by suggesting that acts of ethnic identification might be contingent and circum-stantial. Yet, ironically, by destabilising the identity of so-called Malays and thereby problematising the category of "ethnicity", it actually reified the "Malayness" they were claiming. Analysing the decision to assert one's "Malayness" as strategic presumes that it exists as a coherent and stable subject position, in relation to which one can position oneself. However, as Mayor Suryatati's experiences show, in practice the situational claiming of Malayness can be more difficult than Nagata might have us believe. To understand why, we need begin by revisiting the classical period of Southeast Asian history, the era in which the term "Malay" first began to spread through the maritime worlds of the Indian Ocean and the South China Sea.

Malayness over Time

From at least the 16th century to the onset of European colonialism, the label "Malay" (*Melayu*) was notable principally for its adaptability. It "had no essence," writes Adrian Vickers, but rather was the out-come of a series of "antipathies and interchanges" arising from the "cosmopolitan interweaving of cultures" that characterised the trading circuits of maritime Southeast Asia (Vickers 1993: 56; 1997: 181). It also lacked the depth with which claims to cultural identity are so frequently associated today. "Being Malay" was about surfaces and appearances — forms of dress, demeanour and language to which Southeast Asians lacked deep attachments, and between which they would readily switch. This reflected the mobile, itinerant character of life in Southeast Asia during this period. Many people made their living as seafaring merchants, a profession which led them to voyage across the maritime world and encounter a diverse range of people and practices. Those who stayed in one place were no less exposed to cosmopolitan cultural forms. Political authority in precolonial Southeast Asia was closely associated with the oversight of trade, and so contact with visitors from afar was a common feature of many people's lives. Such encounters led to the exchange, hybridisation, and adoption of different cultural styles without any apparent sense that any fundamental identity was being eroded. Indeed, as Milner (1982) has argued, the aspect of identity to which precolonial Southeast Asians appear to have been most deeply attached was their allegiance to a particular ruler, a relationship that might be transferred several times over the course of their lives.

Denys Lombard (1986) and Adrian Vickers (1987) have developed such findings to propose the concept of "*pasisir* culture" as a shared maritime scale of forms that extended across the Southeast Asian maritime world during the period before colonial rule.[7] Any particular cultural identity, such as "Malayness", was but a local manifestation of *pasisir* culture, and hence was a framework into which new arrivals, who also belonged to the *pasisir* culture, could readily be incorporated. Such behaviour points not only to the malleability of specific cultural identities but also to the possibility of wider relationships between them, operating at the level of the region as a whole (Vickers 1987: 57).

A dramatic change occurred with the introduction of European terms and categorisations through trading relations and subsequent conquest, encounters happening at the time when ethnic and racial consciousness was burgeoning in Europe itself (Andaya 2008: 4; Maier 2011). The notions of "race" (*bangsa*) and its ethnic subdivisions (*suku*), which had not been a component of the *pasisir* cultural

---

[7] The term *pasisir* had a more restricted meaning in precolonial and colonial Java, where it referred to Java's northern coastal regions and, eventually, other Javanese cultural areas outside the royal "heartland" (Florida 1995: 27). Some accounts of Southeast Asian history (e.g. Ricklefs 2007) therefore use the term "*pasisir* culture" to designate the culture of these specific geographic areas, a usage that should be distinguished from the more expansive concept advanced by Lombard and Vickers.

world prior to the arrival of European colonial powers, had by
the late 19th century become well-established concepts in societies
across the region. Racial and ethnic categorisations saturated projects
of colonial rule, from the taking of censuses to the segregation of
schools and urban areas. Indeed, their intrusion into the minutiae
of colonial life made them all the more compelling as prisms
through which the subjects of colonial policies might view themselves.
Although they were often deployed in ambiguous or contradictory
ways by colonial officials and were thus able to be reinterpreted and
refashioned by colonial subjects (Kahn 2006: 17–21), such categories
were bounded, mutually exclusive, and strongly associated with
idioms of "blood" and descent, all in sharp contrast with what had
gone before. Thus, when the ideology of pan-Malay unity began to
gather force in the early decades of the 20th century, it was based
not on political or territorial allegiance, nor on ideas of a shared
subaltern predicament, but on the assertion that Malays everywhere
shared corporeality and bodily substance (Milner 1995: 50–4; Rahim
1998: 13–9).[8]

Striking though it was, this shift in forms of identification
remains poorly theorised. The dramatic contrast between historical
periods has (mis)led many authors into equating colonialism with a
total epistemic rupture. Even Vickers, arguing that such discontinuity
"should not be a taken-for-granted category, as if all traces of local
knowledge had been killed off" suggests that the term "Malay" was
"ossified into [a] strict and exclusive category" by "the one-way street
view of late nineteenth-century colonialism" (Vickers 1997: 181,
203). In this account and others like it, if indigenous models of
Malayness survived at all, they did so only as a "trace".

For late 20th-century Malays seeking to establish what "Malayness" was and should be, however, historical models and definitions
were a crucial resource. This is not to say that they displaced colonial
categories of race and ethnicity but rather that readings of classical
Malayness were brought into productive juxtapositions with contemporary ideas and concerns. For example, 20th-century Malay

---

[8] Less mainstream 20th-century definitions of *bangsa Melayu* echoed the modali-
ties of the *pasisir*, considering "Malayness" to inhere in clothes and manners, and
thus to be a quality that could be lost (Hooker 2000: 121, 216; Milner 2008:
131–2).

novelists grappled with the dilemma of how to balance "modern" ideas associated with Malayness (such as "society", "homeland" and "race") alongside classical concepts such as "aristocracy" and the genre of heroic epics (*hikayat*) in an effort to establish the milieu in which their characters should properly operate (Hooker 2000). Sultanate restoration movements in the Riau Islands (and elsewhere) recruited members on an ethnically exclusive basis whilst at the same time campaigning for the reinstatement of a multiethnic cosmo-politan polity as had existed in precolonial times (Yong 2003: 93–4). In a public lecture given in 1996, the prominent Malay sociologist Syed Hussein Alatas exhorted Singaporean Malays to read classical literature and study its characters in order to determine what kinds of Malay they wish to be in the future (Alatas 1996: 34). Each of these endeavours selectively rejected and upheld aspects of historical Malayness, generating distinct and novel forms of Malayness out of the same raw materials. Just as the process of genetic recombination involves strands of DNA being broken, mixed and rejoined to create a new molecule of "recombinant DNA", so I argue that this process might be helpfully conceptualised as the recombination of Malayness.

Thus, far from being ossified by colonial knowledge practices, Malayness has proliferated in a startling variety of ways. Some sense of this diversity is provided by Anthony Reid (2004) in his account of the different ways Malayness has come to be (officially) defined in three contemporary Southeast Asian states. In postcolonial Indonesia, "Malay" persisted as one among many ethnic groups (*suku*), whilst in Malaysia, this whole collection of 'indigenous' (*bumiputera*) South-east Asian races was classified as "Malay" and elevated to the core *ethnie* at the heart of Malaysian citizenship. In Brunei Darussalam, "Malayness" comes closer to the precolonial sense of the term, in that it is an ideology of loyalty, though also one that seeks to mar-ginalise or incorporate minorities by positing certain practices (nota-bly Islamic worship and use of the Malay language) as pre-requisites for citizenship. Each of these models has been developed in response to specific national circumstances by drawing on selected aspects of the past, yet they are also interconnected, constantly drawing on and reacting against each other. For example, Reid (2004: 23) notes that Brunei's choice to emphasise Malayness has underscored its membership in a supra-national culture, leading to elements of local tradition being sacrificed in favour of a "Malay high culture" that emanates from Malaysia. Just as the precolonial *pasisir* culture was

characterised by regional antipathies and interchanges that gave rise
to specific experiences of being Malay, so the cosmopolitan connections of the postcolonial world continue to spur the creation and
contestation of recombinant Malaynesses.

Such a process has been particularly evident in the case of the
Riau Islands, where the creation of a new "Malay province" led to
public engagement with the idea of Malayness on a scale and to a
degree that had not been witnessed before. Questions of Malayness
and regional belonging have long been present in the islands but
they began to acquire a new urgency and political relevance after the
fall of President Suharto and the passing of laws on regional autonomy as part of Indonesia's new commitment to political reform.[9]
Once "Malayness" was determined to be a fundamental aspect of
the political space they inhabited, Riau Islanders were prompted to
ask more searching questions about what "Malayness" was, or should
be, and how they should relate to it. As they did so, Riau Islanders
drew on a diverse range of sources, from the biographies of local
and international leaders, to stereotypes of Malay fishermen, to the
constitutionally empowered Malays of Malaysia's New Economic
Policy. A host of new understandings of Malayness emerged. One
high-ranking civil servant even went so far as to suggest that "we
have a blank slate here in the Riau Islands. We can make Malayness
anything we want it to be. There's no precedent: this is a new
province, and we can do whatever we want. Whatever best suits the
needs of the province." Tellingly, however, he told me this at the end
of 2011, over seven years after the "new" province had been created.
Working out what they wanted Malayness to be was evidently taking
government officials longer than they might have imagined.

Malayness, then, is not so much an identity as a mass of accumulated knowledge and discourse, a history of ideas upon which
individuals draw in precarious acts of identification. As Milner (2010:
11) has argued, once this point has been recognised, the term

---

[9] When conducting research in 2002, Ford (2003) found that, although the issue
of *putra daerah* (people who originate from a region — which could be understood in terms of their ethnocultural identity *or* simply their place of birth) was
widely discussed in both Mainland Riau and the Riau Islands, Malayness was
far more pressing in Mainland than in Archipelagic Riau. This points to a substantial development in Malay identity politics in the time running up to the
province's official start date in 2004.

"Malay" should not be taken as self-evident but richly contextualised in terms of the specific genealogy of its deployment. However, this emergent new approach to the study of Malayness also raises questions about how Malayness is lived out in practice. It is precisely in this regard that an ethnographic approach to the intricacies and affectivities of being Malay can offer an important contribution.

The Affectivities of Malayness

Although Nagata (1974: 346) found that her informants' situational, strategic claims to Malayness were in no way "a source or consequence of personal stress for the individuals involved", engagements with Malayness in the Riau Islands could be extremely affecting. Insecurity, anxiety and embattled defiance were all common outcomes of individuals' acts of identification and their struggles to reconcile the nuances of multiple ideas about what "being Malay" should entail. Before regional autonomy, Malays and non-Malays had enjoyed equal rights to reside and "belong" in the Riau Islands, premised on their shared status as Indonesian citizens. Once Malayness became integral to the vision and mission of the new province, and as certain groups of Malays began to suggest the virtues of Malaysian-style affirmative action, the relative strength of different claims to belong came into question. This in turn led to a proliferation of further attempts to define Malayness and shore up the basis for political claims. It quickly became hard to know who qualified as a Malay and what, if anything, that designation entitled them to. The early days of autonomy were thus a period of uncertainty and insecurity, in which Riau Islanders found it difficult to feel "at home".

Hence, while the authors of a recent attempt to reset the scholarly agenda for Malay Studies are correct to note that "Malayness is more than just an ambiguous phenomenon ... it has been the basis upon which peoples and communities in Southeast Asia have invented and reinvented their traditions" (Mohamad and Aljunied 2011: xiii), their assertion that the confusing character of the category "exists only in the minds of a select group of scholars and analysts" does not stand up to ethnographic scrutiny. The unsettling ambiguities of the term inform the very processes of (re)invention that they describe in ways of which Riau Islanders are acutely aware, suggesting that the more fruitful way forward for Malay Studies may not be to attend to Malayness's "resilience" (Mohamad and Aljunied 2011), but rather its affectivity.

To understand why the category of Malayness is so frequently associated with anxious and unsettled states of being, we have to move beyond the way in which it is conceptualised to consider how it is communicated within the social world. Noting the violence that can be perpetrated when the rich complexities of one's consciousness and inner life are condensed into linguistic form, Judith Butler argues that:

> The desire to persist in one's own being requires submitting to a world of others that is fundamentally not one's own … Vulnerable to terms that one never made, one persists always, to some degree, through categories, names, terms and classifications that mark a primary and inaugurative alienation in society (1997: 28).

Butler's analysis is instructive because it reveals the power that one person's articulation of a recombinant Malayness could have upon others around them. Being bracketed into, or out of, a definition of Malayness to which one does not fully subscribe can be a tense, even traumatic experience. Suryatati (2007: 52) attests to this herself in the penultimate stanza of her previously quoted poem "Am I A Malay?" (2007), where she expresses her relief that her parents "didn't get to hear/there was a witness who testified/that I was of C H I N E S E ancestry". But the court case she refers to also revealed the dynamism and speed with which dominant understandings of Malayness, and their emotional impacts, can change, something that *longue durée* histories of the term rarely capture. When the legal proceedings generated their own new recombinant model of Malayness, it was Frankim who was faced with the ultimate alienation: a literal removal from society (having been sentenced to incarceration) because his own claims about what makes someone Chinese or Malay had become classifiably defamatory.

One especially important point to emerge from the dispute between Frankim and Suryatati is that affective reactions to claims about Malayness can be the driving force behind changing social and political relations, as well as leading to the articulation of new official discourses about what Malayness is. Although the case was news-worthy because it involved two high-ranking and experienced local politicians, similar predicaments are navigated on an everyday basis by people from all walks of life: from traders to historians, poets to housewives. Having recognised this, it is possible to develop a fresh perspective on many long-standing concerns in the ethnography of "Malay" societies: a timely endeavour when, as Kahn (2006: xxi) notes, public reflexivity towards the nature of Malayness is becoming increasingly widespread across Southeast Asia.

Feeling at Home in the Riau Islands

Whilst it became clear early in my fieldwork that the proliferation of multiple, politicised formulations of recombinant Malayness was having an unsettling effect upon most Riau Islanders, it was not self-evident exactly how or why that "unsettling" was taking place. To make better sense of these consequences of decentralisation therefore requires investigating the psychological and cultural processes that lead to individuals achieving a sense of settledness within a changing world and also into the means by which that sense of settledness can be disturbed. The most influential theoretical model addressing these issues has been that advanced by Sigmund Freud ([1919] 2003) in his attempt to understand what connects the forms of fear, dread and unsettledness that are regularly referred to as "uncanny". Recognising that these can emerge in a broad range of situations — from getting lost in an Italian town, to reading fictional tales of severed limbs that can move or talk — he nevertheless suggests that they represent a "specific affective nucleus", hence their being described using the same term ([1919] 2003: 123). In German, that term is *unheimlich* (literally "un-homely"), which leads Freud to couch his explanation in a broader theory of how people feel at home in the world. Through a detailed investigation of what leads to situations being classified as "homely" or "un-homely", he argues that feeling at home involves two sets of ideas: "one relating to what is familiar and comfortable" but also "one relating to what is concealed and kept hidden" ([1919] 2003: 132). This process of concealment is necessary to sustain the feeling of familiarity and comfort. By contrast, he suggests, "the term 'uncanny' (*unheimlich*) applies to everything that was intended to remain secret, hidden away, and has come into the open" ([1919] 2003: 132). Glossing Freud on this point, Ken Gelder and Jane Jacobs (1998: 23) note that one has an uncanny experience when "one's home is rendered, somehow and in some sense, unfamiliar; one has the experience of, in other words, of being in place and 'out of place' simultaneously".

Freud himself was quick to link this observation to his developing theory of the psyche, suggesting that "uncanny" feelings were experienced when people encountered symbols which evoked anxieties (such as the fear of castration) that they had psychically repressed. While that specific argument is not likely to prove fruitful in understanding why Riau Islanders came to feel uneasy and unsettled in the new province that had been created as their home, some of Freud's other ideas show greater promise. He suggested that there were further "species of the uncanny" that did not involve psychological repression, but rather the societal or cultural suppression of particular ideas ([1919] 2003: 154). This point was later developed by the political theorist Slavoj Žižek (1994), who noted that one of the principal aims of any ideology is the creation of coherent symbolized realities in which people can feel "at home", but that this can only be achieved through suppressing aspects of reality that threaten to undermine the ideology, leaving them unsymbolised in public discourse. These elements of reality, he argues, always have the potential to resurface, and when they do they are disruptive not only because of the challenges they pose to an ideology's propositional force, but also because of the uncanny sensations they evoke.

Žižek's argument offers a helpful initial point of departure for my study of the Riau Islands because it offers a means of conceptualising the causal relations between the political process of creating a "home" (an obvious concern in a newly devolved province) and affective states (specifically those of feeling unsettled or uneasy) that can be put into a dialogue with ethnographic observations. Indeed, a similar post-Freudian approach has already been used to good effect in a study of Australian identity politics by Gelder and Jacobs (1998). Focusing on the predicaments facing postcolonial Australians confronted with parallel Aboriginal and non-Aboriginal claims to sovereignty and land, they argue that to feel truly at home, each group would need to keep the other's claims out of sight. The fact that this is impossible means that Australia is a nation in which "one's place is always already another's place and the issue of possession is never complete, never entirely settled" (1998: 138). This formulation bears a striking resemblance to the experiences of Riau Islanders in the face of multiple parallel claims of sovereignty, membership and belonging, where "Malay claims to place have left many non-Malays with a sense that they have no place to claim" (Ford 2003: 132). Equally, the public invocation of a specific definition of "Malayness" can prove incredibly unsettling and disempowering for those who define themselves as "Malay" according to different parameters. The advantage conferred by using the vocabulary of "the uncanny" to describe such situations is that, by emphasising the simultaneity of feeling both "in place" and "out of place", it helps to draw attention to the ways in which such competing ideologies — and the seemingly distinct and parallel ways of life with which they are associated — are actually deeply intertwined within the domains of lived experience and affect.

Yet although post-Freudian approaches help to illuminate aspects of contemporary life in the Riau Islands, there are limits to what they can explain. They fit well with cases where the resurfacing of an inconvenient or suppressed reality gives rise to feelings of dread, unsettledness, or anxiety — and these were certainly widespread in the Riau Islands. Nevertheless, not every situation that meets the formal criteria for eliciting "the uncanny" seems to engender this particular affective response. It might instead give rise to states of mirth, pleasure, or delight. Conversely, I observed cases where Riau Islanders were not just "unsettled" but intensely distressed by aspects of provincial politics. Such variability in affective states is not incompatible with Freud's original essay — as Renée Bergland (2000) has pointed out — but neither that piece nor the works inspired by it offer a satisfactory explanation for why the response to "un-homely" situations should be so diverse.

Ethnographic research can thus help to develop more powerful theories of how, why and to what effect people experience unsettledness by placing situations that would appear to be quintessentially "uncanny" or "un-homely" in historical, political and biographical context, by examining the forms and degrees of attachment to that which is unsettled, and by examining how "un-homely" affects might be transformed through social and political manipulation. The relevance of such an enterprise is by no means limited to the Riau Islands or Indonesia. All areas undergoing decentralisation in the name of an ethnic, cultural, or religious category share the predicament of how to balance that group's claims with the claims of other citizens. Moreover, while the diverse and colourful history that Malayness has enjoyed — one involving multiple trajectories across four postcolonial states — makes its ambiguity as a category particularly clear, the categories inspiring decentralisation elsewhere in the world may be no more stable or coherent. Indeed, as Rogers

Brubaker and Frederick Cooper (2000: 32–3) have remarked, "activists of identity politics deploy the language of bounded groups not because it reflects social reality, but precisely because groupness is ambiguous and contested". Thus, although the nuances of my account will be resolutely local in their specificity, this book's exploration of how and why distinctive dispositions of unsettledness and bad faith emerge in and inflect the social life of the Riau Islands also sets an agenda for a broader comparative enquiry: one that pays close attention to the affective implications of political change and thereby offers a further way in which, following Hadiz (2010), the study of Indonesia can contribute to a global understanding of what happens when regimes decentralise.

The Structure of the Book

For the people with whom I lived and worked in the Riau Archipelago, Malay identity politics were rarely out of view. In Chapter 2, I explore why this should have been the case. I show how a series of changes in Southeast Asian political economy, local demography and national politics over the course of the 20th century combined to create an environment in which Malayness became a compelling political category, ripe for recombination. The next four chapters then investigate how these diverse understandings of Malayness play out in, and affectively mark, various aspects of everyday life.

Chapter 3 analyses historical consciousness in the region, investigating why history telling should be a domain marked by widespread reticence, fear and perceptions of danger. The "unspeakable" narratives that I uncover help to explain why certain figures' claims to Malayness might have such a powerful affective resonance for other Riau Islanders and suggest that the motivations behind contemporary identity politics lie less in sentiments of ethnic chauvinism and more in perceptions of moral monstrosity deriving from memories of the past.

In Chapter 4 I turn to the economy, and ask why Malays are widely said to be bad at commercial activity when many enjoy considerable success. I trace how processes of historical and contemporary misrecognition have intersected with demographic patterns and specific models of "success" to generate a resilient perception of Malay "backwardness": a stereotype that plays a major role in contemporary debates over the rights that Malays should be allocated in the Riau

Islands province and which, as Chapters 5 and 6 reveal, can have a remarkably unsettling effect on everyday social life.

Chapter 5 examines the dilemmas of living in multiethnic neighbourhoods, arguing that although Malayness can be used as a device to integrate people, its associations with passivity and a "weak will" leads many non-Malays to consider the Malays in their neighbourhood a source of danger. Chapter 6 investigates encounters with mysterious other-worldly creatures and energies. These are frequently described by Riau Islanders as *angker* (spooky) and yet I show that in a multicosmological setting such as Tanjung Pinang, these are often not affectively unsettling but a source of security, pleasure, or of hope. Yet while the beliefs of others can engender intrigue, delight and fun when interpreting mysterious events, the idea that other islanders might be "out there" acting on such beliefs is much more chilling: once again the danger of "backward", "superstitious" Malays proves particularly unsettling.

With "backwardness" such a persistent concern, creating "high quality human resources" has become a priority for the provincial government. Chapter 7 investigates policies implemented to inculcate an "achieving mindset" in Riau Islanders, arguing that these were compromised by citizens' bad faith towards their own capacities. Attempts to harness the cross-border expertise available in Singapore have also foundered, with Riau Islanders struggling to accept the pedagogical hierarchies that pervade such encounters. The result has been to suffuse the context of personal development with affects of angst, resentment and doubt. Chapter 8 explores this further by investigating "cultural contests" in which Malayness is placed at the centre of attempts to promote and support human resource development. While some such contests reveal the uncomfortable limits of the province's aspirations to become a high-achieving Malay region, others have afforded new engagements with Malayness that reflect wryly on the painful and unsettling processes described earlier in this volume, binding people together in pleasurable new forms of "Riau Islands culture", and marking a possible new chapter in the history of being Malay in Indonesia. The book concludes with a discussion of how the Riau Islands material offers a new agenda not only for the study of Malayness and regional autonomy, but also for the conceptualisation of governmentality and affective experience within anthropological theory.

2

Provincial Capital

As one of the officials working at Tanjung Pinang's international harbour, Agam had met a lot of researchers as they embarked on their initial forays into the Riau Islands. It was one of the perks of his job. Describing himself as a "man of learning", he hoped that one day he could become a lecturer in harbour design and used his work as a means of securing the opportunity to share ideas with experts visiting from abroad. But, as he told me over drinks in a foodcourt late at night, he had often been disappointed. The researchers he had met were, in his words, "rubbish".

"But you're not like the others," he added tipsily, patting me affectionately on the shoulder. "You're a real researcher." The son of two Toba Bataks who had moved to Tanjung Pinang in the 1970s, Agam frequently lived up to the Batak reputation for forthrightness. "You know why? Because you're not just interested in Malays. Most of them only want to know about Malays. They get off the ferry and they ask me, 'Where are the Malays?' In fact, even here, people say that this is a Malay town. It's not. At least 75 per cent of the people here are migrants."

Agam was right. Tanjung Pinang prides itself on its Malay heritage and atmosphere. Arriving at the town's harbour by boat, one can see numerous colourful placards issuing a warm welcome to "the heartland of Malay culture", "the land of Malay history", and "the pinnacle of the Malay civilisation" (Figure 2.1). Yet both historically and today, Tanjung Pinang would much more accurately be described as a multicultural town than as a Malay one: in the 2010 census, only 30.7 per cent of Tanjung Pinang's residents self-identified as "Malay" (Minnesota Population Center 2011). So why

Figure 2.1 A harbourside billboard welcoming visitors to "The pinnacle of the Malay civilisation, Riau Islands Province" (Source: author)

should the central predicament facing residents of the town today be that of "being Malay in Indonesia"? This chapter offers a historical and genealogical approach to the puzzle, exploring how the preoccupation with the town's Malayness has emerged as a consequence of its changing demographic composition as well as its shifting political and economic relations with Singapore, Jakarta and the Sumatran mainland.

Founding the Town

Ironically, for a town reputed to be the "heartland of Malay culture", Tanjung Pinang was founded in the late 1780s by Chinese plantation workers. Throughout the 17th and 18th centuries, the island of Bintan[1] had been the site of a sizeable entrepôt. Known as Bandar Riau, this entrepôt was located at the estuary of the Bintan River, in the present-day suburb of Kota Piring, and run by the viceroys of the Johor-Riau-Lingga sultanate (Chapter 3). To guarantee the prosperity of the trading port and its visitors, a steady food supply was needed, but the granitic Bintan soil did not lend itself to rice

---

[1] Prior to Indonesian independence, "Bintan" was also commonly referred to as "Riau Island". To avoid confusion, I refer to it as Bintan throughout the text.

farming. However, gambier, a leaf extract used as a medicine and
for tanning leather, could be cultivated easily on Bintan and exchanged with Javanese merchants for rice at a very profitable rate.
In 1734–40, the second viceroy of Riau, Daeng Celak, decided
to bring Chinese workers to Bintan in order to establish and run
gambier plantations (Trocki 1979: 33–4). His decision paid off. By
the 1780s, over 10,000 Chinese workers were resident on Bintan, and
the entrepôt was noted by European visitors as "one of the most
frequented trading posts in Southeast Asia" (Vos 1993: 149).

That period of prosperity was shattered when hostilities broke
out between the region's indigenous rulers and officials of the Dutch
East India Company in Malacca over how to divide the spoils from
a captured British ship. In 1784, a series of military skirmishes
culminated in a devastating Dutch attack on Bintan, the destruction
of the trading post and the expulsion of many of its inhabitants. The
sultan, Mahmud, signed a contract intended to render Johor-Riau-
Lingga a vassal state (*leenrijk*) in which the Company took control
of all trading operations. Indigenous aristocrats would only be able
to exercise rule at the Company's pleasure, and the Dutch insisted
that some — such as the viceroys based on Bintan — be stripped
of office. However, unlike the Dutch language version of the treaty,
the Malay-language version that the sultan actually signed contained
no reference to becoming a vassal of the Dutch. This led to Sultan
Mahmud being confused and alienated by the direct style of colonial
rule adopted by the Dutch, whose attempts to restrict his sovereignty
he perceived as illegitimate acts of aggression (Koh 2007: 86–96). In
1787, he decided the situation had to change and recruited a group
of Ilanun raiders to overthrow the Dutch. His attempt succeeded,
but the fear of Dutch reprisals and Ilanun demands for rewards
quickly proved overwhelming: Bintan was abandoned (Andaya and
Andaya 1982: 105–6).

Nevertheless, thousands of Chinese plantation workers were left
behind. They relocated downstream, found a suitable location for a
new settlement and established the town now called Tanjung Pinang,
although for many years it was more commonly known as "Riau" or
"Rhio".[2] Initial Dutch attempts to govern the Chinese resulted in a

---

[2] To avoid confusion, I refer to the town as "Tanjung Pinang" throughout the text.

gradual loss of control as colonial officials became pawns in disputes between Chinese leaders, the nature of which they did not fully understand (Koh 2007: 103–42). In 1795, in the early years of what became the Napoleonic Wars, the British took over Dutch possessions in the Straits and adopted a policy of non-intervention in the islands' affairs (Koh 2007: 4). During this period, the indigenous authorities, who had regained sovereignty over the sultanate following the Dutch withdrawal, had relocated to the island of Bulang and were unable to exert anything other than periodic oversight of the Chinese from a location so far away. The Chinese thereby enjoyed "virtual independence" (Trocki 1979: 41). In 1818, the Dutch resumed governing Bintan following a treaty with the British. By this time, the Chinese had become self-sufficient, with their own institutions of political and economic control (Trocki 1979: 41–5). They would continue to be a substantial and autonomous force within the region.

Thus, from its very inception, it would hardly be true to refer to Tanjung Pinang as a "Malay town". The viceroys who ruled Bintan until the indigenous polity was dissolved in 1911 are remembered by some as being "Malay" but, as will be shown in Chapter 3, such identifications are themselves hotly contested. Moreover, even if their claims to Malayness are taken at face value, from the 19th century onwards their authority in the town depended on securing the trust and obedience of the Chinese, who were the backbone of the town's economy (Putten 2001). Census data and travellers' accounts suggest that, demographically, Tanjung Pinang remained a predominantly Chinese settlement throughout the colonial period,[3] with its economy centring on the provision of opium, prostitutes and gambling to Chinese plantation workers (Thompson 1847). A significant minority of South Asian traders also lived in the town under colonial rule (see Chapter 4), as did small communities of migrants from across the Netherlands Indies.

---

[3] In 1852, Chinese accounted for at least 85 per cent of Tanjung Pinang's population, while "natives" (which included those identifying as Malays, Javanese, Bugis and possibly others) comprised a mere 11.6 per cent (Putten 2001: 46). A 1930 census found that 63 per cent of the town's population identified as Chinese, and 33 per cent as "native" (Ng 1976: 20).

Figure 2.2 Artist's impression of Tanjung Pinang in the 1840s (Source: Röttger 1846)

Colonial-era migration to the Riau Islands was nothing, however, compared to that witnessed on the nearby island of Singapore. Prior to the 19th century, Singapore had been just another island under the control of the Johor-Riau-Lingga sultanate — largely uninhabited and freely accessible to Riau Islanders. When Sir Thomas Stamford Raffles, Lieutenant Governor of the British colony of Bencoolen, arrived in Singapore in 1819, he saw in it an opportunity to create a port that would allow the British to challenge the Dutch economic monopoly in the Malay Archipelago. And so it did. Once Singapore had been ceded in perpetuity to the British East India Company, and secured under the British flag by the Anglo-Dutch Treaty of London (1824), its free port became a magnet for British investment and Chinese immigration, quickly becoming the leading entrepôt in Southeast Asia (Wong 1991: 42). By contrast, the Dutch Resident of Tanjung Pinang imposed a heavy customs duty that deterred traders: by the time the Dutch realised the mistake and declared Tanjung Pinang a free port in 1828, commercial patterns had been permanently redirected (Andaya 1997: 495). Henceforth, social change in the Riau Islands would be intertwined with the flows of capital, currency and people to and from nearby Singapore.

Nationalism and Urbanisation

After the proclamation of Indonesia's Independence in 1945, the archipelago's proximity to Singapore made it the destination of successive waves of internal migration, a trend of significant consequence for its urban demography. At first, migrants were attracted by the strong currency present in the islands. Until 1965 the Riau Archipelago did not use the Indonesian rupiah, which from the early 1950s was a rapidly depreciating currency (Dick 2002: 192–3). Rather, they used the stronger and more stable "Straits" or Malayan dollar, which in 1963 was replaced at par by the Riau rupiah. These strong currencies gave islanders increased spending power, allowing them to enjoy the pleasures of luxurious lifestyles and conspicuous consumption, as did a steady supply of foreign goods that had entered Indonesia via extensive smuggling networks (Ng 1976: 59–69). Burhan, a Minangkabau historian who had arrived in Tanjung Pinang as a child in the 1950s, boasted that in those days, Tanjung Pinang had been "so wealthy that when people came home from work they could afford to throw away their clothes and buy new ones for the next day". He paused. "Just look at our clothes now."

While people living in the Riau Islands today tend to emphasise that this period saw a dramatic influx of Minangkabau, Bataks and Javanese, it was not only residents of far-flung provinces who were drawn to the town. Inhabitants of other islands in the Riau Archipelago, many of whom were Malays, moved to Tanjung Pinang to avail themselves of better education, healthcare, and the work and leisure opportunities afforded by an urban lifestyle. Although there had been some inter-island migration prior to Indonesian independence, it accelerated dramatically thereafter. Burhan linked this back to the wealth of the region, and the circulation of the Malayan dollar. "In the 1950s, Tanjung Pinang was known as a city of education. We were so rich that we were able to build our own senior high school. It was the first one in the Riau Islands — before that people who wanted to study at senior high school level had to go to Java. Now people came here to study." The post-Independence past is also remembered as a time of considerable local autonomy. As Burhan put it, "the town was so wealthy that the local government had a lot of influence over what happened", something townsfolk would later lobby hard to reclaim. Moreover, it was a period in which Malays from across the Riau Islands had new incentives to move to the archipelago's urban centre and did so on an unprecedented scale. Whole districts of Tanjung Pinang became associated with Malays hailing from particular reaches of the archipelago. For the very first time, Tanjung Pinang began to have a sizeable Malay presence.

The Riau Archipelago was an appealing place to live, but for reasons that generated concern in the higher echelons of the post-colonial government. The new Indonesian state saw the widespread circulation and consumption of foreign goods as undermining Indonesia's economic integrity, a problem heightened by the extensive loss of export revenue when Indonesian products were smuggled across the border to be sold in Singapore (Poulgrain 1998: 65–9). The problem was particularly serious given that trade taxes, levied via a "multiple exchange rates" system, accounted for around 50 per cent of all Indonesia's tax revenue during the mid-1950s (Dick 2004). When the British authorities in Malaya proved reluctant to intervene, it was interpreted as an act of political hostility. This did nothing to improve the souring relationship between Malaya and newly independent Indonesia.

This relationship deteriorated still further in 1962, when the Indonesian government began to express opposition to the proposed extension of the Malayan Federation to include Singapore, Sabah and Sarawak, dubbing it a "neo-colonial plot" (Cheah 2006: 642). While their opposition was initially expressed through propaganda, diplomacy and covert aid to insurgents in northern Borneo, in September 1963 it escalated to a state of Confrontation (*Konfrontasi*) (Poulgrain 1998). This involved the cutting of all legal commercial ties between Indonesia and Malaysia, and a series of military operations (Mackie 1974). Two years later, the Riau Islands were forced to adopt the Indonesian rupiah, ushering in a period that my respondents described as one of unprecedented hardship. "Suddenly everything became difficult," one Chinese man remembered, "We couldn't sell our things in Singapore. The rubber families all went bankrupt." Maznah, an elderly Malay woman, described it as the most difficult time of her life.

Once normal trade had resumed in 1966 under Suharto's New Order government, self-declared "economic" migrants began to flock to Tanjung Pinang once again. In some cases, their motivation was not economic at all. The Riau Islands were unusual in being spared the severe anti-communist violence that was breaking out across the rest of the country (Wee 2002: 12). Consequently, many Indonesians with communist sympathies — or who feared they might be so accused by their neighbours — came to the Riau Islands in the mid-1960s in order to make a new life for themselves. Other migrants had genuine economic motives. Even though the Indonesian economy experienced a dramatic recovery nationwide during the 1970s (Thee 2002), the Riau Archipelago offered opportunities for better-paid jobs not available in many regions of Java or Sumatra, such as work in higher-end trading, mining, or the service industry. Moreover, travel between the Riau Islands and Singapore had become possible once again, even if border-crossing was more strictly regulated than before Confrontation (Ford and Lyons 2006: 260), and so Singapore dollars began to circulate widely in the islands. Although there was no longer a lucrative black market in currency exchange, the Singapore dollar was seen as a stable currency in which to store one's savings. Proximity to Singapore also gave Riau Islanders — especially those in urban centres such as Tanjung Pinang — easy access to televisions and other electronic goods that were not readily available in many parts of Indonesia at the time. Residents of the town stressed the high quality of their lifestyle during this period, insisting that it was just as modern and developed as that of Singapore, which they had seen depicted in the television programmes they could pick up from across the border (Ford and Lyons 2006: 269n12).

Slowly, however, the shine began to wear off. Singapore, which until the 1960s had relied heavily on the export of primary commodities such as rubber, petroleum and tin, had taken steps to diversify its economy, encouraging investment in manufacturing, oil processing, and financial services (Huff 1994: 299–307). By the 1980s, the benefits of this strategy were becoming apparent as Singapore's economic and social development raced ahead of Indonesia's, leaving Riau Islanders with a sense that they were underdeveloped and shattering their previous sense of a "shared way of life" across the Straits (Ford and Lyons 2006: 261). "The 1980s were when everything changed," explained Pertiwi, an old Javanese lady who had moved to Tanjung Pinang just before the Second World War, "Singapore and Malaysia became so strong. Our rupiah had so little value, but was so hard to get". The Riau Archipelago's relationship with Singapore, its place in Indonesia, and its very identity as a region, were beginning to be thought of in distinctive new ways.

Triangles and Tribulations

Riau Islanders were not the only Indonesians who were rethinking their relations with Singapore during the 1970s and 1980s. The central government, most notably President Suharto and his technology minister, B.J. Habibie, had long taken an interest in the Riau Archipelago's strategic location on the shipping route between Europe, India and the Far East, and its consequent potential for economic development. After Confrontation, it was even hoped that one of the Riau Islands might displace Singapore as Southeast Asia's economic and trading hub. To this effect, from 1970 the sparsely inhabited island of Batam began to be developed into a port under the management of the national oil and gas producer Pertamina (Nur 2000: 147–8). Following Pertamina's bankruptcy in 1976, however, the government was forced to concede that such an ambition was unrealistic. When Habibie became chairman of the Batam Industrial Development Authority (BIDA) in 1978, he turned his attention to developing ways in which Batam could instead take advantage of Singapore's development and expansion (Nur 2000: 149). This culminated in the creation of a regional "growth triangle" scheme, announced in 1989, which sought to combine the comparative advantages of Singapore — namely, capital and expertise — with the natural resources and manpower available in the Riau Archipelago and Johor. Initially called SIJORI (to reflect the integration of its constituent regions: Singapore, Johor and the Riau Islands), at the behest of the economic ministers of all three countries it was broadened to include other regions of both Indonesia and Malaysia, becoming the IMS-GT (Indonesia-Malaysia-Singapore Growth Triangle). Nevertheless, many Riau Islanders continue to refer to it as SIJORI, or simply as "the Growth Triangle" (*segitiga pembangunan*).

The triangle scheme led to the creation of large industrial parks on both Batam and Bintan, funded by investments from Singapore, the Malaysian state of Johor, and the Salim Group, Indonesia's largest conglomerate. Factories belonging to multinational corporations could relocate to these parks from Singapore, enjoying cheap overheads and wage costs whilst retaining Singaporean management (Royle 1997). A second ambitious project involved the annexation of 23,000 hectares of land on the island of Bintan to form a luxury international beach resort, a venture which combined Singaporean management and investment capital (as well as that of the Salim

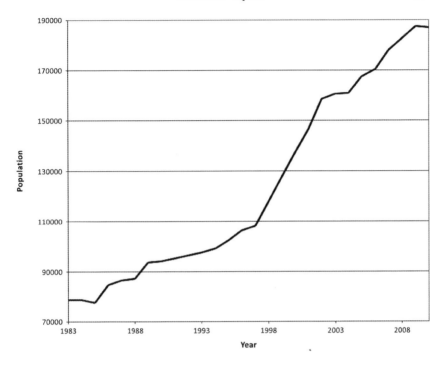

Figure 2.3 Tanjung Pinang's total population, 1983–2010 (Data source: BPS)

Group) with Indonesian land and labour (Bunnell *et al.* 2006). Several smaller tourism and business projects were set up using similar principles.

The news that Batam had become a "development island" or "the next Singapore" — epithets that carried with them exaggerated rumours of employment, modernity and 24-hour entertainment — attracted migrants in droves. The majority of these newcomers went straight to Batam, and the island witnessed a population explosion. In the late 1960s, just 3,000 people lived on Batam; by the 2010 census, that number had risen to over 900,000 (Source: BPS). Though other towns were less affected, they also witnessed dramatic population growth. Tanjung Pinang was no exception (Figure 2.3). Some migrants hoped to work in the Bintan Industrial Park or Bintan Resorts on the northern shores of the island; many others were Batam-bound migrants who had failed to find work and hoped that Tanjung Pinang would offer them a more welcoming and less competitive way of life.

When the Asian economic crisis struck Indonesia in 1997, the archipelago's proximity to Singapore once again proved critical. The Indonesian rupiah tumbled in value: whereas one US dollar had been worth 2,609 rupiah on 1 August 1997, by January 1998 it was worth no more than about 15,000 rupiah.[4] The economic disparities between Indonesia and Singapore had long made Tanjung Pinang, Batam and Tanjung Balai Karimun popular destinations for Singaporeans in search of cheap shopping, sex and drugs. When the crisis made all of these even cheaper, tourism to the Riau Islands became more popular still. However, most of the visitors to the Riau Islands paid for goods and services using Singapore dollars, a currency which had not been badly affected by the crisis. The influx of dollars mitigated the devaluation of the rupiah, allowing inhabitants of the islands to enjoy relatively affluent lifestyles amongst the privations and austerity of what Indonesians soon referred to as not just a "monetary crisis" (*krismon*) but a "total crisis" (*krisis total*, or *kristal*) (Clear 2005: 155). As a result, the Riau Islands were once again inundated with migrants hoping to make a living but their sheer numbers, and the consequent rise in unemployment and petty crime, soon drove Singaporean customers — and their currency — away (Ford and Lyons 2006: 267).

The early 2000s was thus a period that my informants remembered as "difficult" (*susah*) for several reasons. Life was tough economically: it was hard to find work and prices were rising continually. Moreover, Riau Islanders had seen their hopes and expectations for the future shattered. Recent migrants were confronted with the painful truth that they were unlikely to ever enjoy the high-flying white-collar lifestyles to which so many of them aspired (Lindquist 2009). Those who had been in the islands for longer saw their prosperity and security ebb away: a situation that could be directly attributed to the influx of migrants around them. Dissatisfaction and discontent held sway, tainting the pleasures of freedom from Suharto's authoritarian New Order regime and raising doubts as to whether the Riau Archipelago could ever enjoy the development and modernity of which its inhabitants dreamed. Population growth slowed. Word

---

[4] Data from http://www.indexmundi.com/xrates/graph.aspx?c1=IDR&c2=USD& days=5475 [accessed 25 July 2012].

gradually reached outlying provinces that the Riau Islands did not offer much in the way of work, reducing the numbers of hopeful young migrants seeking to make their fortune. Within the islands, some migrants simply gave up trying and returned home.[5]

Although in-migration was slowing down at the time of my fieldwork, the repercussions of the sudden influx of migrants during the 1990s remained a widespread concern. Longer-standing residents of the town told me that it had changed their lives irrevocably and in ways they were only just beginning to grasp fully. This did not just refer to migration's effects on the regional economy. It was said to affect the very material fabric of the town, rendering it "crowded" (*ramai*) not just with people but with buildings. The neighbourhood in which I lived during my fieldwork, Kampung Jawa (see Map 0.2), was held up as an example of what could happen when the economy grew too fast. Pertiwi, who had moved to the neighbourhood in the 1960s, told me that it "used to be beautiful, with large numbers of fruit trees, and wide spaces between houses in which children could play". Over time, however, small concrete buildings had been squeezed into the gaps between older houses as landowners saw an opportunity to secure rents from the ever-increasing migrant population.

The social fabric of the town was also said to have been affected. Accelerating migration meant rising levels of unemployment, which led to paranoia that Tanjung Pinang was filling with thieves, prostitutes and crooks. Even my neighbours were unflagging in their insistence that the street on which I lived was so dangerous that I must come home early at night or risk becoming a victim of violent crime. I did once catch a thief trying to break into my room. He made a feeble attempt at pretending to be from the neighbourhood

---

[5] Lindquist (2009) has argued that migrants to the Riau Islands are kept on the move by the feelings of shame or embarrassment (*malu*) they would feel if they returned home having "failed" on the migration circuit and unable to support their dependents. However, he advances this notion of an "emotional economy" on the basis of fieldwork conducted in Batam during the late 1990s when levels of Singaporean tourism were still high. By the late 2000s, economic pressures forced many migrants to return home, despite any feelings of shame this might engender. Many also managed to offset their feelings of failure by developing more flexible notions of migratory success.

watch before losing his nerve and fleeing mid-sentence. While I was relieved that the criminal face of Tanjung Pinang seemed rather more benign than that of London, the city in which I grew up, my neighbours — somewhat startled that their bleak prophecies had come true — were deeply upset that they could not bring the burglar to justice. I had provided as detailed a description of the man as I could, but nobody seemed to recognise him. This was the problem of living in a town with such high migration and residential mobility, my neighbour Khalid ruminated: you never quite knew who was living around you (Chapter 5).

A much darker shadow than petty crime haunted my informants' imaginations, however: civil conflict. The prospect of communal violence features heavily in Indonesians' understanding of the social world in which they live. In *National Integration in Riau* (Novendra *et al.* 2000), for example, the authors argue that the goal of national unity is threatened by what they term "*masalah kesukubangsaan*", that is, the "problem" of Indonesia's many ethnic groups and the associated concern that territorial or ethnic loyalties might influence citizens more than nationalism (Guinness 1994: 271). This sense of threat, a legacy of the many regional independence movements that sprung up in the newly created nation-state, resurfaced in the Reformasi era as the destabilisation of power structures reignited deep-seated resentments between members of ethnic and religious groups. Maluku, Kalimantan and Central Sulawesi were amongst the worst affected regions, witnessing horrific acts of violence and the deaths of over 10,000 people (Klinken 2007a).

When talking to Riau Islanders, I was struck by how frequently they would refer to these events. "Tanjung Pinang mustn't become another Ambon!" my neighbour Diyah told me, in an imploring reference to the conflict-ridden capital of the troubled Maluku province, before invoking the violent clashes between Dayaks, Madurese and Malays in the West of Borneo: "Don't let the Riau Islands become like Kalimantan!" She had good reason to worry. Minor inter-ethnic skirmishes had already broken out in Batam (Tri Ratnawati 2006: 75–9). Moreover, while migrants in the 1960s and 1970s were usually integrationist in outlook, many new migrants are not (Lyons and Ford 2007: 243). The proliferation of registered *ikatan* (clubs, associations) in which membership is based on ethnicity or province of origin attests to the increasing significance of identities from beyond Tanjung Pinang for residents' lives within it (Chapter 5). Working out how to manage Tanjung Pinang and Riau Islands

Province's highly multicultural societies (Tables 2.1 and 2.2) thus presented a host of "blurred but sensitive issues" for local political leaders to work through (Faucher 2007: 451).

Table 2.1 Tanjung Pinang's population in 2010 by self-declared ethnic group

Ethnic Group	Number	Percentage
Malay	57,484	30.7
Javanese	52,121	27.9
Chinese	25,206	13.5
Minangkabau	17,838	9.5
Batak	12,393	6.6
Sundanese	5,322	2.8
Bugis	3,510	1.9
Boyan	1,607	0.9
Florinese	1,463	0.8
Banjar	1,433	0.8
Other	8,617	4.6
TOTAL	186,993	100

Source: Minnesota Population Center (2011)

Table 2.2 Riau Islands Province's population in 2010 by self-declared ethnic group

Ethnic Group	Number	Percentage
Malay	502,895	29.9
Javanese	414,890	24.7
Batak	206,973	12.3
Minangkabau	162,657	9.7
Chinese	128,567	7.7
Sundanese	50,049	3.0
Bugis	37,144	2.2
Palembang	30,752	1.8
Florinese	28,702	1.7
Acehnese	11,313	0.7
Banjar	11,028	0.7
Other	94,193	5.6
TOTAL	1,679,163	100

Source: Minnesota Population Center (2011)

Foremost amongst these were the questions of what "Riau Islands culture" was, what it ought to be, and to what extent it could (and should) be said to be "Malay". Yet this in itself is perhaps a surprising development: for many decades, as outlined above, the "Malayness" of the town had not been one of its defining characteristics. Emphasis was instead placed upon its Chineseness, its "Straits orientation" or its multiculturalism. I therefore now turn to the question of why the category of "Malayness" should have such a strong hold on the ways Riau Islanders imagine their region — a question that is inseparable from the history of their desire for autonomy.

A Bushy Tale

As one stands on Tanjung Pinang's seaboard looking out to the southwest, a small sandy island can be seen on the horizon. This island, Paku, has bushes growing on it now, but for decades it was barren. People had tried to plant shrubs on it, but they withered and died.

Paku had been green before. After being used as a point of rest for the indigenous ruler Raja Haji Fisabilillah during his naval campaign against the Dutch East India Company in 1783, the island had miraculously burst into leaf. Trees and bushes had grown throughout the 1780s as Raja Haji Fisabilillah had been shot dead off the coast of Malaya, the island of Bintan emptied of his followers, and the town of Tanjung Pinang established. They had grown in the 1820s as the indigenous rulers of the Riau-Lingga polity negotiated with the Dutch and the British for sovereignty over the archipelago (Ho 2002: 26–7; Vos 1993: 204–5), and they had continued to grow over the course of the 19th century as the once thriving entrepôt dwindled under Dutch colonialism to become a quiet backwater. But on 20 January 1959, all Paku's plants turned brown.

When pressed to explain this dramatic change, Riau Islanders noted that whatever its past hardships, Bintan had remained a seat of rule and thus a place that aroused a sense of *marwah*, an emotional complex that bespeaks pride and dignity. Since the 1720s, the Riau-Lingga sultanate had been a diarchic state, with power shared between the sultan, living on the island of Lingga, and the viceroys living on Bintan. Even under Dutch colonialism, these viceroys — who had now relocated to the island of Penyengat, a few miles away from Tanjung Pinang's main seaboard — retained considerable authority and took a leading role in countering piracy, resolving conflicts within the town's population, and supervising the activities of merchants and traders (Putten 2001: 182–7). In principle, the indigenous rulers were still sovereign, with the Netherlands acting as liege lord (Resink 1968: 133). Even when the sultanate was eventually liquidated by the Dutch in 1911 as a response to its increasingly anticolonial character (Andaya 1977), Tanjung Pinang remained the seat of government for the Dutch Residency of Riau and its Dependencies.

Things began to change after the Japanese invaded in 1942. Tanjung Pinang was supplanted as a locus of power by the Japanese headquarters in Singapore, although the Japanese temporarily reinstated the viceroys of the precolonial sultanate in a project of indirect rule. Following independence, the archipelago was subsequently incorporated into the province of Central Sumatra and ruled from the West Sumatran hill town of Bukittinggi. "We got no support from that province," Burhan remembered bitterly, "they gave us nothing." But the islanders kept their *marwah* intact. Convinced that Tanjung Pinang's rightful status was as a capital, and that being in such a large province boded poorly for government spending on its eastern fringes, they lobbied hard for change, proposing the creation of a new province — "Riau" — that would retain its historic administrative centre and encompass both the Riau Archipelago and a section of the Eastern Sumatran mainland, widely referred to as "*Riau Daratan*" (Mainland Riau). In March 1958, Central Sumatra was divided, giving birth to the provinces of West Sumatra, Jambi and Riau. The last of these was to be administered from Tanjung Pinang. The town's residents were delighted, though not for long. Five months later, the Ministry of Internal Affairs sent a telegram to the governor of Riau instructing him to transfer the provincial capital from Tanjung Pinang to the oil-rich mainland town of Pekanbaru.

"Everything that had been fought for was destroyed," writes Sumanti Ardi (2002: 20), in an emotive account of this period. A new Riau province had been achieved, but it was not Tanjung Pinang that would witness the improvements in infrastructure and development that being a provincial capital engendered. After five disheartening months preparing for the transfer, sovereignty was wrested from Tanjung Pinang's grip. Along with the islanders' *marwah*, the bushes on Paku withered away.

"This is a myth, so you can choose whether to believe it or not," Burhan explained as we ate fried noodles by the sea one evening, "but in 1998 Paku Island suddenly started becoming green again. Some people say it was because of something mystical — but I realise that someone probably went there and planted new bushes. Even so, how come the bushes could grow on sand? 1998: that's when they were beginning to plan the new province. And now, just a few years later, Tanjung Pinang has become a capital city again". Riau Islanders' *marwah* had returned.

The Campaign for a New Province

In the post-Suharto period, Riau Islanders' interest in regional autonomy was couched in terms of returning to a state of affairs they had once enjoyed but which had been cruelly and senselessly wrested from them. This sentiment was hardened by the changes affecting the region in the 1980s and 1990s. The growing disparity between the Riau Islands and Singapore, perceived to have been equals as recently as the 1970s, fostered resentment towards the political systems that were preventing the archipelago from developing at a similar pace. The subsequent creation of the Indonesia-Malaysia-Singapore Growth Triangle heightened local awareness of the potential gains to be made from the strategic location of the Riau Islands, but also frustration that the project had led to only very limited development in most parts of the archipelago (Ford and Lyons 2006: 265).

Julius, a Toba Batak who worked in the Development and Planning Office of Bintan Regency, attributed the perceived mismanagement of the Growth Triangle to the political structures of the time. "Why was our region sold out?" he asked me mournfully, "that's what used to confuse me. But it's because we followed the centre too much." Poor central administration was only one of several grievances elicited by the tepid outcomes of the project. A second complaint was that revenue from the Triangle was being channelled direct to the central and provincial governments, where it was spent on nationwide programmes or on development projects in mainland Sumatra rather than being reinvested in the islands. Finally, the fact that migrants to the archipelago appeared to be more successful in getting jobs within Growth Triangle projects than locally born islanders led to frustration that the people of the Riau Islands were being deprived of a chance to taste the fruits of development happening in their own archipelago. This engendered a feeling of resentment towards the incomers, but also a profound sense of inadequacy on the part of islanders, and much soul-searching as to why they were less competitive applicants for these jobs. The blame was attributed to the systemic lack of investment in high-quality education and job training by the provincial government on the Sumatran mainland.

Meanwhile, in Pekanbaru, life was also far from rosy. The presence of an extensive oilfield and its exploitation by the American corporation Caltex had led to massive investment in Mainland Riau, but this had not translated into improved living conditions for the province's population. In 2000, Riau was the second poorest province in Sumatra with over half its population living below the poverty line, despite generating an estimated 20 per cent of Indonesia's wealth (Riza Sihbudi *et al.* 2001: 140). These economic problems were compounded by growing resentment towards centralised rule. The turning point had been the 1985 elections, when the central government overturned the Riau parliament's majority preference to elect a locally born candidate over the incumbent governor (Zaili Asril *et al.* 2002). Whereas earlier efforts to break away from the newly independent Indonesia had failed to garner popular support in either Insular or Mainland Riau (Yong 2003), now regionalist and secessionist sentiments began to become commonplace.

At first, these feelings found their outlet in forms of cultural expression. As part of the "cultural policy" adopted by Suharto's New Order government, every province in Indonesia was associated with a specific ethnic group to the exclusion of others, thereby naturalising a spatial scale in which ethnicity and locality presumed each other, an idea that Tom Boellstorff (2002) has termed "ethnolocality". The principal aim of this measure was to defuse the fissiparous potential of ethnic diversity within individual regions, whilst still appearing to be doing justice to a notion of "Unity in Diversity" across the entire nation (Guinness 1994: 271). The province of Riau, the archipelago included, was classified as a Malay region, but while the cultural renaissance of "traditional Malay" arts served to entrench the New Order's ethnolocal logic, it also provided a vehicle for expressing oppositional sentiments. As Will Derks (1997) argues, "Malay" songs, dances, and poetry harked back to a sultanic era which predated centralised control by the New Order, thereby fostering what James Scott (1985) has termed a "hidden transcript" of resistance against the centre. Such politicisation of Malay culture in the 1980s marked a decisive point in the genealogy of "Malay identity" in the Riau Archipelago. "Malayness" was, at this point, anchored to regionality — a category of provincial identity — and, as such, accessible to citizens of diverse cultural backgrounds. What really distinguished this phase in its genealogy, however, was its imbrication with regionalist sentiments and identity politics through the medium of widely available forms of popular culture. "Malayness" had become a category of political expression on a far grander scale than ever before.

Although the expression of reformist and secessionist impulses was confined to informal or hidden expressions until 1998, they became an open public demand after Suharto's resignation. Activists in Mainland Riau launched the "Riau Merdeka" (Free Riau) movement, an initiative demanding nothing less than the creation of a Federal Republic of Riau (Colombijn 2003; Riza Sihbudi *et al.* 2001). Yet as the vision of an independent Riau began to gain momentum, politicians and activists in the Riau Islands started to ask themselves hard questions. Their place in the Federal Republic of Riau had been assured but, even though they had been uncomfortable with Jakarta's centralised rule, the prospect of a future in which they continued to be governed from Pekanbaru held very little appeal. Led by the regent of the Riau Islands, Hoezrin Hood, a cross-party consensus grew that of the two power centres, Jakarta and Pekanbaru, it was the latter that was the more insidious. Pekanbaru was dominated by Minangkabau and Bataks and had long behaved in a "colonial" way towards the archipelagic heartlands, resulting in the complete marginalisation of island populations, especially Malays. The archipelago could better exploit its natural gas reserves, realise its strategic potential from being located near the border with Singapore, and improve its human resource base if it became an autonomous province and ensured that profits from its resources were directed towards archipelagic needs rather than welfare and development projects on the mainland (Sumanti Ardi 2002).[6] Hood

---

[6] A similar attempt to establish the Riau Archipelago as an independent province had been made in the 1960s, but was thwarted by the political turmoil following the alleged communist coup of 1965 (Thung and Leolita Masnun 2002: 19).

thus launched the campaign for a new province, with the backing of the archipelagic branches of all the main political parties.

As I was told about this campaign by my informants, I often wondered whether there was any latent desire for the Riau Islands to become a fully autonomous republic of their own. When I asked about this, the reaction I received was normally one of shock. "How could you think that, when the nationalist sentiment here is already extremely strong?" asked one of my Minangkabau friends reproachfully. Other respondents suggested that when provinces such as Aceh and Papua had experienced such little success in their struggles for independence, becoming an autonomous province was a more realistic aim. Notable exceptions to this trend, however, were the aristocratic descendents of the viceroys and sultans of the Riau-Lingga sultanate, individuals who strongly identify as Malay. Many of them deny the legitimacy of all political interventions in the region since the 1824 Treaty of London drew an imperial boundary across the Straits of Malacca. Instead they seek to assert the enduring relevance of a "sultanic era" in which an indigenous polity reigned over a unified territory encompassing much of the present day Riau Archipelago, Singapore and Malaysia (Wee 2002). Pak Raja, for example, an elderly aristocrat from the island of Penyengat, was adamant that Indonesia was an illegitimate nation from which the Riau Islands should secede. "I am not Indonesian," he told me, "I am Malay. You write that in your thesis. The people of Riau are not Indonesian!" He even claimed he could not speak or understand Indonesian, only Malay. As this example shows, aristocratic separatism is tightly bound up with the perception that the sultanate was (and is) a "Malay" polity, a view that is widespread in the Riau Islands, if not uncontroversial (Chapter 3). Of course, the aristocrats who advocate such an atavistic outlook are also the people who would stand to benefit the most if the sultanate were restored, and the creation of an independent Riau Archipelago would be an important first step in achieving that goal.

This situation had crucial implications for the character that the new province was to acquire. The aristocrats have remained a powerful political force within the region because of their associations with Malayness and cultural heritage. As a consequence, while they lacked any formal power to govern under the New Order, they often found themselves occupying senior positions in the civil service, despite their professed hostility to the Indonesian state as a "Javanese" incursion into a "Malay" polity. They were classified as *tokoh masyarakat* ("community leaders") and were frequently asked to represent the perspectives of the Riau Islands' population on issues such as planning decisions. Any bid for regional autonomy needed to secure their support if it was to be credible to the authorities in Jakarta. Yet previous attempts to restore the Riau-Lingga or Johor-Riau sultanates had foundered due to a lack of popular support for the aristocrats (Yong 2003; Chapter 3). Becoming an autonomous province — but nothing more — was a convenient way to prevent them from usurping power, ensuring that any of their attempts to do so had to be mediated through the ballot box, but required delicate manoeuvring to ensure their support and to allow them to feel the new province would restore selected elements of the bygone sultanic era (Kimura 2010: 438).

This can help explain the emphasis that the case for a new province placed on Malay ethnonationalist sentiments. Hood premised much of his rhetoric on issues that were likely to resonate with the aristocrats' concerns. He pointed to the greatness of the Malay civilisation that had existed under the viceroyalty, celebrating achievements such as the creation of a wealthy trading post, the creation of a Malay-language dictionary, and the literary masterpieces of the 19th-century aristocrat Raja Ali Haji. Juxtaposing those achievements with the present, he lamented the fact that Malays today remained trapped in coastal villages, living on the brink of poverty in the world they had once considered to be their oyster. Although, as we shall see, the historical and cultural analysis underpinning such claims is problematic, it was enough to bring the majority of aristocrats behind the movement, as well as evoking broader sympathies. Faucher (2005: 135) notes that a number of aristocrats felt excluded from the activities of the Planning Board tasked with forming the Riau Islands Province, and that the process was not conforming to Malay *adat* (or customary law) which, in their interpretation, would have involved such issues as the restoration of the sultanate and the imposition of *shariah* law. This, however, seems to be a dispute over the role the aristocrats should play within the campaign rather than opposition towards the enterprise as a whole. My informants named a large number of aristocrats who, they asserted, supported the entire project.

It was thus agreed that the Riau Islands Province should be, at heart, a "Malay Province". Nazar Machmud (2003: 38), an oil industry expert given the task of formulating the masterplan for the new province, articulated its core mission as follows: "to create the Riau Islands Province as a maritime province, backed up by exceptional human resources, that will pay homage to Malay culture and the pride of the Malay people, and in which the welfare of the entire society will increase in a steady and even manner". Meanwhile, supporters of the secession boosted their subaltern credentials and attracted sympathy by presenting themselves as hard-headed Malays, prevailing over their opposition through sheer determination and grit (Robby Patria 2008).

In 2001 and 2002, Hood travelled to Jakarta to present his demands for provincial autonomy to the central government, doing so "in the name of the Malay people" (Thung and Leolita Masnun 2002: 20). He was accompanied by a group of "Malays", with whom he staged an ethnonationalist demonstration. "After that, the government had to listen," a civil servant confided to me, "but actually, the people he took weren't Malays, they were all economic migrants from Java. They were very happy to help Hoezrin Hood because he paid them a lot of money and took them to Jakarta." Faucher (2005: 142) reports a similar rumour, in which the demonstrators were in fact Malay, but had only bothered to protest because of the payment they had received.

President Megawati granted Hood his new province, although it remains unclear to what extent she was actually persuaded by the arguments presented. The separation of the Riau Islands from Mainland Riau was an effective way to cripple the ongoing Riau Merdeka movement, which simply would not have enough weight or power to be effective if it only contained activists from the Mainland. From a presidential point of view, the demands for Riau's outright secession presented a far more troubling challenge to state sovereignty and national integrity than the creation of a new province in the Riau Islands. This particular transfer of power to the regions — through *pemekaran* instead of straightforward devolution — was thus entirely in keeping with the central government's dual commitment to invigorating democracy at the local level whilst maintaining the integrity of the Indonesian Republic. Ehito Kimura (2010: 439–40) reports that this argument had been made very clear to Megawati in private meetings with Hood, resulting in two intelligence agencies being directed to ensure that Jakarta-based legislators backed the *pemekaran* process, provided Riau Islanders opposed all initiatives proposed by Riau Merdeka. The bill to create the province was passed in 2002, and the Riau Islands Province (Propinsi Kepulauan Riau, popularly abbreviated to "Kepri") finally came into being on 1 July 2004.

A Province Begins

It would be hard to overstate the enthusiasm with which restoration of "capital city" status filled most residents of Tanjung Pinang. Being part of a provincial capital was not only a source of great pride; it also encouraged a new way of seeing the world. This was brought home to me very clearly when a conversation I was having with Slamet, a coffee shop owner, was interrupted by two government statisticians conducting a survey of living costs:

> **Statistician:** We are doing this survey to improve people's quality of life. It is already much better here in Tanjung Pinang, it is beginning to be nice to live here. Although living costs are high, most people are well enough off to enjoy living here. Different from last year. If you had come here last year, Mister, it wouldn't have been like this [*she gestures around*].
>
> **Nick:** Oh really? What was it like last year?
>
> **Statistician:** Not so developed! There wasn't any of this [*she gestures at the road, and the row of shops in which the coffee shop stands*]. This is all new, and it's excellent. There has been a lot of development in Tanjung Pinang since it became the capital of an independent province. Before it wasn't a capital. But now it is a capital, and you can certainly tell it's a capital.

After she left, Slamet confirmed that the area his coffee shop was in (Pamedan) had stood unchanged for the ten years he had lived in Tanjung Pinang. It had actually been built in 1983. In the statistician's imagination, however, the trajectory of decades of development had been compressed into the two years since the Riau Islands formally separated from Pekanbaru. For others, this "time compression" was also projected into their visions of the future:

> **Civil servant:** It's good you're staying here for a whole year. We're a capital city now, so there's a lot of social change for you to research. By the time you leave, I think Tanjung Pinang will have become as big and modern as Singapore.

Town planner: Did you know Tanjung Pinang has just become a capital again? Because of that we're seeing new buildings absolutely everywhere … The new government buildings in Senggarang are still being built, but hopefully they'll be ready soon. The facilities there are really great. It is a long way out of town, but the town is growing so quickly that we have to build the offices there — there wouldn't be space anywhere else. It would get filled up with houses or other buildings.

To this day, however, the municipal projects of which this planner was speaking stand lonely on the horizon beyond swathes of scrubland.

In contrast to the optimistic narratives that I heard so frequently, some residents had a gloomier outlook. Although they had held high aspirations when autonomy was approved in 2002, the subsequent four years had begun to raise doubts. They had hoped to acquire newly found prosperity through the exploitation of gas reserves in the South China Sea, but no such development had occurred. "Human resources" continued to be a matter of great concern, and the Growth Triangle's industrial parks were experiencing an exodus of firms that had found cheaper premises elsewhere. Liau, a Chinese entrepreneur, told me that this spelt trouble for his business. "The province is making no profits," he explained, "so if the government wants money, they have to take it from businesses like mine. Taxes will go up. We're in the Riau Islands, and what do we have to show for it? Nothing. This province is empty."

A further disappointment came in 2004 when Hoezrin Hood, the charismatic leader of the Riau Islands' campaign for autonomy and the man tipped to be the province's first governor, was imprisoned for corruption. It transpired that Hood's campaign activities, including his trip to Jakarta to lobby for the creation of a new province, had been paid for entirely by public money. By 2008, his relationships with local aristocrats had also broken down, to the extent that they actively opposed his appointment as a Guardian of Bintan's Customs (*pemangku adat Bintan*). Aside from personal disappointments over Hood's politics, they argued he was not serious about protecting Malay culture since he had also served as a leader of the Javanese *ikatan* Among Mitro (Candra Ibrahim 2008). Disillusioned Riau Islanders began to suspect that the claim to create a "Malay province" had been a cynical exercise for Hood and his associates to fulfil their own personal ambitions (Faucher 2007: 135).

While some of Hood's supporters remained faithful and greeted him as a hero when he was released from prison, others were not sure what to think. "He has done a great thing for our islands," Pertiwi reflected, "but he's a corruptor. So is he a hero or a criminal?"

Hood's policy promises continued to influence the expectations of the new province's citizens, especially in regard to the prospect of improved welfare for Malays. In the face of vocal opposition among non-Malays to any form of affirmative action, however, and without clear leadership or any strategy to deliver these promises, the new government was faced with difficult decisions as to how to keep people happy. Moreover, questions over how one could or should balance competing definitions of Malayness with the nationalist imperative for multicultural integration did not go away, but continued to present practical and ethical problems for government policy makers and for citizens in their daily lives. The new province may have been formally *instituted* in 2004, but the process of *creating* it was one that Riau Islanders would be engaged in for much longer. To participate necessarily involved positioning oneself in an ongoing debate over both the nature of Malayness and what it should mean to be living in a "Malay province" in post-Suharto Indonesia.

Home and Malay

The historical processes outlined over the course of this chapter have given rise to a situation in which Riau Islanders are acutely aware that they live in a place that is supposed to be "Malay". Indeed, my interlocutors very commonly asserted that the Riau Islands were "*tanah Melayu*" ("Malay land"). Malayness is thus not a quality that is confined to dimensions of personhood; it also extends to political and physical space. The problem of Malayness therefore became not simply one of identifying who was or was not a Malay, but working out how to exist within, relate with, and belong to a Malay place: socially, culturally and politically. To do this, numerous recombinant models of Malayness were produced, circulated and suppressed, but Riau Islanders have struggled to find any one model that can accommodate the full range of the population's concerns. It is for this reason that notions of the uncanny, which emphasise feelings of (not) being at home, prove so apt for analysing elements of affective experience in the islands (Chapter 1).

Riau Islanders do not agree whether and in what ways it matters that the islands are Malay land or how this should inform the policies of the new provincial government. Nevertheless, some trends are broadly observable. While Malays in Tanjung Pinang were likely to comment (negatively) on the high numbers of migrants in the town, migrants typically felt that they were living in a place that was "full of Malays". This could have a strong bearing on their activities. Central Javanese restaurant owners adapted their recipes to be spicier and less sweet, while Minangkabau restauranteurs made their curries wetter and less rich. In both cases, chefs described this as making the cuisine more suitable for the Malay tongue, since Malays traditionally eat sour or salty broths spiced with chilli and black pepper. This was considered to be both a business necessity, since the "large number of Malays" would be their main customer base, and a cultural obligation.

Similar ideas of cultural obligation emerged in the case of migrants' weddings. Even when neither self-defined as Malay, brides and grooms were defiantly insistent that they wanted a Malay ceremony. Simply living in the Riau Islands seemed to be enough to forge a relation with "Malayness". As one Minangkabau bridegroom explained:

> Although we're both Minang, we live on Malay land and so we have to use the *adat* of this region, the Malay *adat*. It's respecting the people of the region ... This phenomenon, of using the *adat* of where you've moved to, is migrant culture (*budaya merantau*).

The extent to which a migrant adopts Malay customs can vary widely. Some migrants remain oriented towards their place of origin, even as they are economically and administratively integrated into the Riau Archipelago (Mack 2004; Sobary 1987). However, for many migrants, integration extends beyond the economic or the cultural. These people appropriate the Malay land label to suggest that geo-ethnicity is generative of ethnic personhood. One neighbour of mine described his household as "multiracial" (*multi-ras*): he was Minangkabau and his wife was Javanese, but their two children were Malays, he asserted, because they had been born in Tanjung Pinang.

Such cases exemplify the logic of what I will henceforth call an "integrationist model" of Malayness, in which Malay identity is encapsulated in a set of customs and dispositions that can be acquired by anybody setting foot on "Malay soil". While migrants may have had their own vested interests in arguing for a notion of Malayness that was inclusive and incorporative, this model appealed to Malays as well. Some were struck by the strong similarities that the integrationist model bore to the *pasisir* culture during the pre-colonial era, arguing that it was important to be true to the historic nature of Malayness. The most prominent exponent of this position is the Pekanbaru-based intellectual Tenas Effendy, widely known in the islands for having written over a hundred books on Malay culture. Arguing that the history of both Mainland and Insular Riau has always been one of military and political cooperation between polities located across maritime Southeast Asia, he contends that "Malayness became an open culture, adopting foreign cultures with the philosophy of 'sift and filter' (keep the refined elements, and throw away the coarse). From that process of acculturation there resulted a Malay philosophy that taught people to live together in friendship, guiding each other and helping each other" (*Kompas* 2010). Indeed, during a public seminar on Malay culture staged in Tanjung Pinang in September 2006, Effendy was adamant that this should remain the "principal mission" of Malay culture in the contemporary era, a proposal which received a warm reception.

If the historical grounds for integrationism were convincing for some, many more were drawn to its practical benefits. As noted earlier, the prospect of interethnic conflict was a constant concern in the lives of Riau Islanders, citizens and officials alike. "'Malay culture" was proffered as a means of offsetting this danger. Bureaucrats in the new provincial government worked tirelessly to promote "Malay culture" in the hope that it might unite the islands' diverse population in shared appreciation of historically Malay forms of song, literature and dance (see Chapter 8). Moreover, such activities might promote the peaceful and tolerant values associated with Malay culture and thereby defuse the potential for communal violence. Many islanders told me that this was already happening simply through migrants living alongside Malays. "It's safe here in the Riau Islands," explained an elderly Malay named Salleh one evening, "and that's because this is Malay land. Following the values of Malay culture has established harmony between all the ethnic groups here — except on Batam."

Batam was frequently noted as an exception, but one which was felt to prove the rule. The fact that Batam had been sparsely inhabited until the Growth Triangle project meant the proportion of Malays living there was quite small (14.4 per cent in 2010), which many people assured me explained its higher levels of crime and violence. Hardi, a Javanese hotel waiter, suggested that:

> Batam has become like another Jakarta, with people there from all over Indonesia. It means it is very dangerous at night, many murders and muggings. But on Bintan, it's okay. There are also people here from across Indonesia, but there are more Malays — they are more cultured; they have more morals than the people on Batam. With so many Malays, you will be safe here.

The appeal of integrationism lay in its ability to balance an awareness of the Riau Islands' multicultural reality with Malay-centric rhetoric that would comfort those who had supported provincial devolution on ethnonationalist grounds. The approach nevertheless invited furtive debate over what precisely the "Malay culture" being promoted should be; while Tenas Effendy's vision of a radical openness appealed to some, others had more circumscribed visions. These debates both drew on and generated many recombinant formulations of Malayness that proved to be of immense salience in both provincial politics and islanders' everyday lives.

One of the thorniest issues was the significance of Islam. The contention that "Malayness is identical with Islam" was widely subscribed to in the islands and underpinned the visions of many of the most powerful non-governmental Malay cultural organisations, not least the highly influential Lembaga Adat Melayu (LAM, Institute of Malay Customs). The head of the Riau Islands branch of the LAM, for example, gave a lecture to a group of senior high school pupils in which he argued that "Islam and Malayness cannot be separated. Malays follow Islam. All of their cultural values and social norms must refer to the teachings of Islam, and are strongly forbidden to conflict with them, let alone violate them." This was no abstract claim. In 2010, for example, it led some members of the LAM to team up with an Islamic association, Hizbut Tahrir, that was likened by many of my informants to the Front Pembela Islam (FPI, Islamic Defenders Front), an Islamist group that in the early 2000s achieved notoriety through its widespread use of paramilitary force (see Hefner 2010: 195–8). Together, these activists protested against a government-sponsored seminar on the customs and traditions of the *orang laut*. "They said that this is a Malay province and

Malayness is identical with Islam," explained a university student who had been hoping to attend the seminar, "and that the province's money should not be spent on researching the non-Islamic *orang laut*. But actually a lot of *orang laut* have now converted to Islam! Ultimately, the people in charge were scared and the seminar was cancelled. It's such a pity."

Needless to say, such events only fuelled the anxieties of other non-Muslim islanders that they themselves might one day be denounced as unwelcome or become the targets of violence. While such definitions of Malayness are still integrationist to the extent that they welcome converts to Islam, they stop well short of endorsing the claims of regional belonging made by migrants subscribing to other religions. One Protestant, the child of two Batak underwear sellers who had moved from the North Sumatran island of Samosir to Tanjung Pinang in the 1970s, was adamant that I describe him in my writings as a Malay. "If people ask me whether I'm a Malay, I say yes, because I was born in Tanjung Pinang," he explained. "My parents are Malay too. To claim an ethnic identity in Indonesia you just need to have lived somewhere for 20 years". But when I asked other Riau Islanders whether such logic had any validity, the answer was usually a straightforward no. "If your friend is Christian, he is not Malay," one Malay man elaborated, "and he is not allowed to say that he is."

Non-Malay Muslims also encountered religious difficulties with assimilation. They often told me that they were confused about what *kind* of Islam was appropriately Malay, and how reformist it should be. Some addressed this by shoring up claims that there could only ever be one true kind of Islam. Members of several reformist movements told me that the Riau Islands Province had been identified as a national problem by Islamic groups based in Java, prompting the arrival of missionaries (*da'i*) whose aim was to re-educate the province. Rejecting the narrative of the Riau Archipelago, and Penyengat in particular, as a major centre of Islamic learning (Matheson 1989), one female missionary from West Java explained that she considered the islands to be an inherently immoral place, due to the innate "weakness" of the local Malays. Their sociable natures and weak wills meant that, in their hands, Islam was in a perpetual state of unbecoming, a situation that required a regular missionary "reset". This, she explained, was why Penyengat Island had historically served as a point of pilgrimage for people in the Riau area who were travelling to Mecca (Matheson 1989: 163); not because of the innate holiness of Penyengat's Malays, but rather as a strategy of Allah's to expose the local population to the more holy exemplars of the pilgrims.

However, others found the concept of "Malayness" gave them ammunition with which to question the more strident versions of Islamism and reformism. For example, while the FPI had supporters amongst high-ranking Malay intellectuals, most of the ordinary town residents I met said they found even its limited presence in the islands frightening and unwelcome. They drew on the stereotype of the peace-loving and conflict-averse Malay to suggest that the FPI was a self-evidently non-Malay intrusion that had "come over from Java" and had no rightful place in the islands' political life. Other reformist movements were similarly disparaged for putting too much of an emphasis on aspects of Islam, such as the restrictions on female dress, that informants told me reflected "Arab influence" rather than the real "essence of Islam" that should characterise Malayness. "The Islam we practice is actually the essence of the Middle East," explained the founder of an NGO devoted to promoting Sufi meditation in the islands. "We need to go back to the original Malayness that we had before the Muslims arrived. That was much more Indian. We should be practising the kind of Sufism that they have in India."[7]

Integrationism can thus be seen to have engendered multiple forms of recombinant Malayness, all responses to thorny questions about what can most effectively unite people, what counts as "authentic" Malayness, and theological debates about the purity and relevance of diverse versions of Islam. Ironically, alternative formulations of Malayness and its appropriate relationship to regionality were devised precisely as an attempt to counter the integrationist position. While integrationism "honours" Malay culture, a considerable number of Malays had hoped the benefits accruing from the creation of a "Malay province" would be structural and economic, rather than honorific. Equally, not all migrants felt comfortable with the prospect of being assimilated, or the rationale that posited they should be. Both positions gave rise to models of what I term "multicultural Malayness", so called because it insists that Malayness is just one of

---

[7] A similar interest in recapturing the Indic, pre-Islamic, dimension of Southeast Asian culture has also been documented in Malaysia (Willford 2006).

many cultures present in the Riau Islands, and that the boundaries between each of these cultural identities should remain intact.

When Malays argued for a multicultural approach, they typically did so as a basis for securing rights and privileges that would not be made available to other ethnic groups. Their model for such a position is the neighbouring state of Malaysia, whose constitution draws a sharp distinction between *bumiputera* (lit. "sons of the soil" — a category that encompasses both Malays and a number of indigenous forest peoples known as *orang asli*) and other Malaysians, mostly Chinese, Indians and Eurasians. Based on the argument that Malaysia "belongs" to the *bumiputera* and that non-*bumiputera* owe them a debt in exchange for the privilege of citizenship, the Malaysian government passed legislation that disbursed this debt by providing Malays and *orang asli* with a range of privileges, ranging from discounts on real estate to quotas in the civil service, in universities, and as shareholders of corporations (Cheah 2002). The possibility of a comparable policy in the Riau Archipelago did not escape islanders' attention. Indeed, a high-ranked member of a government office suggested it already implicitly informed recruitment practices:

> This is a Malay region. Say another ethnic group arrives. I'd say to them, 'No problem! You're welcome here. But it can't be you that's in charge'. It's like that. They've got to respect the people who are actually from the region. But the reality is the more outsiders that come in, the more powerful they become. The best-known cases, pretty much anywhere, are Minangkabau and Bataks. Bataks are hard-headed; Minangkabau are tight-fisted. If Bataks come here, it's going to be difficult — the Malays will lose out against them. So those of us who are on the inside [of the government] have to boost Malays. For example, when we recruit civil servants we have to make sure that the majority of them are Malays. Just a few Bataks. We can't give them an opportunity. If we gave them the opportunity to take off by recruiting them, then we would also be in the wrong. It's nothing personal. We're just making sure this region stays stable, and that everyone respects each other.

While the formalisation of such policies did not explicitly inform the agendas of any of the province's political parties, it was a principal demand of several prominent non-governmental and lobbying organisations, most notably Malays United (*Rumpun Melayu Bersatu*), which formed during 2006 and quickly gathered strength thereafter. At their inaugural event, their leader gave a powerful speech arguing that while it was "only Malays who could unite the Riau Islands, because Malays will accept anyone from anywhere," they nevertheless had to "stand up against migrants" and "prioritise Malays wherever possible". While the criteria for being identified as a Malay remained ambiguous and a point of contention, this event nevertheless displayed in textbook fashion ethnolocality's "ontological complicity with ethnic absolutism and its movements" (Boellstorff 2002: 34).

"It's only since the fall of Suharto that we've had groups like Malays United," explained my Minangkabau friend Rachmad, a teacher at a vocational school:

> They are asking that the leaders all be Malays, and that there are lots of Malays in power and not many migrants any more. And actually, they've felt like that for a long time. But in the Suharto period they weren't brave enough to speak out. Now because of Reformasi they've started to speak non-stop. I just hope that it's momentary and they will forget about this topic and no longer want to make distinctions between Malays and people of other descent.

This, however, is not to suggest that Rachmad supported integrationism. He was virulently opposed. Like many non-Malays, and echoing Agam's remarks at the start of this chapter, he acknowledged that the Riau Islands might be Malay land but that the *town* of Tanjung Pinang, as a distinct social and infrastructural system built upon that land, was not a "Malay town". He considered it a "migrant town" or — reflecting its diversity — a "hodge-podge town" (*kota gado-gado*). Rachmad told me that without the work of migrants, Tanjung Pinang would still be a backwater, indicting Malays as lazy and economically handicapped. Migrants' ability to generate the capital that had, quite literally, built the town up to its current size, equipped them with a right to belong as strong as any Malay's. This argument was widely subscribed to. "These Riau Islands never had good human resources," asserted a Batak luggage porter who worked at the harbour, "Well, they did, but the clever people all went to Singapore and Malaysia when the border allowed free movement. They left stupid people behind. Their heads are empty. All they know how to do is fish. There were no doctors, no nurses, no

teachers. The first ones to arrive were Bataks, and a few Minangkabau. The Malays have always relied on people coming from outside, especially from Mainland Sumatra. We were the ones who
developed this province!"

Interestingly, most of the people who expressed these sentiments also estimated the proportion of Malays in Tanjung Pinang
to be more than three-quarters. What mattered for them in terms
of determining the identity of a town was not the question of its
demographic majority, but the activity and labour that had gone
into making it. As Ford (2003: 140) has argued, they felt "betrayal",
"hurt" and "distress" at attempts to exclude them, sentiments
heightened by the prominence of "*putra daerah*" (literally "sons of
the region" — an ambiguous term that could refer either to Malays
or to anyone who was Riau Island-born) as a master trope of
regional autonomy and decentralisation since the fall of Suharto.

The multiple parallel claims of belonging and exclusion that
exist in such a situation resonate with Gelder and Jacobs' (1998)
notion of an "uncanny" polity in which citizens' daily lives are
marked by a sense of being simultaneously in place and out of
place. Certainly the tensions and contestations that prevail in the
Riau Islands are as intractable, and as deeply rooted in complex
historical trajectories, as the Australian cases that Gelder and Jacobs
discuss. When those debates are translated into the everyday business
of Tanjung Pinang life, however, they take on further complexity
still. Ideas about Malayness and multiculturalism often prove easier
to argue for than to live out in practice, while political, theological,
and intellectual stances are complicated by personal agendas and
the affectivities of lived experience. This is the focus of the next
four chapters.

3

Poisoned Histories

"No, please! Get out!" screamed Rahmi, "I don't know anything! Leave this house at once!" Her frail figure seemed more hunched than ever, and tears began to shine on her cheeks. Her grandchildren cowed against their parents' legs, their faces transfixed. Rahmi regained her composure, stood upright and turned to face me. "I do not know any history," she whined pleadingly, "I am just a simple woman. Please do not talk to me. If they know I have been speaking to you, they will poison me. They will poison me like they poisoned me last time. Like they poisoned my husband ..."

I stood to leave, but felt a hand on my shoulder pushing me back down into the seat. It was Syahrial, her son. 30 years old, he had worked as a tour guide in Yogyakarta, where he had fallen in love with a tourist. Their romance had been sundered when his recently widowed mother fell ill from "poisoning". Syahrial had returned home to attend to her bedside, and had remained in Tanjung Pinang ever since.

"Ma, Mr Nick is not a historian," he said in a commanding tone, "He does not want you to tell him any history."

This stopped Rahmi in her tracks. "Not a historian?" she whispered, "But you said he was a researcher. Then what ...?"

"Anthropologist, Ma," replied Syahrial, "not a historian".

There was a long pause, and then Rahmi began to laugh. It was not the deep laugh of humour, but the shallow, breathy chuckle of relief. Her grandchildren, no longer immobile, also began to laugh. Amidst this, Rahmi apologised profusely. "I am so sorry," she gasped, "please forgive me. I misunderstood. I thought you were a historian. I was so scared ..." I laughed along with her, and the conversation quickly moved on. Yet something about this "misunderstanding" continued to trouble me: why should the prospect of meeting "a historian" be enough to fill an old woman with such terror?

The Problem of History

History matters in the Riau Archipelago. As Chapter 2 revealed, particular ways of remembering, imagining and recounting the past helped establish the Riau Islands' legitimacy as a "Malay province", while Tanjung Pinang based its claims to become the new provincial capital on its long history as a seat of rule and the (problematic) assertion that it was a "land of Malay history". The region's past is felt to be an important resource in attracting tourists and inspiring the province's youngsters to strive for a better future (Chapter 8). Moreover, many citizens turn to accounts of the past in order to understand what "Malayness" could and should be. Given that the principal audience for this history is a body of migrants who have no direct knowledge of regional history, nor easy access to sources with which they might evaluate or contest it, becoming established as a historical authority is a significant means of exercising power and influence. Conflicting interpretations of the region's past, and the broader question of who is authorised to tell "Malay history" (*sejarah Melayu*), can thus be matters of intense debate.

What was surprising, however, was how palpably "history" (*sejarah*) seemed to be associated with a sense of danger for many of the Riau Islanders that I met. Several people simply refused to speak with me when "historical" subjects were raised, sometimes insinuating that their lives would be at risk if they answered my questions. Others gave brief or evasive answers, clearly uncomfortable or distressed that our conversation had taken a historical turn. Even my most loquacious informants would suddenly run out of things to say. Such reactions were widespread amongst those who, like Rahmi, had lived in Tanjung Pinang for more than 50 years. I found their reticence to be frustrating, but also revealing. As much as it signalled that the past (or at least certain aspects of it) was "off-limits" to me as a topic, it also showed how fundamental it was within Riau Islanders' lives. Moreover, their fear and silences worked to suppress certain narratives which could actually help contextualise, frame and interpret the identity politics surrounding the history that *is* made public. This chapter is therefore concerned with analysing exactly what it is that makes history dangerous, the ways in which those fears entrench and subvert particular structures of historical authority, and examining the role that silenced histories continue to play in the Riau Islands today. Such an analysis reframes what is at stake in arguments over who "belongs" in the Riau Islands and helps to explain why parallel claims to "being Malay" or being able to tell "Malay history" should elicit such profound and visceral distress.

Producing Histories

Public interest in the past of both Mainland and Archipelagic Riau surged in the early 1980s, alongside the renaissance of Malay cultural arts and regionalist sentiments discussed in the last chapter. Although local history receives little attention in the school syllabus, which focuses instead on topics deemed of greater significance to Indonesia's national history (Faucher 2006), it flourishes in the public sphere. Newspapers regularly carry articles on local history paired with commentary on their relevance to life in the modern era. Serialised historical essays, memoirs and short stories set in historical periods are also popular. Many of my wealthier and better-educated informants owned book-length collections of such writings, while historical figures are widely invoked in political rhetoric, during the speeches at public events, and as the subject matter of locally produced novels, poetry, dance and film.

The local history put forward in this public culture typically concerns the life of the viceroys (*raja*) of the indigenous sultanate, during both the 18th century, when they administered the trading port at Bandar Riau, and the 19th century, when they lived on the island of Penyengat (Figure 3.1). Popular topics include political and romantic relations within the palace, the viceroys' service to the ordinary people of the islands, and their hostility to Dutch colonialism. Consequently, present-day aristocrats are seen as the most knowledgeable sources of historical information. Indeed, some anthropologists who have worked in the region have suggested that they serve as the lone guardians of the region's heritage. A case in point would be Faucher's analysis of the "centres of power" inhabited by members of the aristocracy, one of which is Penyengat. "Oral tradition circulating from these centres," she writes, "remains the only source for

Figure 3.1 Aristocratic graves on Penyengat attract a regular stream of local tourists and pilgrims (Source: author)

the transmission of local history among the Malays of the Riau Archipelago. Aristocrats living on these islands are thus the main providers of historical memories and mythologies related to the Malay world" (Faucher 2005: 132). As underscored by Faucher's remarks, contemporary Penyengat aristocrats strongly identify as Malay, and argue that the histories that they produce, and the histories of their forefathers, are "Malay history" (*sejarah Melayu*) of significance to the entire Riau Archipelago.

Although, as this chapter will show, aristocrats are by no means the "only" sources of historical narrative, they do hold an effective monopoly over official narratives of history and memory at the provincial level. The town, regency and provincial branches of the Department of Tourism, Arts and Culture are the government offices responsible for producing historical and ethnographic publications to inform the public about "Malay history" and "'Malay culture". Within these offices, many of the high-ranked civil servants are of aristocratic descent and prominently display their titles on their name badges. Although willing to cooperate with non-Malay "cultural experts" for events such as multiethnic dance performances, when matters concern Malayness, the offices — and the rajas within them — enforce a strict distinction between aristocrats and others.

Maznah, an elderly Malay housewife, experienced this when attempting to publish a history of Galang Island. With little written about this part of the Riau Archipelago in official history books, Maznah believed the manuscript would make a valuable contribution to Malay history. Hoping that the Department of Tourism would publish the book, she asked me to accompany her to their offices, where she would present her manuscript. After summarising the manuscript's contents, she was asked by a civil servant whether she was a "Penyengat person" (*orang Penyengat*). She replied that she was from Galang, but that her grandfather was from Penyengat. When it transpired this grandfather was not an aristocrat but a fisherman, however, she was summarily dismissed.

"If it's like that, we're not interested," the official snapped. "If you want to pursue this further you will need to find a sponsor and write us a proposal." The conversation had been so brief that his "if it's like that" could not have referred to anything *but* Maznah's genealogical pedigree and her grandfather's distinctly un-aristocratic credentials. As we were ushered out, the civil servant advised me that if I hoped to pass my PhD, I would be much better off speaking to the aristocrats on Penyengat than I would to women like Maznah.

Redirection to Penyengat was a suggestion I encountered regularly. Most migrants, and Malays who described themselves as "poorly educated", warned me that they knew little of Malay history, which they equated with the term "anthropology". "But the rajas know a lot, so you should talk to them," one woman in Kampung Jawa advised me. Another said she imagined anthropological research involved "spending every day drinking tea and discussing history with the rajas. How lovely!" Stories of academics and students living with the rajas helped boost their prestige and credibility even further; my own decision to live and work in the main township was therefore controversial, and I would periodically hear reports that the aristocratic families were "incensed" (*panas*) because I had chosen not to live with them. Indeed, when visiting Tanjung Pinang in 2005, one aristocrat had been very candid about the significance of having a researcher adopted into the family for entrenching his own hegemony over historical knowledge. "Look at this," he said, gesturing me over to a bookcase and pointing at a series of old manuscripts written in Jawi script, "These are the books my grandfather and his siblings wrote". His finger then moved to the right hand side of the shelf, which was stuffed with soft-bound PhD theses and published academic texts. "These books were written by my adopted children. It shows that it is, and has always been, my family that best understands the history and culture of Riau."

If such evidence supports the contention that Penyengat aristocrats have a privileged historical voice within the Riau Islands, the full implications of such privilege rest on what they use that voice to say. During my fieldwork, three topics stood out as attracting a disproportionate amount of attention both within professional local history and in the historical narratives that permeated everyday life. All of them concern the lives and actions of former members of the viceroyship.

The first principal area of discourse concerns the "golden age" of 18th-century commerce, during which the trading post on Bintan became an international centre for the exchange of opium, tin, pepper, cloth, gambier and spices. The viceroyship grew rich through the imposition of a five per cent import and export duty on all traders entering the area, and this revenue was distributed throughout the polity (Bassett 1989; Vos 1993). This era is still fondly remembered today. Indeed, the very word Riau is popularly theorised as deriving from the antiquated Malay word *riuh*, meaning "boisterous", in reference to the tumult as trade was conducted along the river. Trade is thus projected as basic to the very identity of the Riau Islands.

The second and third main areas of discussion both concern specific individuals. The first is Raja Haji, the last viceroy to oversee the trading post on Bintan, who in 1784 laid siege to the Dutch fort at Malacca. Killed there by the Dutch during the ensuing naval battle, he was subsequently given the title of "Fisabilillah" (martyr). His biography has since been fully incorporated into the fabric of the contemporary town: the official anniversary of Tanjung Pinang's "founding" is in fact the anniversary of the day Raja Haji repelled the Dutch (January 6th); the municipal airport has been named after him, as have several schools and colleges; and in 1998 a large bronze

Figure 3.2 A graffiti mural of Raja Ali Haji. This picture was drawn in September 2011, shortly before the artist left Tanjung Pinang to study in Java. "If anyone ever asks me what I've done for my town," he wrote on his Facebook profile, "I'll say that I painted a picture of Raja Ali Haji, the author of *Gurindam Duabelas*. That's how much I love my homeland." (Source: author)

statue of the raja and four henchmen was erected at a prominent position on the seaboard. Nothing now remains of this monument but its plinth — the "bronze" statue transpired to be made of fibreglass and shattered during high winds in 2005. Nevertheless, it is still referred to as "the Fisabilillah statue" and so, semantically at least, the figure of the raja continues to dominate this portion of the landscape.

The second key historical figure is Raja Haji's grandson, Raja Ali Haji (Figure 3.2). Though never a viceroy, this aristocrat was foremost amongst the Islamic scholars for which Penyengat was famous during the 19th century, contributing to knowledge of Malay language, Malay history and Malay literature through a series of poetic works, most famously the *Gurindam Duabelas* (2002 [1847]), a suite of rhyming couplets prescribing good religious and ethical conduct. The prominence of these works has led to him becoming one of the Riau Archipelago's most cherished historical figures, "his name invested with a capacity to signal Malayness that is beyond compare" (Derks 1997: 712).

Each of these images of the Riau Islands' golden age serves to entrench and valorise the significance of the Malay polity, particularly the post of viceroy, for the region's history. Their political currency and emotional appeal has been heightened by the movement for provincial devolution, for which they exemplified the "Malay greatness" that campaigners sought to recapture. This has had clear benefits for the present-day aristocrats, who are frequently spoken of with reverence and awe by Riau Islanders who have recently migrated to the archipelago and know little of the region's history beyond the cursory information outlined above. Unsurprisingly, such emphasis can lead to resentment on the part of other parties, such as the Chinese, whose own perspective on the region's history is neglected in comparison. However, the most vocal contestations of the aristocrats' accounts focus on a rather different issue. The rajas as self-styled authors and architects of Malay history have come under sustained attack for not being Malay, and the viceroyship for being a foreign intrusion into a Malay polity.

"Bugis": Contesting the Viceroys

In 2007, a group of citizens lobbied the provincial government, asking them to redefine the focus of Malay history. A friend sent me the following account by email:

> Educated but ordinary [i.e. non-aristocratic] Malay people in Tanjung Pinang made a move to bring the discourse of Malay-ness back to the Bintan era [i.e. pre-18th century]. These people proposed that the government switch the centre of attention from Penyengat to Bintan, for example by naming many public places after figures related to Bintan.

The reason this movement had begun, she told me, was that "Malay history" as it stood was "much more Bugis than Malay". This 2007 protest was just the latest incarnation of a frustration that some Malays had been feeling for many years. It was a particular concern for Maznah, the elderly housewife I introduced earlier. She confessed she felt aggrieved (*sakit hati*) to hear so many stories about "the Bugis" in accounts of regional history and that she often fantasised about storming into a government seminar on Malay history, armed with genealogies. "Your poster said this seminar was about Malay history," she wanted to say, "but you're only talking about the Bugis. Where are the Malays?"

The Bugis are an ethnic group identified with the contemporary province of South Sulawesi. In the 17th and 18th centuries, they had a fearsome reputation as seafarers, pirates and mercenaries (Pelras 1996: 305–11). Their relevance to the history of the Riau Islands lies in the early 1700s, when the Malay World had been thrown into turmoil following the assassination of the childless sultan of Johor, Mahmud Shah II, in 1699. A new sultan was appointed from amongst the polity's high ranked officials, but he was unable to trace his ancestry through a mythically powerful line of rulers as previous sultans had done (Barnard 2001: 332). This threw his legitimacy into question, and allowed groups and individuals from elsewhere to claim a stake in the Malay polity.

One such figure was an adventurer from the Eastern Sumatran polity of Siak named Raja Kecik, who claimed to be the posthumous son of Mahmud Shah and thus the rightful heir to the sultanate (Barnard 2003). In 1718, he took Johor by force. Yet by 1721, Raja Kecik had been repelled and a group of Bugis warriors installed as viceroys of the Johor-Riau-Lingga sultanate. Local narratives suggest these Bugis were recruited by the sultan to repel Raja Kecik, their excellent work leading to the reward of the title of viceroy and jurisdiction over Bintan and surrounding islands. In other interpretations, the Bugis conquered the Johor-Riau-Lingga sultanate, defeating Raja Kecik in the process, and retained the sultan as a puppet figurehead to help win the sympathies of the local population (Andaya and Andaya 2001: 82). Ambiguity thus surrounds the arrival of the Bugis; it also bedevils the question of their incorporation into the polity.

It is unclear how harmonious relations were between the Bugis viceroys on Bintan and the Malay sultan, based at Johor, during the 18th century. Several of the Bugis warriors married the female relatives of Sultan Sulaiman (Matheson 1986: 9), but it remains uncertain whether the sultan entered into such alliances willingly or under duress. What is clear is that, despite such alliances, the viceroys and their relatives continued to be identified as "Bugis", rather than "Malay", both by European visitors and by indigenous residents of the Riau Islands (Ali Haji 1982 [1885]; Bassett 1989; Vos 1993). Moreover, sources concur that there was a degree of "anti-Bugis sentiment" amongst the Malays of the Riau Archipelago. Yet while the Dutch captain Jacob van Braam considered this sufficiently serious that he felt his 1784 naval assault on Bintan to be liberating native Malays from Bugis invaders (Vos 1993: 166–8), Raja Ali Haji, himself a descendant of the viceroys, suggested that such views were only held by a small troublemaking faction (Matheson 1979).

Whether driven by the desire to liberate, or by their own political and economic interests, the Dutch insisted that the Bugis no longer hold high offices of state. For several years, Bintan was overseen by a Malay official while the viceroy lived in the trading ports of Kalimantan's west coast. However, once sovereignty over the Johor-Riau-Lingga kingdom was returned to the sultan, the viceroy came back violently to reclaim his place. This conflict was eventually settled in the early 1800s through an arrangement which partitioned the sultanate: Lingga and its dependencies were to be the sultan's domain, while Bintan, Penyengat and surrounding islands would be under the viceroy's control (Matheson 1986: 9–10). Throughout the 19th century, however, the viceroys would move away from defining themselves as "Bugis". They became "champions of Malay customs and traditions and appeared to European observers to be the custodians of pure Malay culture" (Matheson 1986: 6), asserting that they were Malays, albeit Malays "of Bugis ancestry" (Putten 2004). Their descendants continue to make such claims to this day.

Several forms of reasoning can underpin such claims to Malayness. The first would note the viceroys to be directly descended from Sultan Sulaiman's female relatives, although matrilineal descent is not usually recognised in Malay *adat*. A second, which is similar to the *pasisir* logic described in Chapter 1, holds that anyone who adopts the established protocols of a Malay way of life can be thought of as a Malay, and thus be a legitimate participant in or even ruler of a Malay polity. Such a logic might explain both why Penyengat aristocrats in the 19th century showed so much interest in Malay customs, and why they placed such an emphasis on Islam as a prerequisite of Malay kingship, since this was an arena in which the devoutly Muslim Bugis would already appear to be highly compatible with Malay culture (Putten 2004). Finally, present-day aristocrats articulate a hierarchical model of "pure Malayness" (*Melayu murni*) in which rajas of Bugis descent, by virtue of their exteriority to the system, gain authoritative precedence:

> Those who continue to demonstrate dyed-in-the-wool indigeny (*asli*) are seen as less fit to rule than those (the *murni*) who have remade themselves culturally. The more recent the 'arrival', the more legitimate is the right to rule ...

> Sultans, nobles and prime ministers alike are not shy about their less-than-solely Melayu origins. Contrariwise, to be fully indigenous (*asli*) implies that one is born to be ruled (Benjamin 2002: 20).

Such reasoning brings the aristocrats squarely under the remit of Malayness and allows them to be emblematic of it because of, rather than despite, their Bugis ancestry. This has afforded them political advantages in the New Order and Reformasi periods, when the Riau Islands were classified as a "Malay" region, and someone who could not make effective claims to be Malay risked losing power and influence as a result.

As noted in the introduction to this book, however, there are multiple definitions of Malayness in circulation within the contemporary Riau Islands, many of which would see Bugis identity as irreconcilable with Malay identity. These formulations, to which a large number of both Malays and non-Malays subscribe, may stipulate that "race" or "ethnicity" is strictly transmitted down a patrilineal descent line, or that it is geographically tied to one's ancestors' region of origin. Thus it is remarked of Riau Island aristocrats that "they might say they are Malay, but actually they are Bugis". At the most extreme, informants spoke of their region falling victim to "Bugis colonialism" (*penjajahan Bugis*), painting the aristocrats as tyrants and oppressors.

The rajas' response to this has been diluted by their ambivalent relationship to Bugis identity, which is undergoing its own renaissance elsewhere in Indonesia. Historians based in Makassar, the capital of South Sulawesi, have been making active efforts to "reclaim" Riau-Lingga as a precolonial Bugis kingdom. As part of these efforts, the Penyengat rajas have received invitations to prestigious pan-Indonesian events exploring "Bugis history", an opportunity that some find irresistible but which at the same time shakes faith in their "Malay" credentials amongst the broader Riau Islands population who had previously assumed them to be "100 per cent Malay".

The reappraisal of the past in "Bugis" terms is also undertaken by Riau Islanders who consider themselves Bugis, as evidenced when I interviewed Eddy, a Tanjung Pinang-born Bugis, on a series of issues related to urban demography and provincial politics:

> In the 1960s, it was dangerous in this town because the Minang-kabau people started arriving. There were a lot of fights in the

streets between the Minang and the Bugis, because we still remembered that the Bugis had come here to help drive away Raja Kecik who was Minangkabau. Now, the Minangkabau were coming back and starting to control the marketplace. So lots of Bugis were really angry and fought against them. I know the sultanate had become obsolete, but I guess it was a question of *racial pride* [English used]. But ultimately it was Padang[1] that won when the provincial capital moved to Pekanbaru. It meant we were ruled from the Minangkabau lands. Now though, we've won back the province and we have our own government, so the Bugis are in power again.

Eddy's account completely obscures "Malays" in the so-called land of Malay history. An implicit reference to them is made when he says the Bugis "came to help" — for someone needed to be helped — yet in his final comment, the choice of who will wield political power is one between "Minangkabau" or "Bugis". Malays being in power does not appear to be an option. Needless to say, such statements fuel the perception that the Bugis are a colonial presence amongst their Malay detractors.

Yet while figures such as Maznah argued that their opposition to Penyengat historians was an attempt to safeguard the history of the "genuine Malays", this in itself did not seem to account for the black humour and spite that infused their language as they discussed "the Bugis". Previous efforts to address this issue also raise more questions than they resolve. Both Virginia Matheson (1986: 31) and Will Derks (1997: 713) found that Malays who could trace their ancestry back to the sultans of Johor-Riau-Lingga described feeling "superior" to the descendants of the viceroys on Penyengat. Derks' respondents also seemed resentful of the Penyengat aristocrats' contemporary standing, which he suggests is because the sultan historically held a higher rank. This raises the questions of why such a distinction is still a live issue in the present day, why it should lead to the outright exclusion of "the Bugis" from the realm of Malayness, and why Malays without sultanic ancestry should also feel such hostility to Penyengat aristocrats.

In Derks' analysis, the implicit motivating force behind Malay identity politics appears to be self-aggrandisement and a desire to

---

[1] The capital of West Sumatra, the province associated with Minangkabau.

claim superiority, painting Malays as "difficult to unite" and riven by "local chauvinism" and "tribalism" (Derks 1997: 714). His argument resonates with a more general consensus on how regional and ethnic movements should be characterised in post-Suharto Indonesia; Quinn (2003: 164), for example, describes how "commercial and political opportunism, not to mention brute personal ambition ... have ridden on the powerful tides of local history, identity and chauvinism". This characterisation may apply in some cases — such as that of the historians in Lingga who compiled their genealogical charts in ways that generated a ranking of Malay kingdoms, with Lingga as the greatest (Matheson 1986: 36). As a general theory, however, it gives too simplistic an account of the actors' motivations. The "powerful tides" Quinn refers to have enough counter-currents that they should not be taken for granted. Instead of positing Malays, Indonesians, or human beings as inherently factional, it might pay to consider more carefully why so-called "Bugis" aristocrats are disparaged with such vitriol. The dangers that surround history telling offer a powerful perspective from which to do so.

The History that Dare Not Speak Its Name

If you lie, even just a little,
It may be compared with having cancer of the mouth.

(Ali Haji 2002 [1847]: 7)

This couplet from Raja Ali Haji's *Gurindam Duabelas* was often invoked when discussions with my informants moved onto the topic of whether or not particular accounts of the past were true (*benar*). In the Riau Islands, inaccurate information is summarily dismissed as "lies" (*bohong*) and the moral integrity of the liar roundly condemned. People are therefore at pains to place their accounts one or other side of a division between "history" (*sejarah*) and "story" (*cerita*). The crucial distinction is the narrators' confidence in their accounts. History is expected to be a statement of factual truth, in which one has complete confidence. When telling "history", my respondents often focused on seemingly objective and widely agreed information, such as the genealogical relationships between members of the sultanate, or the dates in which important events such as the Japanese Occupation or Confrontation had occurred. Since I was also keen to collect information on what life had been like in the region throughout the 20th century, many informants also offered eyewitness accounts of things that they had seen and could remember clearly, telling me that these were "history". Some also offered second-hand accounts of "histories" they had been told by their parents, assuring me that they completely trusted their parents as a source and were therefore certain these accounts were true. A *cerita* could encompass more hazily remembered events from one's past, as well as accounts that one had heard from sources whose reliability seemed to be in question. This could include friends and distant relatives; usually it also included the life histories of sources featured in television documentaries, books and newspapers. The ultimate arbiter for deciding whether a source was reliable seemed to be personal discretion: most of my respondents erred on the side of caution and insisted that, unless they had experienced something themselves and therefore knew it to be true, it was a *cerita*. Though informative, *cerita* are not to be written down, and, I was warned, not to be discussed, let alone presented as "history", in anything I published. The publication of a *cerita* in an academic book as anything other than a "folktale" (*cerita rakyat*) would imbue it with the flavour of truth — and if such a claim were unjustified, terrible consequences would follow for both source and reporter.

Mochtar Zam was a retired civil servant with distant links to Penyengat and a passion for local history. As with many residents of Tanjung Pinang, he enjoyed the practice of meditating upon the alphabetic composition of words and names in order to detect their deeper meanings. One day he turned his mind towards the name "Tanjung Pinang", usually translated as the "cape of areca palms" in reference to the trees lining the coast in the 18th century. Mochtar Zam's ruminations revealed a different logic and he quickly called the *Tribun Batam* newspaper to publish his insights. The word *nang*, he had realised, was Hokkien for "person". Meanwhile, *pi* was a contraction of the Malay *api-api*, meaning "fires". For Mochtar Zam, the name of Tanjung Pinang referred to the period in the late 1780s when the town was empty of Bugis-Malays and occupied predominantly by Chinese. Their fires at night would have lit up the skyline, and thus the settlement was eventually known as "Tanjung Pi-nang"; not a reference to areca palms at all, but to the "cape of the fires of the Chinese people" (*Tribun Batam* 2005).

A month later, Mochtar Zam was dead. "He said that Tanjung Pinang derived from the word *nang*," exclaimed one elderly Malay informant by the name of Agus, "and it was a lie! All lies! It was all created by Mochtar Zam himself, it came from his own head. But then he lied in the newspaper, and immediately after that, he was dead!" The triumphant and conclusive delivery of this pronouncement made it clear that Agus understood the death to be a direct consequence of the historical dabblings. Indeed, the suddenness of Mochtar Zam's death gave added weight to claims of his argument's implausibility. Drawing on a similar logic, Maznah contested the Penyengat school of history by noting that one of its most prominent proponents, Raja Hamzah Yunus, had died in his fifties. As she ruminated, "it makes you think why that could be".

In the case of Mochtar Zam, informants were disposed to attribute his death to a punishment from Allah for spreading what he knew to be falsehoods. This is first a question of genre: his reflections would have been permissible had they been presented as a linguistic commentary, or an ironic observation, but he had gone too far in claiming they were "history". Mochtar Zam's mistake was not that he intentionally sought to deceive, nor his hubris that his interpretation of Tanjung Pinang's etymology was superior to that which had stood the test of time. Rather he had sinned by stating as historical fact something that was false. The lethal consequences of such a mistake discouraged many of the Riau Islanders whom I met to share anything but the most widely accepted histories: if one was in any doubt about a historical tale, it was better to simply not tell it at all. Assura, a 49-year-old Bugis-Malay civil servant explained this attitude in the following way:

> It might be that I tell you something, saying it is history, and it turns out not to be true. I am not a historian. I only know a little bit from what my parents told me, they didn't tell me much. So I don't know that what I say is correct, and if you then write it in your book… [*he trails off and looks at me anxiously*]
>
> Nick, when I was young, I read *Gurindam Duabelas*. It says quite clearly that liars will get into trouble. It's better if you talk to the real historians. I will give you their names.

This particular danger of history telling worked to entrench the dominance of aristocrats and other historical "experts", and to suppress the subjugated histories that might circulate as rumour and hearsay: *cerita*. Since most townsfolk were recent arrivals who did not consider themselves to have historical expertise, they felt it wisest and safest to deflect enquiries towards the Penyengat rajas living amongst ruins and manuscripts. Such deferral absolved interviewees of responsibility for sharing a history that might be incomplete or inaccurate when they knew that sources of more comprehensive and exact information lived just a boat ride away. Allah, however, is not the only arbiter who may intervene in the field of historical narration — and even relating histories known to be "true" can be a dangerous undertaking.

Maznah Writes Another Book

A few months after her unsuccessful visit to the government offices, Maznah told me of her latest publication plans. She had chosen to take a single chapter of her previous work and expand it into a small book of its own, *Lancang Kuning and the Galang River*. She hoped that the shorter length might facilitate the circulation of the text without requiring government support. The book related the tale of the *Lancang Kuning*, a sailing boat made out of yellow wood from the *keledang* tree (*Artocarpus lancifolius*), which has become a well-known symbol of the Riau region. Maznah claimed her text offered the true history of the boat, as it had been passed down generations of her family, and that it should be read as such, rather than as a folk story.

Maznah's book recounts how a sultan and a team of workers constructed this beautiful boat on the island of Galang, near a forest of *keledang* trees. Once it was complete, the sultan ordered his men to push the boat into the sea, yet however hard they pushed, the boat would not budge. The sultan consulted a soothsayer (*ahli nujum*) who explained that the boat would only descend to the sea if it was rolled over the bodies of seven women who were pregnant with their first child. The sultan's men snatched seven pregnant women from the nearby *orang laut* population, women who were non-Muslim and who had strong magical powers. As they were crushed to death by the boat, their bodies liquefied into blood and the boat carved a river, the Sungai Galang, along which it could travel to the sea. Left behind were their seven children, who grew up to be powerful local leaders, the "Panglima Galang", and to have many descendants. The majority of people in that region of the Riau Archipelago were descended from one or more of the Panglima. The word *galang*, used to describe a roller over which boats can be hauled, just as the Lancang Kuning had rolled over the seven *orang laut* women, was thereafter adopted as the name of the island.[2]

Maznah felt a strong moral imperative to publish the story. "For years, I have been wondering whether I should write this," she explained, "and I have decided that I should. I know some people say I shouldn't. But Nick, what will happen if in 30 years' time, someone wants to know the stories and history of Sungai Galang? There will be no source of information. Everyone who knew the history will be dead. What a shame for this region! I have to write this book. I know the history, so it would be irresponsible of me not to write it. If I don't write this book, all the histories like it will disappear and only the stories of the Bugis will be left. And..." At this point she checked herself. During Ramadan, one must fast not only from food, but also from speaking ill of one's enemies.

The impending distribution of the pamphlet had proved controversial, but it was not "the Bugis" who opposed Maznah's project. She had received angry responses from the people of Galang, in whose interests she claimed to be preserving the information. Maznah's husband Tahir explained that Galang people became angry when they heard the history, but that this was not a rational anger based on having reasons to disapprove of it. Rather it was because hearing the history invoked a possession (*kesurupan*) prompting a wild, other-worldly fury in which their bodies would be taken over by mysterious non-human creatures known as *makhluk gaib*.[3] The risk of such possessions meant that the history was considered too dangerous to tell and the people of Galang were anticipating its eventual forgetting.

---

[2] Maznah's version differs significantly from published versions of the tale, which are set on the island of Bengkalis and leave no survivors (Fredrick 1992; Nurana 1985). Wee (1985: 503–6) also collected two oral versions of the tale that involved Galang. One is similar to Maznah's, but with the pregnant women surviving their ordeal. The other casts the Panglima Galang as shipbuilders fleeing a cruel sultanate in Peninsular Malaysia.

[3] Some of Wee's informants reported that "one's hair stands on end" when uttering the names of the Panglima Galang (Wee 1985: 504). Her Galang informants, when asked to name their ancestors, broke down in "traumatic weeping". Wee (1985: 429–31) interprets this as resolving a psychical conflict deriving from a taboo surrounding ancestors' names, but gives no explanation for the taboo's existence.

Tahir explained that the *orang laut*'s mysterious disappearance in the story points to their having strong black magic and alliances with powerful *makhluk gaib*, probably *jin* affiliated to the Devil. These *jin* — understood in Islam to be fire-based creatures endowed with superhuman powers — were so tightly bound up with the women's bodies that they also passed into the cells, genes and gametes of their children, the Panglima Galang, and from there proceeded to pass into all of their descendants. Many people in Galang and the surrounding islands therefore unknowingly contained powerful *jin* within them — and were at risk of violent possession. Historical narrative was thought to stimulate the creatures, inducing them to crystallise out of the flesh into which they had been incorporated and take over the subjectivity of their hosts, which would be dangerous to everyone but above all to the body they were inhabiting.

It was not especially dangerous for Maznah herself to speak of the Lancang Kuning because she did not trace her descent to the Panglima Galang and had therefore not inherited such disruptive forces. The licence this permitted her as narrator presented the dilemma of balancing the potential dangers to Galang people of telling the tale against the importance of preserving truly Malay history. Historical narrative became an ethical project in which both political and tangible stakes were high. She thought her book represented a happy compromise: it would be read silently, rather than spoken aloud like an oral history, so that the *jin* would not be angered by hearing their names uttered. Moreover, she had deliberately not given a full account. "There are things I know that I have not written down," she confided. "Because the *orang laut* had powerful dark arts (*ilmu hitam*), elements of the story are highly charged with dark arts and should not be openly narrated. I know the names of the Panglima Galang, but I have just written their titles. If you say the name, the possession is always extremely violent. I daren't write the names down because of what readers might do with that knowledge."

Other historical narratives were restricted for similar reasons. Ripin, a Tanjung Pinang Malay now working in Singapore, explained that he and his contemporaries had been "told about many mysteries like the origins of the name Bintan by mystical creatures in our dreams. Of course, the people in the villages of Bintan will have been told more than we have, because it is their home. But we must all obey what the creatures say, and they tell us that if we share what we know then we will be punished." By this logic, non-human creatures act as arbiters over who may possess historical knowledge; jurisdiction over this era's history does not lie with the human narrator. This was often linked to the prevalent "mysticism" of the early past, as an elderly Malay woman named Zahra explained:

> The problem is that in the era of those stories, there were very few Muslims in the area. It was only when the first sultan arrived from Aceh that he brought a version of the Muslim faith.

For Zahra, it was the arrival of a sultanic system, and (a "version" of) Islam, which gave rise to historical events that could be spoken of without fear of mystical reprisals. Although the sultans were often impious Muslims, they brought with them enough of a faith to temper and control the forces of troublesome non-human agents, allowing the history of those times to be spoken of in some detail. By contrast, the "indigenous" realities that preceded or existed on the margins of the sultanate were best revealed through non-human, rather than human, endeavour. Of course, this cosmology enforces the notion that the historical topic most properly discussed by humans is that of the polity, and that individuals whose control over the mystical realm made them the safest placed to do so are those descended from the ruler.

Yet does such an explanation account for the fear that individuals such as Rahmi felt when I ventured into their homes? The prospect of a "historical interview" with a foreign ethnographer who may not be aware of these subtleties and might blunder into topics that would be dangerous for the interviewee would certainly be unsettling. On the other hand, as long as no such history is actually told, the informant remains safe. These dangers might, then, explain the unease and awkwardness surrounding some of my historical interviews. The cases of true terror, however, require an alternative explanation.

Poisonous Preoccupations

Minangkabau man: Indonesians aren't like Westerners. If Indonesians don't like somebody, they are still very friendly towards them. But behind their backs, they hate them and want to use dark arts. Teachers are afraid to give low marks. If someone has a certain position, others will definitely be jealous, and will want

to send dark arts towards the person who got the position they
wanted. There is a lot of danger and one must always be on
one's guard.

The Riau Archipelago has histories that people refuse to tell because
of fears of revenge by sorcery.[4] This could take many forms. Informants often expressed their fear of being exposed to "poison" (*racun*)
or other dark arts,[5] leading to rapid death or the gradual development of a crippling, if not lethal, illness. Rahmi's husband, for
example, had died following a rapid decline in health only a few
days after he had revealed details of a corrupt transaction to the
authorities. She was convinced that his actions had led someone to
employ poison or magic to shorten his life. Such reprisals are a
widespread fear in the Riau Islands, although some informants also
suggested to me that claims of sorcery might be used as a cipher for
more martial reprisals. Fadli, a Minangkabau English teacher whom
I got to know well during my fieldwork, explained how under the
New Order, free speech risked incurring the wrath of the government, including Suharto's followers (*anak buah*) in the local bureau-
cracy. In the worst cases, this could lead to arrest, abuse, or even
disappearance. With state "punishments" unable to be discussed,
Fadli identified the seemingly "superstitious" language of sorcery as
one way in which such dangers could be articulated. As I conducted
research in the midst of Reformasi, my informants would occasionally
be very explicit that this was a danger of which they were afraid.
Assura, for example, suggested his parents had always refused to tell
him the region's history, for precisely this reason:

> There were many historical things my parents knew, but they
> would never tell me because they were afraid of being taken away
> by Suharto or his henchmen. I really don't know enough to help
> you, and I'd rather not discuss it. Why don't you go to the rajas
> on Penyengat?

---

[4] Anthropologists have conventionally defined "sorcery" as the directed and inten-
tional use of dark arts to harm others, in contrast to "witchcraft", in which harm
is inflicted by the witch without his or her knowledge or intent (Douglas 1970).
[5] In the Riau Islands, the category of "poison" encompassed both mundane and
magical toxic substances. Such poisons could be poured or sprinkled (usually
into food or drink), but also "sent" to victims by supernatural means. Even resolutely non-magical varieties could be classified as being amongst the "dark arts",
perhaps reflecting the hidden and indirect means by which a poisoner realised
his or her wishes (for a similar case, see Ferguson 1999: 118–21).

Most allusions to sorcery, however, were much vaguer in their identification of the threat, at least while in the presence of a foreign
researcher. Loose reference was usually made to there being "somebody" who presented a threat, rather than a sorcerer being identified
by name.

Nevertheless, certain groups were widely reputed to have a
heightened propensity for sorcery. Migrants were figures of suspicion,
as they had unknown backgrounds and may have come from areas of
Indonesia where the dark arts were thought to still be very strong,
such as Central and East Java. *Orang laut* were widely feared because,
as seen earlier, their animism could bring them into close, almost
symbiotic relationships with powerful non-human *makhluk gaib*.
Surprisingly, given their own self-definition as pious Muslims, aristocrats were also widely implicated as being skilled in the dark arts.
Whilst sultans and rajas were acknowledged to have introduced Islam
to the islands, they had brought an impure variant:

> **Tahir:** All the Islam was mixed with dark arts. This was a
> sultanate, so people were competing to take control of it. People
> were fighters. If you wanted to be the ruler, you had to be
> strong; you had to be able to defeat your rivals, kings from other
> sultanates who came to defeat you. Raja Kecik for instance —
> that was a war! So of course the sultans had to be strong, and of
> course they used dark arts and *jin* to achieve that.

Thus, just as the Panglima Galang had transmitted unruly *jin* through
their sperm, so it was believed that other *jin*, and arcane knowledge
of dark arts, had travelled down the supposedly pure and pious aristocratic descent line.

Sorcery can occur for two reasons. It may be simply the pre-
dations of the wicked: such attacks are indiscriminate but usually
directed at those who are vulnerable and easy targets, such as newly-
arrived migrants. The second category consists of reprisals after a
social relationship has broken down, spurred by situations such as
insults, jealousies, workplace rivalries, spurned romantic advances or
unpaid debts. My interlocutors' allusions to sorcery suggested that
the telling of history could be similarly destructive to social relationships, in this case between the narrator and an unspecified other, by
revealing something that the sorcerer would want to be kept secret.
For example, occasionally my friends would share with me their
"secret" for detecting whether food had been spiked with poison or

magic powder, a very useful skill, I was told, if spending time with *orang laut*. I heard the same advice from numerous sources, but each was extremely anxious that I should not pass on the information to anyone else. If the *orang laut* discovered that the secret had been exposed, they told me, they would become so angry that they would hunt down and silence the source. Similar fears seemed to bedevil at least some of my prospective interviewees when I asked them to share tales of the past. "If people know that I have been talking with you," one old man explained, "they might think I have told you certain things, even though I have not. That is too dangerous for me."

Although it might seem that this process of silencing works to entrench the authority of the dominant narratives that *can* be spoken, it can also be interpreted as a tactical and strategic attempt to manipulate the memory of the past, and to challenge the institutions and people with which history is associated. Sorcery allegations imply that the history known by the informant in question is being held in check by a powerful and deeply immoral form of violence, undermining the sanctity of accepted public narratives and suggesting that they are shot through with personal interests. Consequently, claims to victimhood cannot be taken uncritically and the question of whether sorcerous or military action would ever actually be taken in response to the telling of historical narrative must remain an open one. Nevertheless, as I now seek to demonstrate, such claims can shed an illuminating new light on the Riau Islands' history industry and the politics of Malayness.

Apriliyani Gets Carried Away

During a fieldtrip to the island of Karimun, I met a man named Firaz who invited me to interview his 90-year-old grandmother, Apriliyani. The old lady was excited to receive a visitor and, sitting in her front yard, talked at length about her experiences growing up as a child under the Dutch. Her daughter and Firaz joined us, encouraging Apriliyani to elaborate on interesting points and drawing comparisons between the affluence of the Dutch period and the poverty of contemporary Indonesia.

About an hour into the interview, as Apriliyani was discussing her life as a young woman in the 1930s and 1940s, Firaz and his mother began to withdraw from the conversation, exchanging edgy looks. Their apparent unease only intensified as Apriliyani enthusiastically described how a large number of Singaporeans had moved to

Karimun during the war and had set up farms where they grew sweet potatoes. Firaz's mother started to send a barrage of text messages from her mobile phone. A few minutes later, an unknown man on a motorcycle pulled up at the house. Firaz lifted his grandmother up out of her chair and placed her on the back of the motorcycle, telling her not to struggle and that she had "already said enough". The motorcyclist then rode off, taking a bewildered Apriliyani down the hill and out of sight.

An awkward silence filled the front yard. Firaz explained that his mother had needed to arrange for Apriliyani to be removed because they had both been scared that she would say something she should not. This was not strictly a "secret", but information that it would be better for me not to know because if she had told me, there would be "danger". I replied that if this were the case, I would not ask them what the information was, but would like to be told more about the danger, lest I unwittingly expose myself or my interviewees to it again. After a brief hesitation, Firaz decided to elaborate:

> It's like this. Grandma was about to talk about the Japanese period. We could tell, because she was talking about the 1940s. And we knew that you are recording the interview and might use what she says to write a book. We were scared. What would happen if she told you some of the things that happened during the war? People in Japan would read your book, and they would be so angry about what had been revealed that they would re-invade Indonesia.

His tone did not strike me as being sincere. I countered that plenty of unflattering research into the Japanese Occupation had already been conducted, much of it by Japanese scholars. The risk of invasion seemed negligible. Taufik, a Malay friend who had joined me for the day, nodded his assent. Firaz, looking more uncomfortable than ever, decided to change the tack of his explanation:

> I can see you are a true scholar and I admit I just lied. Since I am a scholar too, I will now be honest with you. If you want to know the history of this region, there is a woman who knows it all. She has all of the manuscripts in her living room. The Dutch period, the Japanese period, all of it. Many manuscripts with information nobody else knows. She has told me the true history of Riau. She has shared her manuscripts with me, and I have told my grandmother about them. But I must not tell anyone outside my family.

This woman has very powerful mystical abilities (*ilmu*). She is 120 years old, but you would think she was much younger. She is watching me all the time. When I pray in the mosque she appears to me and reminds me of my duties. She tells me if I am being a good Muslim, and she reminds me that if I tell anyone the history of the islands, then she will kill me. She will do it if anyone learns the secrets of her manuscripts. She will kill me and all my family. So now you understand. If my grandmother had spoken to you any more, we could all have been killed.

If you want to learn the history of the Riau Islands, you should look for this woman and persuade her to let you see her manuscripts. She lives in Tanjung Pinang, just like you, and she does not live far from all that history. But I have already told you too much, and she will be angry. Sorry, I cannot tell you any more.

This story, certainly the most dramatic and overt description of a sorcerer that I encountered during ethnohistorical interviews, presents numerous interpretive challenges. The level of detail means it cannot be simply dismissed as a superstitious belief as some of my Indonesian friends were wont to do regarding other cases where informants made reference to fears of poisoning or sorcery. Moreover, the sheer amount of effort taken to halt Apriliyani's narrative mid-flow shows that silencing her was a serious concern for her daughter and grandson. Whereas some informants' protestations of danger could be interpreted as a shield hiding the fact that they actually knew very little history, Apriliyani was evidently thought to know too much. It seemed from Firaz's remarks that the troublesome knowledge was associated with the 1940s: his initial explanation was explicitly linked with that period, and while his second was a more general commentary on the dangers of talking about the past, this fear had not been present when he and his mother had discussed the 1920s and 1930s. Ultimately, I will never know what troublesome information Apriliyani might have told me. But recounting my experience to people I knew in Tanjung Pinang was revealing in itself.

Interpreting Firaz's explanation became a perfect example of what James Holstein and Jaber Gubrium (1995) term "active interviewing", a process in which researcher and respondent searched for "horizons of meaning" together through collaborative exploration of the nuances of the tale. Several informants were quick to dismiss it as a lie or an attempt on Firaz's part to halt any further questioning.

Others, more credulous, suggested the contents of the tale could themselves be useful clues. Taufik, who had been present for the entire episode, told me I was wrong to be sceptical about Firaz's tale. He himself had once had a similar experience when he was working as a garage apprentice in Batam. A mysterious mentor, steeped in knowledge of both the dark arts and Islam, had used mystical abilities to appear to Taufik whenever he prayed, and these apparitions had inspired him to forego the lifestyle of drink and drugs he had turned to after being dumped by his first girlfriend. Fadli told me that he "almost couldn't believe the story", but conceded that while the abilities the sorceress was professed to command were rare, they were not unknown. What puzzled him most about the account was that, having grown up in Tanjung Pinang, he had never heard of this female historian. That, to him, suggested an isolated residence far from the town centre. Both Fadli and Taufik suspected that the reference to "living near all that history" was an allusion to Penyengat.

Maznah, by contrast, immediately wondered whether the woman in question might be her own mother, also said to be 120 years old. She interrogated her sharply as to whether she had been using mysticism to disseminate historical narrative, a charge the old lady denied. "He's either lying, or it's Penyengat he's talking about," Maznah concluded, "It wouldn't surprise me if it was Penyengat. They have plenty they want to hide."

In these moments of spontaneous interpretation, the raja community is no longer a collection of benevolent experts with whom it would be nice to drink tea. Guarding knowledge that cannot be shared, these aristocrats employ sinful, frightening, and possibly violent means to subjugate those who might disseminate this information; a parallel to their institutional manipulation of publishing contracts and printing presses. But how could such a possibility be so readily entertained when it contradicts all the hallmarks of what it means to be a "pure Malay"? What happened in the 1940s that Penyengat aristocrats might want to hide?

The Silent War

M.S. Suwardi *et al.*'s *History of Resistance to Imperialism and Colonialism in Riau* (1984) remains the most comprehensive account of how societies in Archipelagic and Mainland Riau dealt with successive encounters with foreign occupying forces. Yet there is a puzzle in

its coverage of the Japanese Occupation. The Riau Islands are conspicuous by their absence. In 11 pages devoted to discussing anti-
Japanese resistance movements, locations in the Riau Archipelago are
not mentioned once.

When Vivienne Wee conducted ethnographic research with
Penyengat aristocrats, she encountered a sanguine attitude towards
the Japanese. Her informants viewed the period of occupation as, like
the Dutch era and the archipelago's incorporation into the Republic
of Indonesia, a "mere episode within the larger historical context of
zaman sultan [the era of the sultanate]" (Wee 1985: 119). If anything was notable about this period, it was that people had been
won to the Japanese cause, the Japanese were regarded as allies, and
the Japanese presence presented distinct military opportunities for
re-establishing the sultanate:

> The Japanese commander had an attitude of sympathy (*bersifat
> simpatis*) and formed a battalion consisting of the indigenous
> inhabitants of Riau. Older respondents who were in this battalion
> still speak of it with fond memories. Apparently, the officers
> were mostly aristocrats while the rank-and-file were mostly com-
> moners ... It was headed by Raja Muhammad Yunus, who held
> the rank of major. Evidently, the existence of this military bat-
> talion lent some military substance to the hope that the Riau
> sultanate could be revived (Wee 2002: 2–3).

A rather different perspective is offered by Shigeru Sato (2000) in
his analysis of a Netherlands War Crimes Investigation Team report.
Interviewing forced labourers (*romusha*) who had been brought to
the Riau Islands, Dutch investigators uncovered tales of extraordinary
brutality:

> One day in a timbering site in Tanjung Pinang, a small amount
> of beans were stolen from the garden. About 300 coolies and
> foremen were assembled and two Japanese and a couple of
> *Heiho* [Indonesian troops assisting the Japanese] beat every one
> of them, nine times on average, to draw the thief out. The thief
> was eventually caught and was beaten anew with rattan sticks.
> He was then tied to a tree in a sitting position with his hands
> tied behind the back, and left in that position for seven days and
> nights. He was given some drinks but no food. When he was
> let free, he could not walk, and was carried by other workers to
> the clinic, where he died about ten days later. [...]

One day a Javanese coolie called Kartasan bought a jacket from his friend. A Japanese called Osaka suspected wrongly that Kartasan stole it, and as punishment, he tied Kartasan's hands behind the back and hanged him from a tree in such a way that his toes just touched the ground. Osaka then sprinkled petrol on Kartasan's head and set fire [to it]. Kartasan's hair flared up instantly, causing him to shriek out of pain. Soon his head swelled up and became like a pig's and blood gushed out of it. Kartasan was then taken down and untied. Once his head was cleansed by his friends, Osaka approached him again and slapped his pig-like face many times with full force. Still unsatisfied, he pumped water into Kartasan's stomach until it swelled up like a balloon. (Sato 2000: 7)

Similar atrocities against Riau Islanders, both civilians and those enrolled in Japanese forces, are reported in several eyewitness accounts preserved in the Oral History Collection at the National Archives of Singapore. Acts described range from beatings and bayonettings to demanding hard labour on a starvation diet. The islands were afflicted with structural hardship as well: acute food shortages wracked the archipelago, necessitating smuggling, tax evasion and black marketeering in and around Karimun (Twang 1998: 94–100). These accounts are hard to reconcile with Wee's assertion that the Japanese were viewed as allies and their presence remembered fondly. It is also puzzling why such hardships, which Indonesian history books describe and discuss in some detail for areas other than the Riau Islands, remain cloaked in silence.

The silence persisted during my field research. Informants were strikingly reluctant to elaborate on the Japanese period and the accounts of those who had lived through it displayed a marked degree of uniformity. They would rehearse the dates when the Japanese entered and left the Riau Archipelago, the "Nipponisation" of local place names, and transitions in the region's currency, but when I asked them for personal stories or memories of the period, they typically said they did not know, could not remember, or that I was better placed asking someone else. Those who did reply invoked the generic trope that times were "difficult" (*susah*). This "difficulty" was always linked to the shortage of rice and other staple commodities:

Elderly woman: We had to eat sago, there was no rice. Only ever sago. It's not filling, and we had no rice, so we were always hungry.

Elderly man: Eating was difficult, cloth was difficult, and as for rice — there wasn't any! We just ate tubers and sago, which we grated so it could be like rice. It was like eating pig food. Sometimes, if we wanted meat, we had to eat pork [a meat forbidden to Muslims] in our dinner.

Though these descriptions of wartime diets were interesting and evocative, they lacked the personal feeling of accounts that the same informants would give of their experiences and their families' activities under Dutch rule. The Japanese Occupation seemed to be remembered as a set of economic conditions, or a set of dry, objective facts.

I decided to try a different approach in my enquiries. Bringing along a printed copy of Wee's (2002) paper on ethno-historical narratives in the Riau Islands, I read out (in translation) the sections on the Japanese and how "Riau Malays" had "fond memories" of the Japanese battalion, waiting to gauge the response. The effect was electric:

Maznah: We had to eat rats! Can you have fond memories of eating a rat?! Lies. They are lying! Who is it who has written that history? It must be Raja Hamzah. His father helped the Japanese.

Though Raja Hamzah Yunus was not the author of the article, Wee does openly acknowledge him as her "mentor" during her fieldwork (1985: iv). A high-ranked bureaucrat in the Ministry of Culture and Education, Hamzah Yunus remains a revered figure for many Riau Islanders. Yet Maznah's reaction suggests there are equally many for whom Hamzah Yunus and the alleged "lies" that might account for his untimely death are despised.

Hamzah Yunus' father, Raja Muhammad Yunus, was the figure flagged as a hero and admired leader by the "Riau Malay" informants whom Wee interviewed. My own interviewees painted a rather different picture of a man whose collaboration with the Japanese allowed him to live a disproportionately comfortable lifestyle whilst intensifying the suffering of the Malays he had claimed were under his indigenous jurisdiction. As Maznah recounted:

Every day Muhammad Yunus arrived at eight in the morning and looked for my older brothers, men that could serve in the [Japanese] army. My grandmother asked him, 'What do you

want? Why are you disturbing us, there are no children here!'
But she was scared for her grandsons. For them to be safe they
had to hide in the jungle. Abas and Hasan were 15 years old,
and Djonal was already big, fully adult.

Every day he went to islands and took men to enter the
Japanese army. If they didn't want to go, he tortured them. Perhaps he hit them in front of their mothers, or used some other
torture. Everyone was terrified when they saw him arrive.

I still remember my friend Batin Osman from Karas Island.
They — the people from Penyengat — came and took him, even
though he had just married. The henna was still red on his
hands![6] But because he didn't have a chance to run away he was
taken by them, and sent to Tanjung Pinang. His little brother
was sent to Thailand.

Thailand was a particularly odious destination, since it meant the
prospect of working on the construction of the Thailand-Burma
railway, sometimes known as the Death Railway in recognition of
the tens of thousands of labourers who died during its construction
(Hara 2004). Agus, a Malay who had been 21 when the Japanese
invaded his home island of Karimun, told me of his own narrow
escape:

> There was a man from the Japanese police who asked me how
> it would be if I went somewhere else. I was scared, so I said
> nothing. He said I had to choose between going to Riau — in
> those days, Tanjung Pinang was still known as 'Riau' — to work
> in the police force or being sent to Thailand. But I knew if I
> went to Thailand, it would be to build railways in the jungle,
> and there were lots of people who had died there and never
> came back. There are huge snakes in Thailand. They all died of
> snake bites or from other diseases.

Maznah elaborated on the ways Muhammad Yunus recruited healthy
young men to work as forced labourers. She explained that he came
to the small islands near Tanjung Pinang in a party of three, together
with another Malay called Pak Aziz, and a Japanese officer armed

---

[6] In Malay weddings, the bride and groom typically have their hands decorated
with geometric designs in henna.

with a gun. The Japanese officer was necessary, she explained, because without him nobody would have been in any way afraid of the two aristocrats. Nevertheless, it was the raja who was in charge; the Japanese soldier was following his orders, and he was controlling all negotiations:

> They took away my older brother, who was about 19 years old. He was tall, strong, his skin was very pale. He was very handsome. And he was taken away by that raja. I was already suffering trauma, so I wasn't thinking, and I followed them, crying, asking, 'Please! Please don't take my brother away! Please, Sir!' Finally, Muhammad Yunus turned around and gave me one Japanese dollar. After that, they all went away...
>
> Muhammad Yunus is a man who wanted to sell people (*menjual orang*), and he certainly sold the Malay people. We were all sold! And maybe someone like that, who sells people, could be happy in the Japanese era. But if you didn't sell people, it was extremely difficult. Meanwhile, he was eating delicious food, and we were eating sago and tubers!

Accusations that Penyengat aristocrats collaborated with the Japanese are corroborated by secondary sources. Lynette Silver and Tom Hall (2001: 149–59) record how a "Penegat [*sic*] headman" betrayed the location of several Australian soldiers in exchange for seventy dollars. Island Malays that had assisted the Australians then sought sanctuary on Penyengat, only to be handed over to the Tanjung Pinang torture room. Oral histories of wartime evacuees in the National Archives of Singapore also report "Malay chiefs" bringing Japanese soldiers to the houses of Chinese women, who were then raped. Such complicity led to the widespread resentment of certain Malay aristocrats amongst their "subject" populations.[7]

In 1946, after the Japanese had withdrawn, Raja Muhammad Yunus had tried to re-establish the Riau-Lingga sultanate as an entity that was "separate and distinct from Indonesia", with himself as ruler (Wee 2002: 5). The movement failed to garner popular support,

---

[7] Robinson (1995: 75) describes a similar situation in Bali: "Unless [elites] made clear efforts to protect their community from [Japanese] extractions ... they came to be viewed increasingly as agents of a predatory and brutal state. Yet they knew that if they failed to comply with the demands of the Japanese, they could easily be replaced, exiled, or worse".

and in 1950 Muhammad Yunus fled to Johor. For Tahir, the nub of this failure was that the ordinary people could remember what Muhammad Yunus had done under the Japanese and did not want him to rule them. "He was truly hated at the time of the occupation," underscored Agus, "For the ordinary people of the Riau Archipelago he is famous for being an evil man."

When I asked around more widely about these allegations, the questions invariably made my respondents very uncomfortable, but nobody suggested the information was false. Rather, most conceded that they had "once heard such a thing", but that it was "better not to discuss it". There are nevertheless several possible reasons for there to be such widespread silence over such a dramatic period in the archipelago's history. A lack of certainty about exactly what happened in the 1940s may have made some people uncomfortable about stating as "history" what they have only heard as rumours or *cerita*; one of my more candid middle-aged interviewees noted that although terrible things happened during the occupation, it was difficult to know who was forced into siding with the Japanese, and who actually volunteered. Equally, the fear of reprisal on the part of the aristocrats seems a plausible explanation for at least some of the informants I spoke to. In other cases, the painful or traumatic nature of the memories associated with this period may be enough to explain why it was rarely discussed. Yet it was clear from my interviews that the Japanese Occupation was still vividly remembered. This sheds a new light on the politicisation of the past, and what is at stake in debates over whether the aristocrats are "Malay" or "Bugis".

Rethinking the Bugis

Debates over aristocratic Malayness often hinge on whether one should give more weight to the identity that is inherited via lines of patrilineal descent, or that which is performed through adherence to cultural, linguistic or religious precepts. Yet other ways of thinking about identity might be relevant to the debate, as highlighted by recent anthropological work on the concept of monstrosity. Researchers working in Amazonia have highlighted how the performance of violent acts, such as exhibiting anger or committing a murder, aligns an individual with the "monstrous". As Luisa Belaunde elaborates, for the Airo-Pai of Peru:

'Anger' is not solely an emotional state, but a transformational force of key sociological and cosmological significance. It is synonymous with death and acts as an operator of radical alterity … An angry person quite simply is not a true person or a kinsman, but an enemy, a monster, a predator who fails to recognise his or her own kind and therefore treats them as though they were prey (2000: 209)

Similar ideas are expressed amongst the Chewong of Borneo, but in this case monstrosity is expressed not through idioms of predator and prey but rather through apparently "ethnic" classifications. To be "truly human" like the Chewong, one must reject anger. Anger's presence in the neighbouring communities of Malays and Chinese means that, for the Chewong, these groups are not truly human (Howell 1988). The categories of "Malay" and "Chinese" thus connote not only "ethnic" or "cultural" difference from the Chewong but also a more fundamental alterity flagged by their violent or angry behaviour. Building on Howell's analysis, I would suggest that the contemporary "ethnic" identity politics surrounding the history of the Riau Islands is fuelled, at least in part, by the monstrous alterities exposed in memories of the violent wartime past and their affective residues in everyday life.

The sultanate into which the Bugis warriors were incorporated in 1724, and to which their descendants continue to declare allegiance, operated on a different basis from the nation-states found in Southeast Asia today. Milner (1995: 24–5) warns that "we must be cautious even of using language which assumes the subject's distinct and separate identity … individual Malays were seen almost as portions rather than subjects of kingship". To kill the ruler would bring utter confusion to both community and individual: treason was "a type of psychological and spiritual suicide" looked on with "bewilderment". The corollary to this deep intertwining of ruler and polity was that the ruler was obliged to ensure the welfare of his subjects and never to treat them badly. Though able to prey upon those who became sufficiently rich as to be threatening, the Malay ruler was expected to protect his subjects, alleviate their suffering, make sure they could earn a living, and promote a situation in which they would be happy. Mutual pledges of loyalty to this effect were an important component of Malay political discourse, and are repeatedly noted in indigenous histories of Malay polities (Ho 2002: 17; Milner 1982: 23–4).

Such, at least, was the ideal-type Malay polity as propounded in elite texts, the functions of which are likely to have included buttressing the ruler's authority and mystifying the less romantic dimensions of ruler-subject relations (Walker 2004). Regardless of the extent to which the model reflects the historical experience of Malay subjects, it has survived into present times as a template of what a Malay polity ought to be for Riau Islanders: not just a state but an ethical and moral sphere based on the co-dependence of ruler and subject. Moreover, since the precondition of being a Malay was incorporation into such a polity, observance of these principles was a fundamental element of what it meant to be Malay.

A figure such as Raja Haji Fisabilillah, at least as he is popularly remembered, would thus appear to have been a good Malay. By shrewdly administering trade, fostering prosperity and defending his subjects against Dutch incursions with military insight, he epitomises the glorious Malay ruler so well that his Bugis ancestry is irrelevant. This is doubtless one reason why he has become such a romanticised and widely celebrated figure in recent times. Rulers who violate these norms and obligations, however, fall outside the realm of being truly Malay and into the realm of the "monstrous",[8] no longer to be respected or revered (Milner 1995; Schulte Nordholt 1996: 100–10).

Such reasoning would also apply to the Penyengat rajas following their alleged collaborations during the Japanese Occupation. Though they themselves describe their actions as working in the interests of "Malayness" by restoring an indigenous polity through channelling Japanese support, arms and military expertise (Wee 2002), this came at a heavy price: their complicity in wartime atrocities, the brutalisation of Riau Islanders and the forced consignment of Malay labourers to mainland Southeast Asia. By travelling from island to island in search of young men to hand over to the Japanese occupiers, Muhammad Yunus and his entourage enacted their sovereignty over the archipelago to both themselves and the Japanese, yet they had dissociated themselves from the very principles that were

---

[8] This "monstrosity" might be expressed through accusations that a ruler is *jahat* (evil; wicked), *kejam* (cruel), *sadis* (sadistic) or *horor* (horrific; "a horror"). It can also manifest in the hatred and disdain with which a ruler is spoken of, as when Maznah disparaged Muhammad Yunus as "a man who wanted to sell people".

supposed to underpin Malay sovereignty. This is seen perhaps most poignantly in Silver and Hall's (2001) accounts of fishermen who, falling foul of Japanese ire, sought sanctuary with the Penyengat rajas only to be handed over to torturers.

To call this "monstrous" behaviour takes no account of the ways in which the aristocrats might have been manipulated or coerced by the Japanese. Yet these were not considered mitigating circumstances by those Riau Islanders who did eventually speak to me about the war. Instead they saw the aristocrats as having dissociated themselves from the Malay society they were supposed to represent and defend. They had shown themselves to be outside a moral system by "selling" their subjects for their own self-interest, whether that be comfort, status or simply survival, and by perpetrating arbitrary violence against them. Moreover, by living in grand colonial buildings and eating rice, they were perceived to have differentiated themselves from a population suffering from extreme hardship. This revelation of immorality, violence and the lack of concern for ordinary Malays now placed the aristocrats outside the ethical system of the Malay polity. Hope and moral leadership instead came from figures located in the region's deep past. Many islanders, for instance, prayed at the grave of Wan Seri Beni, who had ruled as queen of Bintan prior to the founding of Malacca, in the hope that their children might return from Thailand and Burma unharmed (Massot and Kalus 2012: 45). Not coincidentally, it is precisely such figures as Wan Seri Beni that contemporary activists feel would be more appropriate foci of local history than aristocrats of "Bugis" extraction.

In the contemporary period, when the intricacies of betrayal, collaboration, and disillusionment are still difficult and even dangerous to talk about, these concerns with wickedness, monstrous alterity and historical injustice find at least partial expression in the ethnicised language of "being Bugis". Claims of aristocrats being "non-Malay" — at a time when the Riau Islands Province's identity is increasingly premised upon ethnonationalist Malay rhetoric — marks their difference, distance and alterity. The alleged predatory actions of 20th-century aristocrats even came to influence claims about the more distant past. Thus Riau Islanders such as Maznah and Tahir did not see Raja Haji Fisabilillah as an exemplary Malay ruler but as an extractive and exploitative "Bugis coloniser", his reputation tainted by the way they viewed and related to his descendants.

The Riau Islanders to whom I have referred in this chapter were not driven by regional or ethnic chauvinism, let alone a stubborn conviction that the sultan should outrank the viceroy, belief that Malayness inheres in biology and descent, or xenophobia against Bugis per se. Maznah and Tahir, for example, were very affectionate towards the Bugis man who had married their youngest daughter. Rather, I suggest, they felt compelled to disparage the aristocrats as "Bugis" because of painful periods in their own life histories. They felt that wartime events had stripped Penyengat aristocrats of the right to represent or speak authoritatively on behalf of the Malays that they had betrayed. When these same rajas then presented themselves as "Malay", earning privileges and status as a result, a further injustice was being perpetrated. This is not to say that chauvinism and factionalism do not have a place in the identity politics of the Riau Archipelago. They do. But there can be more to life in the islands than the chauvinistic or opportunistic seeking of advantage: passions for justice, long-standing grievances and thirsts for revenge. These desires and feelings have burnt into the psyches of Riau Islanders whose lives and families were shattered during the war, explaining the passion and ardour with which they fight to advocate their own understandings of Malayness and Malay history, and to keep Bugis elements out.

History, then, is not only dangerous to tell. It has also created a special danger for the new province: a seemingly irresolvable conflict between two categories of "Malays" that throws the question of what "Malayness" is open to public scrutiny. For as long as the Riau Islands remain a "Malay" province over which the aristocrats maintain their influence, the category of "Malayness" will remain bitterly contested and thus a precarious and unsettling basis on which any Riau Islander might advance claims of citizenship and belonging.

4

Marketplaces

"Malays are not very good at commerce."

This myth was subscribed to by virtually everyone I met in the Riau Islands. Malays themselves attested to it and non-Malays were quick to use it to underscore their own contributions to the economy. From a historical perspective, such a pronouncement is certainly surprising — as the cosmopolitan trading class of many of Southeast Asia's major port cities had, historically, always been classified as Malay (Reid 1988b: 7). Moreover, given that one of the justifications for Riau Islands Province was to restore status and dignity to the region's hitherto marginalised Malays, it also raised a set of political conundrums. Should the Riau Archipelago's Malays be the beneficiaries of affirmative action policies such as those implemented under Malaysia's New Economic Policy? Were government attempts to foster a business mindset among young Malays effective or a waste of money? Could Malays ever be trained to succeed as entrepreneurs or should the state just offer subsidies to alleviate their poverty? These were questions that elicited vigorous and often vitriolic debate.

Malays' supposed "economic problem" pushed at the limits of integrationist models of Malayness by articulating a fundamental cultural difference between Malays and others, doing so in ways that gave little incentive to be assimilated into "Malayness". Yet the multiculturalist alternative was rife with competing claims of whose interests should be prioritised by the new provincial administration. Malays felt embittered that immigrant groups had assumed economic dominance. Non-Malays felt that they deserved extra rights and recognition for their hard work: faced with the prospect of discriminatory measures being taken against them, they felt unappreciated and aggrieved. Malays' apparent difficulty with commerce thus lay at the heart of a situation that led to many Riau Islanders, both Malay and non-Malay, feeling "out of place" in their province.

My interlocutors often said they hoped my anthropological study would either inform, or better still resolve, the question of who should be prioritised for government assistance. Some hoped that I would be able to identify an effective way to help the Malays learn how to be better at business. Others were convinced my research would confirm that Malay values were fundamentally incompatible with capitalism. What nobody expected me to discover was that Malays were actually thriving as traders and entrepreneurs.

Whilst living in Tanjung Pinang, I encountered scores of Malay businesses which appeared to be extremely successful. Their owners worked hard and their businesses enjoyed good turnover and profit margins. This was not an idiosyncratic finding. Wee (1988: 205–6) also recorded a strong trading ethic amongst Riau Malays during her fieldwork in the 1970s, noting that they regularly traded goods in Singapore, Jambi and Tanjung Pinang, using "just about any means available to keep their petty entrepreneurship going".

Yet any attempt I made to suggest that Malays could be commercially successful was met with disbelief or even angry denial. Several people dismissed my evidence as "impossible". One woman went so far as to warn me that if I wrote such a thing in my PhD thesis I would certainly fail because "everyone knows" that Malays are inept when it comes to commerce. Perhaps the angriest response came from a 15-year-old Malay schoolgirl whom I met at a seminar dedicated to "improving the Malay work ethic":

> Look Nick, maybe a few Malays have a government job or a business, but you just have to look at the marketplace (*pasar*) in this town. Where are the Malays? There are shops there and they are all run by Minangkabau, or Javanese, or Chinese, no Malays at all. That is a fact. I know there are some Javanese and others who also lack a work ethic but if you look at the reality, that is a fact and it's a big problem. You say you are here as a researcher — you must have seen this in your research!

In light of such remarks, the phenomenon that requires explanation is not the economic marginalisation of Malays but why it is taken as a fact despite seemingly compelling evidence to the contrary. There are two dimensions to my argument. First, the ambiguities and slipperiness of Malay identity conspire to generate a widely shared cultural memory of the 20th century in which the economic marginalisation of Malays is both overstated and rendered inexplicable in any terms other than those of cultural difference. Second, given that local parameters of success emphasise the location and spatiality of trade, I will suggest that Malays' commercial activity goes unnoticed — or is undervalued — because of *where* it occurs. Consequently, a myth of Malay inadequacy that was first propounded in colonial times has not only been maintained but actually exaggerated in ways that affect Riau Islanders of all walks of life.

Locating Success

In Tanjung Pinang, the spatiality of commercial activity plays a central role in determining how "successful" it is considered to be. Residents of the town often exhorted me to "look at the marketplace" as evidence that Malays had difficulties with trading. The Indonesian term employed was *pasar*, which can refer to both "the market" (an abstract noun characterised by trading, in its broadest sense, as a form of labour) and "the marketplace" itself, which in Tanjung Pinang refers to the district surrounding the harbour and docks, this being the most concentrated location of shops, pitches and itinerant stalls in the whole town. At the time I presumed that the alleged absence of Malays in the marketplace was being offered as an example of the more general problem identified by my interlocutors, namely that Malays lacked the right skills, values, or attitudes to succeed in business. Retrospectively, it became clear to me that the marketplace was serving as more than just an illustration. The absence of Malays from the central marketplace was what defined them as unsuccessful.[1]

I often asked informants why it was better to have a business in the marketplace than in other parts of the town. For Malays, the answer was usually framed historically. "Because long ago, the marketplace was all Malays — Malays together with Chinese," explained Fatimah, "But now it has become Chinese and Minang! And those

---

[1] This emphasis on location stands in contrast to Alexander's (1998) characterisation of the Javanese "*pasar* system", which is defined only by a particular type of labour, and could take place anywhere.

wicked (*jahat*) Minang have only been here since the 1960s!" Malays trading in the marketplace would thus be reclaiming what was once theirs, showing they were able to compete with the migrants who were striving to oppress and exclude them.

The prominence of the central marketplace also reflects Sumatran attitudes to urban space, challenging the Javanist bias that underlies many accounts of Indonesian cities. A case in point is Peter Nas and Welmoet Boender's (2002: 12) theory of "focal urbanism", according to which urban space is arranged around the court and palace within which a potent ruler resides as symbolic fulcrum of the universe. Potency, in this characterisation, is obtained through intense asceticism and detachment from material concerns, a pre-occupation with the spiritual over the mundane (Keeler 1987). Con-sequently, the marketplace, a site of commercial bustle and unrefined haggling, has been considered inherently problematic, a "self-contained universe" outside the values of both gentry and peasantry (Geertz 1963: 43–4). Similar characterisations of commerce have been reported in many parts of the contemporary Malay World.[2] However, conducting research in the West Sumatran city of Padang, Hans-Dieter Evers and Rüdiger Korff found that:

> Sketch maps drawn by informants invariably focus on the market.[3] All other quarters, places or buildings are depicted in relation to the main *pasar*. The market rather than the governor's office is the 'exemplary centre' on which attention is focused...
>
> The town square and the town hall also occupy the geo-graphical centre of town, but they are culturally not defined as central, except in official documents. The central market is the structural core of the town, [even though its] physical location shifts with urban development (2000: 123–4).

Although Evers and Korff (2000: 124) suggest that the market is so prominent because its "throng creates a feeling of community, close-ness and belonging that symbolises Indonesian city life", my infor-mants were rather more disposed to emphasise its modernity and its prestige. Thus one Minangkabau shopkeeper told me that:

---

[2] See for example the accounts offered by Banks (1983: 119), Brenner (1998: 29), Carsten (1989: 117), Peletz (1998: 182–3) and Wilder (1982: 112).

[3] In Bali and Java, sketch maps focused on courts and palaces (Nas and Sluis 2002).

In Sumatra, the palace (*istana*) is nothing special — unlike in Java ... The only people who are interested in palaces are the aristocrats themselves. Here in Sumatra it is the marketplace that is special and that is where people want to be. In my opinion, it's because of how television promotes modernity. Indonesians watch television without a filter. We see all the central business districts and malls in the films and think it's great, and what we want to be like. The marketplace is the area most like that, most modern, so it's a good place to be in.

Another Minangkabau shopkeeper suggested that "as you move away from the marketplace, the area is seen as less and less modern, and more like a village. People are ashamed to say that they live in those kinds of outlying areas, let alone work there." But if the "modern" materiality of the marketplace helped make it attractive, then so did the modernity of the activity that was carried out there. In their ruminations upon development, informants often unfavourably contrasted Brunei — which they imagined to be "a high rise city with many computers" — with cities such as Singapore and Hong Kong. "Brunei is rich," explained Syamsuddin, a Malay coffee shop owner, "but not modern. Brunei would always have been a comfortable city because it has oil. Singapore is truly developed (*maju*) because it has no resources and yet has become wealthy through commerce and trade. If people want to trade anything, or if they want to go shopping, they go to Singapore, not Brunei!"

Such contrasts reflect a distinction between modernity and wealth. Although the former was hoped to generate the latter, it was the means by which it did so that mattered when evaluating "development". "Modernity", for my informants, meant distinction in innovation, creative thinking and entrepreneurship. The wealth that modernity brought was wealth generated through the labour of exchange, creating value through human endeavour. This stood in sharp contrast to wealth produced by the "backward" labour of exploiting primary resources, whether those be the fish surrounding a Malay coastal village or the oil fields in Brunei. Trading on all scales was therefore a hallmark of modernity and success.

These ideas featured prominently in government rhetoric and in educational programmes. At seminars and assemblies for school students, bureaucrats from the Departments of Education and Culture exhorted the youth of the Riau Islands to follow the examples of the 18th-century spice merchants that once frequented Bintan Island and make a name for themselves in commerce. One such seminar, dedicated to fostering a strong work ethic, saw the keynote speaker insisting that "since Malays had once been merchants it is no good letting them think that the civil service is an acceptable profession" and receiving a spontaneous burst of applause from all the students present. Such a viewpoint was widespread. Raja Jaffar, a businessman from Penyengat, explained its basis as follows:

> The civil service is bad for Malays because it is a very lazy place to be. Malays go straight to their office and they sit there and do very little. Perhaps they make plans for their policies but they can't do anything without money, and they have no idea how to raise funds for themselves, so they just take money from the government. It doesn't promote a good way of living.

Business and economics — epitomised by the flow of money — are here seen as the route to better citizenship and better life. The marketplace, as a hub of such activities, was thus an extremely desirable and prestigious place in which to operate a business, especially since it was also known to be a competitive environment in which only the most successful businesses could survive.[4]

The absence of Malay traders from the marketplace thus became a compelling indicator of their backwardness and marginalisation. Even at the smallest scale — such as selling simple snacks at night in the Melayu Square foodcourt — not a single Malay could be counted amongst the vendors (*Dëtik Kepri* 2006). This inflamed passions but also begged for explanation, prompting Riau Islanders to develop their own elaborate sociological and historical explanations for why Malays had either been unable to break into the marketplace or had found themselves driven out.

Historical Accounts of Malay Marginalisation

Marketplace histories that circulate in Tanjung Pinang invoke a "golden age" of commerce, in which Riau Island Malays were world

---

[4] "Competitiveness" itself is often cited by Riau Islanders as a desirable characteristic of modernity.

famous for their trading (Sumanti Ardi 2002: 4; Suwardi 2002: 62–5). The claim that large numbers of Malays were subsequently expelled from the marketplace by Chinese, Minangkabau and other traders over the course of the 20th century is widely deployed as "evidence" that contemporary Riau Island Malays have become bad at commerce. However, as I shall argue, a closer examination of the historical material suggests a rather different account for the dramatic shift in marketplace demographics that the region witnessed in the 1950s and 1960s.

It remains an open question as to how active in trading "Riau Malays" ever really were: although the Riau polity prospered from its free port, Jeyamalar Kathirithamby-Wells (1993: 140–1) argues that the region lacked "an indigenous class of merchants and long-distance shippers comparable to that which developed ... in Surat, Bengal, and the Coromandel", and that it was foreign entrepreneurs that held "a distinct advantage". Yet as Reid (1988b: 7) notes, such individuals may nevertheless have been classified as "Malay" on the basis of a secure command of the Malay language and an Islamic faith. They are certainly remembered as such by Riau Islanders today.

According to the dominant narrative in the Riau Islands, the first blow to the Malay trading spirit came with Dutch colonialism. In the islands, as elsewhere in Southeast Asia, colonial officials bemoaned the "lazy" character of the indigenous Southeast Asians, who seemed to be markedly lacking in motivation and work ethic, especially in comparison to the industrious immigrant populations of Chinese and Tamil that lived alongside them. Yet over the past three decades, postcolonial scholars have emphasised that this "laziness" was not an innate attribute but a response to colonial rule. One of the most influential analyses is that offered by Alatas, who suggested that "indolence" on the part of autochthonous Southeast Asians should be read as a silent protest against the "slave labour" of colonial coolie capitalism (1977: 70, 80). Sumatran historians of Mainland and Insular Riau (e.g. Isjoni Ishaq 2002a; Suwardi 2002) take a different tack, suggesting that Malay reluctance to be involved in coolie labour was a sign that their pride (*marwah*) had already been crushed through the indignity of conquest. The Dutch had allegedly excluded Riau Malays from powerful positions in government and business "because if Malays were given opportunities, the Dutch government would feel scared and undermined" (Tarigan *et al.* 1996:

73). Since military resistance was impossible, "Malays 'sulked', withdrew themselves, and became passive and apathetic" (Isjoni Ishaq 2002a: 53). This disposition then became engrained into the Malay character across generations, giving them an "unmotivated" outlook (Isjoni Ishaq 2002b: 55). The result was that in the 1950s, when migrants began to arrive in the Riau Islands from other parts of Indonesia, the Malays trading in the marketplace were, in Fatimah's words, "easily tricked out of their land and their jobs" and "so stupid that they let it happen".

This narrative is a powerful one in Tanjung Pinang, and the cornerstone of efforts to inspire youngsters to become commercially successful like the Riau Island Malays of yore (Suwardi 2002: 66). It is, however, highly problematic when compared with the available historical evidence. Certainly the Riau Archipelago was once world-famous as an entrepôt, but as noted earlier, its traders were principally itinerant merchants rather than local Malays (Bassett 1989). This was with good cause — any wealthy local trader could become a dangerous rival to the polity's ruler, and thus success in trade needed to be discouraged (Milner 1982). Riau Malay subjects were instead provided for by the ruler via the distribution of import and export duties charged to traders using the port.

The high colonial period saw a stagnation of trade and industry in the Riau Islands, although once again the role of Malays was far from clear-cut. When Tanjung Pinang was first established as the commercial centre of the Riau Archipelago, it was almost exclusively Chinese (Trocki 1979). Chinese economic predominance continued well into the 19th century, leading Resident Netscher to worry in his 1863 Political Report that this was preventing the few Malays that lived in the town from establishing a foothold (Putten 2001: 178). Yet the Chinese are *not* painted as the villains in contemporary accounts of Malay marginalisation. Responsibility for the ousting of Malays from the marketplace is placed squarely with the Minangkabau and other Indonesian migrants who moved to Riau during the 1950s and 1960s.

So if Chinese monopolised the colonial marketplace, then where were the Malays who were supposedly ousted in the 1960s? Bakri, who grew up in Tanjung Pinang during the 1930s, told me there were never any Malays trading in the marketplace while he was a boy. "Malays lived in villages on the edge of the town and came in with coconuts and pineapples," he explained. "Then they bartered the fruit for rice and other foodstuffs with Chinese and Keling shopkeepers." Likewise, Maznah emphasised the absence of Malays when she first arrived in Tanjung Pinang from the island of Galang in 1948:

> I remember there were many Chinese, and also many Kelings. You couldn't see any Malays. I remember asking, 'Where are all the people like us? These aren't our people here — they're all Kelings!' There were really very few Malays indeed until the 1960s.

It is therefore tempting to conclude that the "marginalised Malays" of popular discourse are largely imaginary: traders posited to have existed because Tanjung Pinang is Malay land (*tanah Melayu*) and therefore must have been "full of Malays" but also posited to have been marginalised because Malays are not visible in the marketplace today. To an extent, this may hold true, but matters are not quite so simple, nor are Riau Islanders so easily misled. Bakri and Maznah's comments point towards a trading population entirely missing from popular discourse and published histories of the Riau Islands, as well as from Tanjung Pinang today. It is through their story that one might best explain how and why the conviction that Malays had been excluded from the marketplace remains so entrenched.

The Vanishing Keling

"Keling" (*orang Keling*) is a term used across the Malay World to describe individuals of South Asian descent, who have traded and lived in Sumatra and the Malay Peninsula since at least the second century CE (Dhoraisingam 2006: 2). Tanjung Pinang's Kelings were predominantly male Muslims from Bengal, Coromandel and Malabar who came to Bintan during the 19th and 20th centuries in order to establish commercial premises where they sold Indian sari-style cloth, spices, or cooked food.[5] Some migrated directly to Tanjung Pinang.

---

[5] Informants also recounted Hindu "Keling" labourers recruited by the Dutch to work on construction projects, although these seem to have been fewer in number.

Others came via Malaya and the Straits Settlements; having moved to the British colonies to assist in kin-based retail firms, they saw Dutch territories as a promising new market in which they could set up their own store.

Though census records suggest it was numerically small,[6] the Keling population appears to have played a substantial role in both the marketplace economy and the wider township from the 19th century through to the 1960s, although records of Keling activity remain sparse. Even though official histories play down the presence of Kelings in the region, there is general agreement amongst everyone in Tanjung Pinang that the town's very first mosque was entirely funded by Indian merchants living in the town and was therefore known as the Keling Mosque (Mesjid Keling). In 1864, H.C. Klinkert, a Dutch Bible translator living in Tanjung Pinang, wrote home to his Bible Society complaining of the disturbances caused by "drum beating Bengalis performing their dances" outside his lodgings in the centre of town (Putten 2001: 51), thereby attesting to a vibrant Keling presence in the marketplace by the middle of the 19th century. My own ethnohistorical research suggests that Keling coffee parlours remained popular well into the 20th century. Many informants recalled with particular fondness their memories of after-school trips to the *Gelanggang Klenteng*, a large covered bazaar in the centre of the marketplace which was full of Keling-run stalls selling snacks and ice cream (Figure 4.1). More generally, the repeated claim by my older interviewees that the marketplace had been "full of Kelings" during the 1940s and early 1950s confirms that they were a significant and highly visible trading minority.

At least some Kelings maintained a strong sense of their identity as Indians during this period. In a description of Tanjung Pinang's 1953 National Independence Day celebrations written for his school magazine, M.S. Siau (1953: 160) notes that "it seemed to be the happiest day for [*sic*] the whole year here ... Indonesian, Chinese and *Indian flags* were waving all over the street" (my emphasis). Yet "Keling" was also a category of some ambiguity, used to denote

---

[6] The 1852 census records 94 Kelings, the 1930 census records 74 (Ng 1976: 20), and a 1950 census records 314 (Anon. 1957). The basis of categorisation in all these censuses is extremely unclear, and many Kelings may have been classified as "Malays" in census records (see below).

Figure 4.1 The Gelanggang Klenteng in 1956 (Source: Ikatan Alumni Toan Hoon)

both Indians and their mixed-race descendants. Kelings arriving in the Riau Archipelago during the 19th and 20th centuries were predominantly male Muslim migrants. Having settled in the islands, they married local women of the same religion as themselves, the overwhelming majority of whom were Malays. The Keling population living in Tanjung Pinang would therefore have been predominantly composed of individuals with a mixture of Malay and Indian ancestry.

Research in Malaysia, where "Keling" carries a similar dual meaning, has highlighted how this situation creates both ambiguities and strategic opportunities for Kelings regarding both their "Indianness" and their "Malayness". Halimah Mohd Said and Zainab Abdul Majid describe the Keling as someone who is "a Malay and yet not ... a Malay" (2004: 42), while Nagata argues that the physical similarities between Kelings and Malays in Georgetown allow the situational and strategic performance of ethnicity. The Keling, she writes, "seems to partake of two ethnic worlds" (1974: 336). Indeed, the ambiguous nature of the Keling came through very strongly in life history interviews, as in the instance cited above, when Maznah described her realisation that the figures she had seen in the Tanjung Pinang marketplace (whom she had presumed to be dark-skinned Malays) were not "her people" but "all Kelings".

Such ambiguity also raises the possibility that the "Malays" who are remembered as being marginalised from the marketplace were in fact Kelings. This contention seem even more probable given that the 1960s — a period associated with the "ousting of Malays from the marketplace" — saw the disappearance of virtually all Keling businesses in the Riau Islands and the concomitant establishment of Sumatran migrants as a formidable trading force. But why did this happen and why has it been remembered as having happened to "Malays"?

The post-independence years saw the sudden disappearance of South Asian communities across Indonesia (Bachtiar 1993: 137). One of the most important reasons for this was the growth of anti-Indian sentiment on a national scale. To some extent this reflected broader geopolitical concerns. B.D. Arora (1982: 123) explains that relations between Indonesians and Indians deteriorated across Java and Sumatra as the latter "fell victim to the wrath of the pro-Chinese and pro-Pakistan elements represented in the PKI [Indonesian Communist Party], NU [Nahdlatul Ulama, a major Islamic organisation], and other Muslim parties and groups". In Tanjung Pinang, anti-Indian feelings became most evident during 1960 and 1961, when several Keling storekeepers were murdered on suspicion of being British spies (Hasan Junus n.d.). In this case, the Indian dimension of Keling identity appears to have carried unpalatable associations with the British authorities in Malaya, with whom Indonesia's relations were rapidly deteriorating.

At a domestic level, the strong economic role played by Indians clashed with the nationalist desire to see native-born Indonesians flourishing in the market. Indians were castigated as "exploiters of Indonesian wealth ... no better than the Chinese" (Arora 1982: 122–3), and were subject to new government restrictions imposed on "resident aliens". These measures — usually understood as attempts to curb the economic dominance of the Chinese — included a head tax imposed in 1957, and a retail ban in rural areas two years later (Coppel 1983: 37; Purdey 2006: 12). Although authorities in the Riau Islands (principally the navy) were lax in imposing anti-alien regulations (Mackie 1976: 96–7), informants who had lived in Tanjung Pinang during the 1950s told me that the hostile political

climate led many Indians to fear that the worst was yet to come,
causing them to leave while they still had the opportunity.[7]

By the 1960s, living as an Indian had become unappealing and
untenable in both Tanjung Pinang and Indonesia as a whole. Even
today, Indian descent carries a stigma and many "Malays" I met
revealed their Keling ancestry with hesitation and shame. Tanjung
Pinang's Kelings found themselves being reframed as Indians, resident
aliens and as unwelcome outsiders. By contrast, other nations in
the region offered much less problematic opportunities to exist as
a Malay-Indian hybrid (*peranakan*). As one man of Indian descent
explained, "compared with staying here, Singapore and Malaysia, or
even going home to India, were appealing options." Those Kelings
who did stay took all opportunities to play down their Indianness
and redefined themselves as Malay.

The 1950s and 1960s brought other difficulties for Keling
businessmen. Drawn by the prospect of a market buoyed by the
Singapore dollar, Minangkabau and Batak migrants were beginning
to arrive in Tanjung Pinang as cloth traders. These migrants brought
new competition but also formed a new consumer base with its own
distinct tastes in textiles, which Keling retailers struggled to satisfy.
Luqman, a Minangkabau who had migrated to Tanjung Pinang in
1957, told me what he remembered of his Keling rivals during his
first few years in business:

> There were a lot of Kelings once, but they were not competitive
> enough to stay in business. Like the Malays, they found other
> ethnic groups were more advanced (*maju*). The Kelings sold only
> Indian cloth and sari-style dresses. It was too narrow a market.
> They couldn't compete with what the Chinese and Minang
> traders could offer, especially the Chinese. They had links to
> Singapore and China so could bring in all sorts of fashionable
> clothes, and often bring in very cheap clothes from Thailand.
> Minang traders also started trading in these kinds of clothes.
> That was what everyone wanted to buy, not sari-style dresses, so
> the Kelings quickly went out of business.

---

[7] Since these informants were mostly Chinese, it is possible they were projecting
their own sense of political disenfranchisement, of which the 1959 retail ban is a
prominent symbol, onto the Kelings.

Food retailers experienced similar difficulties. Sumatran migrants did not like Indian food and were quick to open rival food stalls. Matters were made worse in 1959 when the municipal authorities knocked down the *Gelanggang Klenteng* and replaced it with a flower park, thereby physically destroying many Keling trading stalls.

Although Luqman painted the Keling failure to adapt as a problem with their own backwardness, they also faced structural difficulties. Heavily reliant on trade networks with Malayan and Singaporean Indians for access to goods, they found their principal source of supplies severed by the Confrontation. While many traders suffered during the period of Confrontation between Indonesia and Malaysia (1963–66), Kelings were affected especially badly. Local historian Burman told me that this partly reflected a historic disparity in trading strength. "The Indians were never as strong as the Chinese," he commented, "because the Chinese were very rich. Not all of them, most were very poor, but there were also lots who came here as political exiles (*perlari*) from mainland China and they had a lot of wealth and a lot of connections". Such connections proved crucial during Confrontation. Some Chinese businessmen were able to draw on kinship and ethnic networks with Chinese elsewhere (principally Hong Kong) to ensure a steady supply of commodities. Others went bankrupt, and were replaced by a new category of Chinese trader known, for reasons that remain obscure, as "*ang-pai*" ("red badges"). At once adventurers, smugglers and businessmen, these *ang-pai* ensured access to goods by paying local military officials to let them cross the otherwise impassable "war front" (Ng 1976: 51). Minang and Batak traders worked through ethnic smuggling syndicates that had been established during the colonial period (Ng 1976: 62; Tagliacozzo 2005). Though they remembered this period as one of constant fear of capture and shame at their crimes, they nevertheless managed to stay in business. Keling traders had no easy access to networks of this kind, while buying smuggled goods from others inflated their prices to an excessive degree. They found themselves faced with two options: bankruptcy or departure.

The Keling exodus vacated the northern area of the marketplace where they had once been dominant. "The Chinese became much more dominant after the Indians left," Burman explained, pointing to the fact that many vacant premises were swiftly occupied by Chinese businesses. Others were taken up by Minangkabau migrants, who have retained a concentration of businesses in the area to this day, largely owing to a "migration ideology" inculcated in young Minangkabau, that "when migrating, Minangkabau must be united". This has led to recruitment practices that discriminate strongly in favour of kin, individuals originating from the same region of West Sumatra, and other ethnic Minangkabau. Kelings, meanwhile, either left or retreated to residential areas, where they became accustomed to identifying and presenting themselves as Malay. Ironically, even though the reasons for their departure were linked to the Indian dimensions of their identity, they were remembered as a group who had been outcompeted because of their passive and uncompetitive character — as Malays.

With Minangkabau and Chinese firmly established in the marketplace, and both groups displaying a tendency to keep businesses in the family, it is not surprising that later Malay migrants to Tanjung Pinang struggled to establish premises in high-premium market locations and chose either to enter alternative professions or to conduct their commerce elsewhere. Indeed, re-reading the history of the marketplace through the history of the Kelings, one could take it as an injunction not to lament the inadequacy of Malays before 1960, but to celebrate their successes since. However, the discriminatory recruitment policies of Chinese and Minangkabau cannot in and of themselves account for why only a few Malay businesses managed to secure a location in the central marketplace, something my interlocutors in the Riau Islands would continue to cite as evidence that Malays are simply not very good at trading. In fact, I met some very successful Malay traders in the Riau Islands but their own constructions of economy and space led to their profitable businesses being either denigrated or rendered invisible.

Inadequacy Today

> **Javanese fishmonger:** I've seen what real Malays are like on Senayang Island. Those are Malays in their original environment, as fishermen, not as townsfolk. And it's true that they are very lazy (*malas*). If they have enough money for one day then they won't do any more fishing until it has run out. How will they ever advance?

For many of my informants, it was unthinkable that Malays might be good at trading. By holding this view, they were reinterpreting the stereotype of the "lazy Malay" as it had been developed by and British colonists (Alatas 1977), and subsequently reiterated in the thought and policies of Malaysia's fourth prime minister, Mahathir bin Mohamad (1970; 1986).[8] This stereotype used the term "Malay" as a generic reference to all autochthonous "Malayan races", but in the Riau Islands it was used exclusively for those who identified as members of the Malay ethnic group (*suku*), to the exclusion of Javanese, Minangkabau and others. While intellectuals and officials in the region desperately tried to argue that Riau Malays' indolent disposition was a consequence of colonial conquest, and so correctible given due diligence and motivation, the majority of the population saw the Malay problem as absolute and insurmountable. Echoing the framework adopted by both colonists and Mahathir, they couched their explanations in frameworks of climatic, ecological and physiological determinism. "It's not about the values Malays have, nor the way they think," one civil servant concluded, "it's about what they are."

For these people, "laziness" was the outcome of Malays having evolved in a marine environment, especially in a tropical climate characterised by such abundance that hard work was not required. It was widely believed that the Malay was, at heart, a fisherman — and fishermen were lazy. "Fishermen don't work hard," sniped one man, "they just throw the net then sit in their boat and smoke for two hours. Then they haul it in. How is that hard work if you compare it to a farmer? Lazy!" This idea did not go unchallenged: several other people whom I met were prepared to concede that the long hours and strenuous travails of fishing expeditions constituted "hard work". For these people, what made Malays lazy was not their lack of diligence but their predisposition against using it for capitalist accumulation. A primordial engagement with the material culture of fishing, which yields a product (fish) that can be used right away, had left contemporary Malays without the mental attributes needed

---

[8] Mahathir implemented a series of positive discrimination policies, arguing these were necessary to overcome the disadvantages Malays faced relative to the Chinese. Their indolence, low energy levels, and lack of motivation were foremost amongst these handicaps. After 20 years in office, he told reporters, "I am sad that I will have to leave without succeeding to change the culture of the Malays. For the Malays, working hard is a good value but in reality they do not. It is not because they can't but they don't want to" (Cheah 2002: 186).

to plan for the future. This was contrasted with workers in agrarian societies, who are used to having to wait before they can reap the fruits of their labours, or capitalists, who must develop long-term strategies to maximise profit.

When Malays attempt business, it is therefore expected that they will be held back by their "fisherman's presentism". Even Malays believed this. Amin, a self-described Malay "community leader" from the town of Kijang, spoke at great length about the ways Malay fishermen had been subordinated to the business interests of their Chinese bosses. "It's getting a bit better now," he added. "There are already some Malays who own their own boats. Maybe they are already more developed in their thinking than the Malays who just want to get enough money to be able to eat and drink well for the time being. But I also see that the Malays who are forward-thinking have names like Suryanto, meaning they have a little bit of Javanese blood in them. Suryanto might already own four boats. He thinks differently from a typical Malay. But if a Malay's name is Amat, Awang, Syamsuddin, and so forth [all traditional Malay names in the Riau Islands] — no chance."

The future-orientation of non-Malay ethnic groups, in other words, was thought to make them better at business. Yet even here, there were nuances. Many of my interlocutors asserted that, were a Javanese to become a fisherman, he would be hardworking and catch a surplus of fish. Perhaps he could even afford his own fleet of boats (as in Amin's example above). However, because a subsistence farming background did not equip him with strong trading skills, most of the catch would end up rotting. Only Chinese or Minangkabau, who had a "culture of business" would be able to dispose profitably of a large haul of fish. Framed in this way, it was hardly surprising that Malays would not be able to fight their way into a marketplace dominated by the Minangkabau and Chinese.

Although few contemporary anthropologists would subscribe to such explanations, many published analyses of Malay trading in other regions of Southeast Asia offer a subtler version of the same approach. The apparent shortage of Malay entrepreneurs is taken at face value, and the reasons for this located deep in Malay culture, such as the reluctance to ask relatives to work without wages (something that is common in Chinese businesses), or a squeamishness about making profits when selling to one's neighbours (Hefner 1998; Li 1989).

In contrast to these models, I suggest that in Tanjung Pinang, the problem that (some) Malays have with commerce is not with trading or capitalist rationality per se, but with its visibility and its emplacement in a central marketplace location. Indeed, many Malay traders chose to eschew the marketplace even though they knew it would be a higher-status place to trade. Often they did so because of the very features that were said by others to make it appealing: its centrality, its modernity and its bustling throng. By reflecting upon several such case studies, I will show how the multiple meanings of the marketplace influence trading strategies in ways that complicate any presumed relationship between Malayness and success in business.

Invisible Trade

Tahir and Maznah married in the 1950s and enjoyed a comfortable lifestyle during the period in which the Riau Islands still used the Malayan dollar. With a young family to support, the household economy was hit hard by the transition to the unstable rupiah in 1964. Hyperinflation left them out of pocket and in need of a new source of income. While Tahir continued to work in his office, Maznah turned to trading. "1964 was the most difficult time of all," she recalled, "How could we make a living? Even though I was pregnant, I was forced to sell coconuts and timber so my children could go to school!" Her next strategy of taking in a lodger backfired when he stole the family's jewellery and fled to Singapore.

Then Maznah hit upon an ingenious idea. She and a group of other Malay women began to purchase garments wholesale from Minangkabau traders, selling them in the nearby islands, such as Dendun and Galang. Garment trading proved lucrative. These islands had few or no clothing retail outlets and travelling to Tanjung Pinang was expensive, time-consuming and less convenient than purchasing clothes from a travelling vendor. The enterprise ran until the early 1980s, when her youngest daughter fell ill with a haemorrhaging sickness. Maznah then realised that she had too much work to do as a mother and housewife to allow her to continue trading in this way.

Amongst her family, Maznah spoke of her commercial achievements with pride. In public, however, the matter was not broached. In the wider urban society of Tanjung Pinang, she preferred to cultivate an identity based around her kinship connections as the wife of a civil servant and the daughter of a *batin* (village headman in the colonial period). She used these connections, as well as her expertise in local history, to garner respect in everyday interactions. Indeed, she urged me to draw upon these aspects of her identity when trying to establish whether my other informants knew her. "Ask them, 'do you know Ibu Maznah binti Abdullah, the historian, daughter of Batin Abdullah and wife of Tahir bin Osman?'" she instructed. "If they have met me they will definitely know who you mean."

Although this formulation was often successful, it met with blank stares on the very islands to which she had travelled to sell clothes during the 1970s. For example, despite having assured me that she travelled to Dendun "at least once a month", had "many friends there" and that "everyone over forty would remember her," when I went to this island and asked about her, nobody could identify the woman I was referring to. Maznah was very disappointed when she heard this, but soon discovered the problem. On these islands, she was not known as a family woman: she was known as a merchant. She had told them her name, but not that she was the daughter of a headman. They knew she had a husband, but not who he was or what he did. Their knowledge of Maznah the friendly garment trader would never have matched with the well-connected historian I was describing. Nor would Maznah the trader be known to any but her closest friends and family in Tanjung Pinang. She explained the paradox as follows:

> With Minangkabau, if they give you something, it's always because they want to get something back. You can see lots of them here in the marketplace … It's very different with Malays. Malays don't want to sell there [the market] because they will have bad luck and feel ashamed (*malu*).
>
> We [Malays] don't want people to think our husband is sitting around at home, or spending his wages irresponsibly, while his wife is selling in the marketplace. But that isn't a problem for Minangkabau. It's for that reason that there aren't any Malays selling in the marketplace: they're selling in the islands. There we won't be seen by people from the town, and the island people don't know us. Actually, we do make friends with them, but as a seller rather than as a wife.

Maznah's reasoning draws on an ideology of Malay marital roles in which the husband should "provide spiritual and material sustenance to his wife" who should in turn be "obedient and loyal" (*patuh*) and "respectfully receive what her husband gives her, however small, and endeavour to use it as fruitfully as possible" (Sasmita *et al.* 1996: 16–7). A wife's need to work, as evidenced by her labour, violates these norms, suggesting the woman is headstrong or, more usually, the man is incompetent or lazy (Novendra *et al.* 2000: 32). This pattern of gender relations is surprising given that women, including those from high-status families, have historically played a substantial economic role in societies across the Malay World, and continue to dominate in local markets in other parts of Indonesia (Koning *et al.* 2000; Reid 1988a). While Riau Islanders identified it as the "traditional Malay" system of organising a household (though not everyone acknowledged it as such), it seems likely that it was influenced by New Order visions of domesticity, which similarly "marked women as domestic denizens first, workers second" and associated being a housewife with the desirable status of being middle-class (Blackwood 2008: 18). Since Tahir worked as a civil servant, it may have been especially important for him and his wife to be seen to incorporate New Order values into their own ways of being Malay.

Maznah was not hampered at commerce by her Malayness. Indeed, the lucrative niche she identified was opened to her precisely because her life history as a Malay gave her knowledge of outlying islands and an affinity with their populations, in contrast to many Sumatran migrants who saw such locations as "backward", "primitive" and just the kinds of environment they had migrated to avoid. However, she felt that a wife "needing" to trade could be seen as a shameful indictment of her husband's conduct, so she restricted her social identity as a trader in order to protect his reputation. The social separation of islanders from urban society, coupled with the islands' geographic distance, worked to disguise Maznah's trading activities. Her story is not atypical. I met several Malay women who described having conducted similar itinerant trade for the same explicit reasons, that the throng in the marketplace exposed them to the eyes of all, and so could bring shame upon their husbands.

Nor was travel the only strategy used to conceal labour. In Kampung Jawa, my unemployed female neighbours all contributed to informal cake-making cooperatives: small groups of women who then either sold their cakes directly in the marketplace or to cafés, shops and other cake vendors. In either case, though Malays were active in making cakes, it was always a non-Malay member of the group (usually Javanese) who was selected to sell them. My Malay neighbours said they did not wish to embarrass their husbands by selling the cakes, while the men often confessed feelings of deep shame that their wives even had to be involved in the activity. The result of such a predicament is that the cake-making groups draw on the power of the commodity fetish to divorce the cake from the Malay labour that produced it. If the cake is associated with anyone, it is the hardworking Javanese seller, whose Malay neighbours are presumed to be idly sitting at home. Ironically, by carefully balancing their multiple roles so their husbands are not perceived as "lazy Malays", such women hide a substantial amount of Malay commerce from view, reinforcing the perception that Malays as an ethnic group are lazy and ill-suited to capitalist ventures.

For other Malays, the marketplace had further negative connotations that meant trading from their neighbourhoods became the wisest choice within their own attempts to live a "modern" capitalist lifestyle.[9] Syamsuddin, a middle-aged Malay from the Mainland Riau town of Dumai, migrated to Tanjung Pinang in the early 1990s. He first worked in a local hotel, but resigned after a disagreement with his manager. He then endured a long spell of unemployment, during which he scraped a living as a motorcycle taxi driver. Frustrated by this lifestyle and its poor earnings, he decided to open his own business. He tried farming catfish; the profits were too low to support his family. Next, he sold free-range chickens (*ayam kampung*), sourced from the surrounding islands. His eyes lit up as he remembered his profit margins. Soon, however, the demand for the chickens outstripped his capacity to supply them. Sourcing enough birds to fulfil big orders became a constant source of stress. He decided to start again, opening a coffee shop selling drinks and light snacks in the Sungei Jang Housing Estate where he lived. He bought some aluminium tables and chairs and converted the front yard of his house into a dining area. Food was prepared in a small garage-like structure to the side of the house, keeping Syamsuddin in full view of his customers and allowing for lively exchanges with them. Custom was quieter than the bustling restaurants and coffee shops of the town centre, yet Syamsuddin estimated he was making a

---

[9] Cf. Singaporean Malays, who specifically avoid trading in their home communities (Li 1989).

reasonable profit of 1.5 million rupiah each month, equivalent to the salary of a junior civil servant.

One year into his business, Syamsuddin began to consider opening premises in the marketplace, but the rental overheads for a marketplace outlet were a source of concern. Small coffee shops in the marketplace cost at least 15 million rupiah per year. By contrast, his current premises cost him nothing and therefore seemed a less risky option. Even if the centrally located coffee shop were busy enough to offset this figure, it would require the constant serving of customers. By comparison, the slow trade in his suburban outlet had distinct advantages.

Civil servants often take "coffee breaks" shortly after arriving at work. These breaks, often denigrated as typical civil service indolence, offer a forum in which new policy ideas and collaborations are explored; "coffee shop politics" has been an informal domain of administration since at least the 1960s (Hasan Junus 2002: 34–9). With many government offices located in the Sungei Jang area, Syamsuddin's coffee shop offered a convenient location for such meetings. Moreover, civil servants argued that the quiet, secluded "neighbourhood" feel of the front yard setting offered advantages over crowded locations in the middle of town, allowing complicated matters to be discussed in detail and relative privacy. Although the suburbs lack the hum of commerce and modernity associated with the marketplace, and are therefore a less prestigious place to trade, sometimes it is also this tranquillity that attracts custom. Through operating in a seemingly less competitive location, Syamsuddin's coffee shop soon developed a competitive advantage over his rivals in the marketplace.

An active member of the Islamic PKS (Partai Keadilan Sejahtera, Prosperous Justice Party), Syamsuddin found his suburban business allowed him to pursue a broad range of interests even when he was working. Although neighbours dropping in for a convenient snack usually occupied tables in the garden for private conversations, those visiting for "coffee shop politics" chose the tables next to Syamsuddin's kitchen, allowing him to converse with them whilst preparing food. This allowed him simultaneously to generate profits through trade and to play an active role in local decision-making, from sharing his opinions on how to raise the standards at the local Islamic Institute of Higher Education to helping draw up budgets on proposals for cultural performances. Doing so forged social ties that would guarantee regular custom, and allowed him to draw upon and develop the social and political interests that are so often portrayed as inimical to Malay economic success (Tarigan *et al.* 1996: 45–55).

Syamsuddin decided not to relocate. There were too many benefits of trading from home, all of which stemmed from the nature of the suburbs and their advantages over the teeming, competitive marketplace. Yet while his slow, socially involved approach to retail represented for him a profitable compromise between economic activity and developing other areas of interest, his business was caricatured by Minangkabau and Javanese in the neighbourhood as run by a "typical Malay" who preferred socialising to hard work. In economic terms, Syamsuddin ran a successful business, but for his neighbours and clients, much as they enjoyed his food, his outlook and reluctance to move to the market was confirmation that Malays were backward and lazy.

Surya, an ambitious Malay hairdresser who dreamed of "making it big" in the salon world, also found there were practical advantages to trading from the suburbs. Surya was a *waria* (*wanita-pria*, woman-man), an identity that has variously been understood as a form of "transvestitism", "transgender", or "third gender". Surya himself defined *waria* as being "a type of man [hence my use of the pronoun 'he'] who has the soul of a woman inside his body"; he wore androgynous clothes, sported a feminine haircut and make-up, and had sex with men. He also faced discrimination, stigma and misunderstanding: all problems that held him back in his entrepreneurial ambitions.

Born into a wealthy family, Surya had once run his own salon in the marketplace but had since decided to sell up and work from home. Trade in that salon had been good, especially during the 1990s, when many Singaporean tourists came to Tanjung Pinang. Yet the salon had done little to raise his social status. "*Waria* are seen as the lowest of the low," he explained, "and salon is not a respected profession, much lower than singer or dancer [other stereotypical *waria* careers]". The problem of respect was augmented by the salon's marketplace location. The marketplace carries connotations as an area where anything could be commodified and transacted, a perception underscored by the area's history as a centre of prostitution. Surya felt that working there had threatened his reputation and heightened public awareness of the transgressive potential in his own gendered identity. The matter was worsened further by the principle that on commercial premises one is obliged to serve any customer, even prostitutes, which would have cemented the problematic association he was so desperate to avoid.

Working from home, Surya combined low-paying neighbourhood work — creating hairstyles for events such as weddings and circumcision ceremonies — with more prestigious contracts in Singapore and for the Riau Islands government. The flexibility of working from home allowed him to pursue these different lines of business, building up his reputation, whereas running a salon would have required him to be in his commercial premises every day, limiting his chances to take high-status government contracts. Working from the suburbs presented a second advantage. By letting customers into his house, which was decorated with Islamic verses and imagery, and exposing himself to neighbourhood surveillance, he could overcome the negative perceptions and expectations associated with him as a *waria*, and perform himself in keeping with the moral strictures of the neighbourhood (see Chapter 5). This in turn increased his chances of future work:

> The only people who visit my house are foreign friends or housewives. I never bring back guys; if I do, I know there will be stories.
>
> I've already become somebody here, and I don't want to be seen as leading an immoral lifestyle like a normal *waria*. I can succeed because everyone in this neighbourhood thinks, 'Yes, he is a *waria*, and that's strange, but he's not immoral like the rest of them, he's a good man, who respects us, and helps us with our hair and make-up' ... I have to keep it that way, because it's those housewives who provide me with work. Besides, would the government want to contract me again if there was lots of gossip about me?!
>
> It has to be like that if you want to be a success. If I was like the other *waria*, I'd still just be working with prostitutes in a regular salon. Besides, my family have already given me a lot of money to help me pursue this route, so I must be careful and always guard my reputation. The other *waria* probably wonder why I care so much about my job, but they don't realise how important it is for the future ... I won't have any children to look after me. As a *waria*, I have to be financially independent.

Surya did hope to go back to the marketplace: his ultimate goal was to open a high-class salon, trading on his reputation to sell expensive hairstyles to the wealthy women of Tanjung Pinang. Meanwhile, it was a more sensible long-term economic strategy to render his commercial (and sexual) activity invisible by working in the depths of the suburbs, or in Singapore.

What Syamsuddin and Surya's cases illustrate, albeit in different ways, is that the marketplace contains certain forms of "glass ceiling" that hinder the development of both businesses and businesspeople. For Surya, becoming a truly successful salon owner necessitated leaving the market to escape the stigmas it would impose upon him. For Syamsuddin, working in the marketplace might help his self-performance as an entrepreneur, but only at the expense of developing his broader interests in policy and politics and with no guarantee of substantially increased revenue. Though these considerations apply to traders of all ethnic identifications, suburban trade is a particularly suitable choice for Malay traders who, for the historical demographic reasons discussed earlier, tend to be concentrated in outlying districts of the town.

These complexities are overlooked, however, in dominant discourses of commercial success that stress the importance of Malays being in the *central* marketplace and which therefore consider trading from home to be "second-best", as opposed to a creative strategy adopted by Malays who migrated into Tanjung Pinang when the *pasar* was already dominated by other groups or was an inappropriate place to be seen. From this perspective, the success of the traders I have discussed counts against them, because it is not acknowledged that their success might be a result of their avoiding the marketplace. Rather, success in the suburbs suggests that these are Malays who could be extremely successful in the marketplace but are too backward or lazy to try.

The Marketplace of Malayness

What then of Malay traders and entrepreneurs who do decide to launch themselves into the marketplace and establish a business there? Whilst such individuals are less visible than the Chinese and Minangkabau majority, they do exist. One reason they are overlooked is a persistent tendency to deny their own Malayness. Concerned that the Malay identity carries associations of backwardness and failure, Malays working in the marketplace tend to self-define as "Indonesian" (Faucher 2005: 137–8) or make claims to a different ethnic identity. The implications of this trend are not clear. Do such strategies entrench the idea of Malayness-as-inadequacy? Or do they cast Malayness as an incorporative identity that is able to absorb the very best elements of the plural cultures that abound in the islands?

For some informants, the denial of Malayness in entrepreneurial contexts clearly reflected a personal lack of faith in their capacity to be commercially successful as Malays. Their claims were not just pandering to a prejudiced audience but also reflecting an ongoing struggle to purge themselves of Malayness and appropriate the skills and dispositions of their more commercially successful counterparts, both in the islands and in neighbouring Singapore. Fatimah, who had ambitions of opening her own private tourism studies course, explained that in order for this to succeed, she would need to learn how to stop herself from thinking like a Malay:

> Not in social terms, or with family — then I will still be a Malay. But in business terms, I will be like a Chinese. When I open my course, I won't be like usual Malays or other Indonesians. I have watched the Chinese, and I have learnt from their experience. I had to do that if I wanted to succeed. When I run my course I will behave exactly like a Chinese.

For Fatimah, becoming a successful entrepreneur involved a delicate balancing act between "Malayness" and the inculcation of non-Malay ways of being deemed more appropriate to economic action.

This balancing process was often complex. Raja Jaffar, who had established a successful chain of English conversation clubs, described how the critical moment on his path to success was when his mother insisted he undertake further study in Singapore:

> I was kind of altered by the environment. People in Singapore live for work, and treat everything business-like — they don't live for living like people do in Tanjung Pinang. I began to learn not to worry about making mistakes, to try lots of new things. Look at me now: I'm always wanting to try something new! Now my attitude is completely different from the other Malays, who are all lazy. I am concerned with my career rather than with family. The other Malays I knew in school — I wouldn't say that I'm better than them, but they want different things. They're happy just to have a job and stay in it, and have a wife and a family. But I can't sit still!

Yet for all Jaffar had reinvented himself as "Singaporean" rather than "Riau Islands Malay", he did so in the spirit of honouring his Penyengat genealogy. Success in business was an achievement tantamount to that of his ancestors ("we don't have sultanates any more," he told me, "but we do have business") but also promised him an important enough voice in society to promote the historical significance of the heirlooms (*pusaka*) left to him by his grandfather, including ornamental daggers and a series of books that he claimed contained information with which one could "rewrite the history of the Riau-Lingga Archipelago". He had held back from presenting these artefacts to anybody since he feared that, until he became a successful businessman, he would not be taken seriously by the authorities and thereby fail in honouring his obligations to his grandfather and "Malay history" writ large. The "Malayness" of being a Malay businessman was thus simultaneously problematic for him and integral to his project of self-formation.

While Jaffar was quick to declare himself a successful entrepreneur, others were less generous in their evaluations of his business acumen. In particular, he was criticised by his detractors for spending too much of his profit too quickly, a trace of residual Malay presentism leaking through. This highlights a paradox faced by all those Malays who, like Jaffar and Fatimah, tried to become a successful entrepreneur through imitating a non-Malay exemplar and internalising their values and practices. As Homi Bhabha (1984: 126) has argued with reference to colonial situations, "the discourse of mimicry is constructed around an ambivalence: in order to be effective, mimicry must continually produce its slippage, its excess, its difference." A Riau Malay who tries to think like a Chinese or a Singaporean will never quite manage to become either of those things; they will always be identifiably Riau Malay, and thus haunted by the prospect that aspects of their Malayness might subvert their attempts at self-reinvention. Entrepreneurial Riau Malay subjectivities thus contain an inherent tension between the local "Malay" dimensions of the self that will stymie a business and the "non-Malay" aspects that will allow it to grow — a point underscored by the ways in which Riau Islanders remember and refer to Tanjung Pinang's Kelings. When recalled as a successful trading community, they are "Keling" or "Indian". When remembered as a group that was ousted, they are "marginalised Malays".

Nevertheless, other entrepreneurs try to reclaim Malayness as an identity of which one could be proud. Ali, a retired Malay head-master, had worked for 11 years (1971–1982) managing a clothing factory in the marketplace before eventually being asked to rescue a failing school. The factory was staffed predominantly by Hokkien Chinese and made good profits, allowing him to build a brick house. He always spoke of this house with pride, because he had "made it himself from the profits of his business". However, his success in the factory led to other Malays suggesting that Ali was actually Javanese.

> **Ali:** [Malays] don't have good hearts, they are evil and haughty. They feel annoyed if another person is better and higher up than them. They are jealous. When a Minang is promoted, all the Minangkabau gather together to celebrate, because if you migrate, you must be united. But not Malays.
>
> You can see it with me. When I was successful, the Malays in this town said that I was not really Malay, because my mother came from Java, near Semarang. But she stayed here a long time, and considered this home, I was born here. Besides, Malayness is not [matrilineal] like Minangkabau, it's patrilineal and my father was Malay. As far as I'm concerned, if you follow Islam and your father is Malay, then you are a Malay. When I was young they said I was Malay. But now they say I am Javanese.

By accepted Malay customary law (*adat*), Ali clearly qualifies as Malay. The accusation that he is Javanese represents a complex renegotiation of "Malayness". Although his maternal ancestry ("Javanese") is invoked as what makes him "non-Malay", Ali was convinced the real reason was because he had become successful, even by the standards of the marketplace parameter. Managing a profitable clothing factory, with Chinese working for him, it was inconceivable — or perhaps inadmissible — that he was "really Malay".

It had been painful for Ali to realise that he had worked hard to show what he could do as a "Malay" only to be stripped of any claim to that identity by those around him. He explained to me that he subscribed to a "Malayness" different from that of "other Malays" who he claimed to be arrogant, jealous and evil-hearted. More in-clined to sympathise with the Minangkabau ideology that celebrated the achievements of others, he admitted his experiences had con-vinced him that Malays actually did suffer from inadequacy — now framed in terms of social solidarity — when compared to the other ethnic groups in Tanjung Pinang.

Conclusion

The economic marginalisation of Malays — and the template of Malayness that underpins it — are two of the most emotive ideas that circulate in the Riau Islands, fundamental to both personal and party politics. They are crucial to understanding whether one feels at home in one's place of residence or even within one's own skin. However, by thinking about Malayness in terms of a "history of ideas", I have argued the notion of the inadequate Malay is a myth that has been sustained by anachronistically imposing contemporary categories onto historical materials. Present-day ideas about Malay identity reconfigure Keling bodies as "Malay" at the point of their departure from Tanjung Pinang's marketplace while the idea of regional Malayness that has been so prominent in provincial political rhetoric presumes the town was full of Malays since time imme-morial. It also finds contemporary support through a distinctively circumscribed parameter of economic success, and the deliberate or inadvertent concealment of profitable Malay trading.

The stereotype of Malay inadequacy nevertheless remains an established part of Riau Islands life. As Syamsuddin, Surya and Ali all discovered, even if they themselves circumvent it, they are still vulnerable to having it applied to them, stripping them of their claims to success, or of their right to identify as Malay. When both these categories matter so much in the context of a province seeking to slough off its "backwardness" and make a mark on the encompas-sing global economy, contests over them have a tremendous impact on people's political views, sense of self-worth and ability to feel settled and "at home" in the place where they live.

5

Neighbourhoods

Obliged to interact with and live alongside masses of anonymous, culturally distinct and potentially hostile strangers, urban dwellers enjoy new opportunities but also face new dangers. Residents of Tanjung Pinang are no exception. The town offers them jobs, services and "modernity" — attractions potent enough to draw in a steady stream of diverse strangers from elsewhere — but the transient and multicultural urban population that results can itself be a source of anxiety and danger. In this chapter, I examine how the experience of living side-by-side in urban neighbourhoods gave rise to feelings of both safety and insecurity for Riau Islanders, and the distinctive role that ideas about "Malayness" played in shaping how readily they could feel at home.

Living in close proximity to other people is an inevitable aspect of urban life, but also challenging, as confirmed by a wide body of theoretical and ethnographic literature. Slavoj Žižek (2005: 140), for example, has argued that there is a "fundamental violence" in the fact that we, as human beings, are forced to live alongside people whom we will never completely be able to know and who, for all that they might seem like us, might actually be something "monstrous". Yet the ambivalence and anxieties that suffuse particular cases of urban relations need to be understood in terms of the broader social imaginaries, panics and fears that characterise particular moments in time and space. Robbie Peters (2012), for example, has charted two distinct ways in which "newcomers" became objects of anxiety, suspicion and surveillance within the East Javanese city of Surabaya. In the late 1990s, residents living in the district of Dinoyo began to intensely distrust the strangers entering their streets. Food vendors, pigeon racers and "madmen" were all suspected of being assassins of the kind that had recently terrorised other regions of East Java, while longer-term residents were feared to be the informants that had given them entry to the neighbourhood, allowing its destruction from within (Peters 2012: 140–55). In the late 2000s, by contrast, it was the police who was most wary of newcomers. Fearing that they might be terrorists (an anxiety heightened by a string of suicide bomb attacks in Bali and Jakarta), they conducted regular raids, and sought to inculcate a similar level of vigilance amongst the residents of the city (Peters 2012: 203–18).

In the Riau Islands, neither assassins nor terrorists proved to be the main sources of anxiety for residents. Both were spoken of as shocking problems affecting Indonesia, but they were considered external to the province. Nor were police raids or patrols a feature of neighbourhood life. As noted in Chapter 2, the more immediate concerns for Riau Islanders, citizens and officials alike, surrounded petty crime and the possibility that interethnic violence might break out. Many of my respondents linked this concern to the profusion of *ikatan* within the province's towns.

An *ikatan* is an association whose membership is restricted, usually on the basis of ethnicity and/or region of origin. Tanjung Pinang alone has more than 100. Just as classic anthropological studies of urbanising environments noted that new forms of association, based on novel and resolutely urban conceptions of "ethnicity", "regionalism" or "tribalism" arose as a means of navigating the social complexities of the city (e.g. Mitchell 1956), so *ikatan* offered migrants to the Riau Islands various opportunities on the basis of ethnic and regional ties. These included access to jobs, apprenticeships and credit, as well as opportunities to consume the much-missed arts and sports of their home region, which are staged by *ikatan* for the benefit of their members and other townsfolk alike. However, some *ikatan* also offered members physical protection in times of trouble, a fact that many Riau Islanders found alarming. In 2001, a personal dispute over a gambling debt between a Batak and Minangkabau living on Batam escalated into a series of interethnic skirmishes as each party mobilised members of their own ethnic group to attack the other (Tri Ratnawati 2006). Although this conflict was quickly settled, it served as a sobering reminder for Riau Islanders of the potential of their multicultural society to tear itself apart. The idea that one day, one of the larger *ikatan* might be mobilised as a force in interethnic conflict was particularly alarming, and one that was sometimes used as a tactic of intimidation in inter-personal disputes. Growing numbers of Riau Islanders therefore felt compelled to join an *ikatan* for their own protection, inadvertently exacerbating the overall problem. Suparman, a young Javanese migrant who had grown up on Bali, explained that:

> It's only when I go back to Bali that I will be able to find peace … I've been in Tanjung Pinang for maybe eight years, but I still can't rest easy. Until now, there's been no trouble, but how much longer will that last? You saw what happened in Kalimantan and in Ambon and Sulawesi. How much longer before it happens here?
>
> There have already been small conflicts in Batam, and in Tanjung Pinang it is very tribalist. Anything you might join, like the martial arts association, is actually about tribalism. There are a lot of *ikatan* here. I myself am a member of three! But it's for my own security. If I need help, I can go to the *ikatan*; if some-one else makes trouble for me, then the *ikatan* can defend me.

With *ikatan* having become a seemingly indispensable part of urban life in the Riau Islands, the primary fear surrounding one's neigh-bours was thus not that they were terrorists or assassins, but that they might put the interests of their *ikatan* above their commitment to the national principle of "Unity in Diversity". If interethnic con-flict broke out, would neighbourly ties be able to win out against ethnic and regional loyalties? Many had their doubts.

However, the ethnically diverse neighbourhoods of the Riau Archipelago's towns were also recognised by citizens and officials alike as sites in which to foster a sense of shared citizenship, belonging and community that might mitigate sentiments of ethnic or religious difference. It was to this effect that Djasarmen Purba, a Batam-based representative of the Riau Islands Province in the national Regional Representative Council (DPD), named neighbourhood leaders as one of the first groups to be targeted in his attempts to increase aware-ness of the "four pillars of nationalism" — one of which is "Unity in Diversity" — within the Riau Islands.[1] He described himself as trying

---

[1] The other three "pillars" he identified are the constitution, a commitment that Indonesia must remain a unitary state, and the national philosophy of *Pancasila*, which declares a commitment to five principles: belief in a supreme being; humanitarianism; nationalism; representative government; and social justice.

to refresh a "glue that is currently dried up and almost worn out", arguing that "the fragmentation or integration of the nation" was at stake (*Tanjungpinang Pos* 2011). His metaphor of glue may have been more apt than he was intending, for when one examines how multiethnic living plays out in Tanjung Pinang's neighbourhoods, "national integration" turns out to be messier and stickier than its proponents typically assume. The processes of mutual accommodation and tolerance that are involved in shared neighbourhood life can in fact lead to an unsettling awareness amongst Riau Islanders of the "cultural differences" that they are "tolerating", an awareness that may in turn precipitate their engagement in ethnically grounded identity politics.

Defining the Neighbourhood

Residents of Tanjung Pinang used two main terms to identify and circumscribe the "neighbourhoods" in which they lived. The first of these, *kampung* (which translates as "village" in rural settings), has attracted a lively press in anthropological studies of urban Java, where it is usually taken to refer to a low-income residential district (e.g. Guinness 2009; Peters 2012). Similar usages have also been documented in Singapore (Loh 2013) and in parts of urban Malaysia, where it often denotes a "squatter settlement" (Bunnell 2002). Yet the term can have multiple meanings. Whole districts of Tanjung Pinang carried the title "Kampung", as in my own residence of Kampung Jawa, but this was rarely the scale at which residents were operating when they talked of their own kampung. The term could certainly have associations with urban poverty, as I discovered when friends of mine who lived in expensive new housing estates (*perumahan*) told me with pity in their voices that Kampung Jawa — one the poorest areas of the town — was "well and truly a kampung" (*betul-betul kampung*). However, these same people would also frequently refer to their own luxurious housing complexes as their "kampung", and it was this casual usage of the term to denote the context in which one resided that was by far the most widely used amongst residents of the town. Noting a similar trend amongst urban dwellers in Yogyakarta, Barbara Hatley (2008: 15) suggested that kampung could be glossed as "home community", but it should also be stressed that this "community" had topographical correlates. In Tanjung Pinang, homes within a 40-household radius from one's place of residence were a particularly significant space of social action, and came to mark out the neighbourhood to which people were referring when they spoke of "their kampung".

The second term widely translated as "neighbourhood" is the civil-administrative category of the *rukun tetangga*, or RT, which has its origins in the neighbourhood associations set up during the Japanese Occupation on the model of the Japanese *aza* (Dick 2002: 164). While the boundaries of kampung are informal and flexible, the RT is a clearly demarcated unit created by carving urban topography into multiple regulatable "neighbourhoods" of approximately 40 households. Every citizen must live in a building registered within an RT, whereupon they enjoy certain rights and protections, enshrined in their relationship with directly elected leaders from the lowest level of the RT head (known as Bapak or Ibu RT) all the way up the civil-administrative hierarchy. Unregistered buildings are subject to demolition at any time (Lindquist 2009: 13). The RT is an administrative unit, but the term *rukun tetangga*, which translates as "harmony between neighbours", underscores how, like the kampung, it is a unit of social relations, and one involving a prescription for "harmonious" interaction (Guinness 1986). RT members are expected to work together in enterprises such as cleaning the streets, building new facilities (such as sports pitches) for the neighbourhood, and operating neighbourhood security vigils. Those who do not participate face social sanctions, and warnings and fines from the RT leader (Gatot Winoto *et al.* 1995: 13).

Scholars continue to be divided over whether the RT's emphasis on "harmony" and "community" reflects "an ideology ... institutionalised ... as a means of imposing order" (Murray 1991: 64) or "an indigenous construction expressing an identity independent of the state" (Guinness 2009: 22). The answer may vary according to the context. *Rukun*, or "harmony" has often been identified as a prized feature of Javanese social life (Guinness 1986: 131–2), but its export to other parts of Indonesia may well have involved the suppression or impoverishment of alternative kinship- and *adat*-based patterns of socio-spatial obligation (e.g. Galizia 1989; Kato 1989). Both positions in this debate, however, tend to presume that "households allocated to [RTs] will tend to develop new ties and form closely knit groups corresponding to the *rukun tetangga* unit" (Sullivan 1992: 145–6). Things were not so straightforward in the culturally diverse neighbourhoods of Tanjung Pinang, especially at a time of heightened ethnic and regional awareness. For all that figures such as Djasarmen Purba hoped that the RT would foster the feelings of interethnic harmony needed for social integration, a more complex and multifaceted set of relations emerged in practice.

"Integration" in the Neighbourhood

Many of my informants asserted that enforced regular participation in RT events drew together neighbours who otherwise would be preoccupied with their own social networks of ethnicity, kinship or work. Moreover, through this enforced contact, neighbours would realise how much they had in common, the traits most widely cited being national values of *Pancasila* and a shared devotion to Islam. National and religious unity were thus believed capable of overcoming any potential lines of conflict between ethnic groups, or between more settled and more recently arrived migrants. Through shared living and citizenship, Malayness in the Riau Islands would be incidental, not fundamental to everyday life. Everyone would be able to feel at home.

In 2006, Fadli had been put in charge of organising Independence Day celebrations for his RT. This was a predominantly middle-class district in the Pamedan area, where most residents had lived for at least ten years. The entertainments included a dominoes tournament for the men, a cookery competition for the women, novelty races (each of which carried a prize) for the children (Figure 5.1), and a karaoke contest open to all. His description of the celebrations opened with the assertion that it illustrated "the difference between Eastern culture and Western culture. Here neighbours are more important than your own family. Here we are all very close." Working in Yogyakarta, Barbara Hatley (1982: 60) maintained that "kampung competitions and performances appear to celebrate an egalitarian, participatory notion of what it means to be Indonesian, perhaps reflecting the experience of nationalist struggle and revolution, coalescing with the age-old, survival-oriented, cooperative patterns of peasant life." Fadli, however, argued that Independence Day festivities were not reflecting closeness but actively creating it:

> A big reason for our being close is all these competitions. Actually, if there weren't any competitions, we would probably rarely meet. But if there are Independence Day celebrations, it's

Figure 5.1 Independence Day races in Fadli's neighbourhood (Source: author)

already certain that for several weeks we will often meet, get to know each other, become close, and then it is nicer when we meet again. If there weren't any celebrations, it would probably be much harder to become close.

Direct observation, however, challenges the extent to which "closeness" can be seen as the outcome of these activities. I was struck by the ill-feeling that emerged during an Independence Day headscarf-tying competition, in which women from a single neighbourhood had to compete with each other to tie their headscarves as prettily as possible, in the shortest time they could manage, without the use of a mirror. The presiding government official explained to me that she hoped the contest would encourage more women to wear the headscarf, something she considered a religious obligation,[2] and to experiment with new ways of tying it, which she hoped would boost their creativity. She also hoped that the competition would "motivate" the women to be more ambitious and higher achieving in

---

[2] For an overview of how Indonesian women have engaged with this proposition over time, see Brenner (1996).

their lives (Chapter 7). However, she stressed to the participants that the contest was "just for fun". It was, she reminded them, supposed to be comic (*lucu*) and they should not be heartbroken (*patah hati*) if they did not win. The thunderous faces filing out at the contest's end suggested her exhortation had not been heeded, whilst accusations of improper judging and denigration of the victor's headscarf-tying skills flew thick and fast during follow-up visits to the entrants. This combination of "novelty" RT activities being comic to watch and taken with deadly seriousness by competitors was very familiar to me by the end of fieldwork (cf. Hatley 1982: 58). Yet, rather than threatening neighbourhood relations, as Beatty (2005: 70–1) observed in East Java, the rivalry that saturated Independence Day competitions in Tanjung Pinang actually helped to build them.

Neighbourhood rivalries and the competitive desire to win prizes generate interest in the outcome of events. Likewise, the comic nature of the contests attracts crowds seeking entertainment. RT contests thus typically attract large groups of spectators who, although divided by allegiances over who they hope will win, can also be perceived as the whole neighbourhood turning out in force. The gathering together of large numbers of people (*keramaian*) is greatly enjoyed by Indonesians: one boy watching an Independence Day volleyball contest gestured towards the crowd of spectators and told me, "it was for this that we fought for independence".

The process of competing and the outcomes — rankings, victories and defeats — create a web of competitive relations amongst RT members who might otherwise have little in common, given their disparate backgrounds and divergent urban lifestyles. Moreover, neighbourhood competitions orient citizens towards the RT. When neighbours strive to become the RT champion, the RT is reinscribed as a unit that matters, which further entrenches neighbourhood ideologies. The RT becomes a space that enables particular kinds of achieving selves, and the awareness and memory of this sustain the RT as a meaningful concept beyond the moment of the contest, demanding the appearance of harmony on both symbolic and practical levels. Informants expressed similar sentiments as they described their pleasure at moving through streets they had swept, or seeing children playing on volleyball courts that they had laid out during periods of communal labour. Such affinities and emotional responses cannot exist within other RTs, only within one's own. This helps cultivate a sense of "belonging" to the RT, the parameters and

Figure 5.2 A neighbourhood *arisan* (Source: author)

boundaries of which come to feel "natural" in everyday experience. Moreover, once the RT has been naturalised as a site of "belonging", such that its social relationships matter, the ideal of neighbourhood harmony is one that all its residents have a stake in maintaining. They may well know it to be false, but they also know it is what the RT is supposed to be all about.

Arisan are regular social events in which friends, co-workers, or neighbours gather together and draw lots to win a pot of money to which they have all contributed a small amount (Figure 5.2). The process repeats, usually every month, until all women have won the pot. They are popular within the RT, especially among female heads of household. Clifford Geertz (1962: 243–5), who first documented the phenomenon in Java, dismissed his informants' claims that the primary attraction was "not the money received but the creation of harmony (*rukun*) which occurs", arguing that these remarks concealed a strident economism. Yet Novendra *et al.* (1996: 28), in their study of neighbourhood life in the multiethnic Mainland Riau town of Tembilahan, argue that *arisan* serve to "increase intimacy between citizens". Similar explanations were often offered by my informants, claims which should be taken seriously for what they reveal about desires for neighbourhood harmony, as well as for what they might conceal. As we watched one *arisan*, a Minangkabau migrant named Zal interpreted the occasion for me, articulating both the received wisdom of RT events and his own hopes for acceptance in the Riau Islands: "Even though they are from all over Indonesia, Padang people, Malay people, Javanese people, they can all come here and be one group. It's what makes Indonesian culture very special".

In Tanjung Pinang, individual interpretations of the *arisan* are diverse. Mohamad Sobary (1987: 13) noted that Javanese migrants in the town during the 1980s saw the *arisan* as a means of preserving a distinctly Javanese tradition while they were away from home, an attitude I also encountered on several occasions. Some Riau Islanders viewed the event in more economistic terms, often in response to sudden or unexpected circumstances: one woman in Kampung Jawa assured me that if I lent her some money, she would be able to persuade her neighbours to rig a forthcoming *arisan* so that she would win the pot and could pay me back. Others told me that the *arisan* was about integration, but spoke of this almost grudgingly. "Bataks are really very strange," remarked one Malay participant of her fellow *arisan* attendee as everyone was leaving. "She is lucky the Malay people here are so welcoming." For this woman, the harmony represented in the *arisan* was neither inevitable nor embedded in citizenship duties, but was linked to Malayness and its incorporative, integrationist nature.

In contrast to family and workplace *arisan*, which were gossipy, relaxed affairs, RT *arisan* tended to be formal, with participants wearing their "best" clothes, and placed a strong emphasis on shared ritual activity, typically Islamic. Unifying factors such as religion and the propinquity of the RT were emphasised while other labels, such as those of class, employment and ethnicity, were downplayed. Yet as I discovered, away from the event, *arisan* were enrolled in a series of potentially conflicting narratives: preserving Javanese culture; a Malay cultural tradition of (grudging) hospitality and incorporation; or forms of cultural acceptance and cosmopolitanism that were framed as "traditionally Indonesian". Each of these ideas constituted a different understanding of what "integration" within the RT involved but, just as Beatty (1999: 39) has argued of the Javanese *slametan* ritual, RT *arisan* were able to contain this ideological diversity within a common frame.

As these analyses of RT competitions, collaborations, and *arisan* reveal, the ability of the RT to "integrate" is not, as is often assumed, a testimony to its power to dissolve problematic categories — "migrant", "Malay", "local" — and sublimate them under either a nationalist ethic or a sense of local "community" (cf. Novendra *et al.* 1996; Sullivan 1992: 145–6). Instead, it lies in its capacity to cloak such diverse interpretations of *rukun* through ambiguous practices that are oriented towards "cooperation," "integration" and "harmonious relations", but which can nevertheless accommodate highly situated rivalries, enmities and tensions. Yet these tensions can sometimes boil over. When they do, ideologies and discourses of the integrated and harmonious neighbourhood reveal that they have a dramatic capacity to exclude.

Chandra, the Bad Neighbour

Amongst the residents living in the boarding house (*kos*) that I stayed in for part of my time in Tanjung Pinang was a Chinese man named Chandra. A migrant from Mainland Riau, he now worked as a petrol pump attendant. He told me that his work was very strenuous, so when he came home he liked to read, watch TV, or listen to music on his own in his room rather than make small talk with other people nearby. Despite this, Chandra was active in the RT, contributing every month to communal labour (*gotong royong*) and regularly giving assistance to households who were having difficulties with their electrical appliances. He seemed, in many ways, a model neighbour.

One night, Chandra was thrown out of the neighbourhood by Khalid, the neighbour charged with supervising our house. Khalid alleged that Chandra had invited another man into his room that evening, closed the door and then dimmed the lights, which he was confident "could only be for one reason". After the "guest" had departed, Khalid confronted Chandra and demanded that he leave the neighbourhood immediately, leading to a violent quarrel. The next morning, I awoke to discover that Chandra's room had been vacated. Khalid refused to discuss the incident, while Chandra himself told me he had moved to the Pamedan area because the landlord in Kampung Jawa was "too passive" and had not responded adequately to Chandra's complaints about the facilities.

The next afternoon, I joined a group of neighbourhood women gossiping in the porch. Erna, an elderly widow who lived in the boarding house, was sitting on the steps as Qisthi, the youngest, knelt behind her and checked her head for lice. Diyah, Khalid's wife, was eating lunch. Chandra's departure was the breaking news. Though Diyah began by pretending his contract had expired, she eventually admitted there had been a "conflict" with her husband, and confessed that she was glad to see him go. "He had an un-suitable character," she began, pointing accusingly to an empty lager can in the gutter. "He would drink into the middle of the night until he was drunk, and that is unsuitable in an area like this. He had guests who visited late at night, and when that happened he shut all the windows and doors so nobody could see what was being done in the room. It's not surprising people viewed him suspiciously. He was too closed-off, a little dishonest. And he was noisy. We weren't very happy having him living here. It's better if he finds somewhere else." Erna was more blunt:

> He's a *banci* [a contemptuous term for a male homosexual]. He likes men in the way that a husband likes a wife. If my grand-children visit, I always keep the door open so nobody can think I'm doing anything immoral. But Chandra performed so many immoral acts (*kenakalan*). I was scared when my grandchildren came to visit, or when he talked to me after he'd been drinking. He wasn't a normal person (*orang normal*, a colloquial term for a heterosexual). We want a normal person next time. Chandra should live in a different area. By the seaboard [a location known to be used for male homosexual cruising late at night], that's the place for him!

Qisthi, keeping silent, looked disapproving and tugged a little more sharply than was necessary at Erna's grey hairs. She was perhaps remembering the time that Erna had embarrassed her by publicly denouncing her own husband for sexual impropriety with a younger woman.

So what was actually at stake in Chandra's eviction? The "problem" — or at least the final straw — was an alleged act of homosexual intercourse. First, we should ask what it was that ren-dered this problematic. Second, given that the evidence against Chandra was highly circumstantial — and he himself denied the allegations very strongly — why was he not believed? The crux of the issue, I suggest, lies in a failure of neighbourship. While Chandra was an exemplary neighbour within the context of the RT system, he had failed to comply with other models of kampung neighbourship that were strongly informed by Islamic moral geographies. These models placed obligations upon both Chandra and Khalid, meaning that when Chandra transgressed them, Khalid had no choice but to evict him.

While Islam is not the only Indonesian religion to look harshly upon homosexuality, it has a distinctive approach to sexual sins that influences life in a predominantly Islamic urban area such as Kampung Jawa. With the exception of some schools of self-styled "liberal Islam", which remain controversial in Indonesia and are not prominent in Tanjung Pinang (Hartono 2005: 214–38), Islam classifies homosexual intercourse within the category of *zina* (illicit sexual practices, including any pre-marital or extra-marital sex) and considers it to be a serious sin. Moreover, if people are in a position to know whether *zina* was being committed within their neighbourhood, but fail to intervene, the punishment for the *zina* is extended across a radius of 40 households from where the act takes place. In other words, the sin implicates an entire kampung. Such logic inscribes the kampung as a location that not only has significance for one's earthly happiness but also for one's spiritual security and afterlife. "I know in the West, you are very individualistic, and believe that sex is a private matter," explained one civil servant, "but in Islamic culture it's different. When you think about it, there are good aspects to our beliefs. They give people a reason to care about the kampung. It allows *social control* [English used]."

Muslim kampung dwellers thus felt an obligation to monitor and survey the households around them in both their own and the collective interests, punishing or expelling problematic residents. On the one hand, such feelings of obligation demonstrated the force within everyday life of what M.B. Hooker (2008) has termed "*syariah* values": an attachment to certain principles of Islamic law, and an informal legal process surrounding them. Yet on the other, Tanjung Pinang's distinctive moral geographies suggested that more was at stake than absolute principles of morality and law: the implications of *zina* were different depending on where it took place.

Although Diyah and Erna spoke of Chandra and his alleged transgressions with hostility and contempt, their principal objections were not to what Chandra had done but where he had done it. He was described as "unsuitable for this area" and "better off somewhere else", such as the seaboard. This point was clarified by Maznah's daughter Nurul as she spoke of her former neighbour, also evicted after a homosexual encounter. "I feel sorry for him," she said. "Of course he wants to do it and it is his human right. But why did he have to do it here?" Few informants had much sympathy for Chandra. His offence, they said, was being too bold (*berani*) in how he chose to conduct his (alleged) sexual affairs. Much better, they suggested, if one wanted to have homosexual intercourse, to do so in a hotel or, at the very least, far away from one's own kampung. *Waria* hairdresser Surya, all of whose sexual activities were *zina*, also agreed. "If I want to do something that [the rest of the kampung] will think is immoral," he told me, "I always make sure I do it a long way from this kampung, and definitely never in my own house." Homosexual intercourse in a distant kampung is still *zina* and still puts people in a radius of 40 households at risk of divine punishment. But those people are not one's own neighbours. Chandra's transgression inheres not only in an sinful act that has been committed in the wrong place, but a revelation that, for all his RT neighbourliness, he was not thinking of his neighbours when planning his tryst.

As a Chinese Buddhist, Chandra had no reason to know these principles, but for the fact that they were inscribed in a system of "*kampung* rules [English used]". All newcomers to the kampung in which I lived were asked to subscribe to these "rules", which formed a recited set of guidelines as to how one should behave. They combined the obligations of RT participation with further prohibitions that one must not be intoxicated or commit *zina* offences — as an attempt to guard against the latter, members of the opposite sex were not allowed in one's room. At the time of my own admission to the kampung, it was a source of great concern that, being a Westerner and thus most likely accustomed to a lifestyle of wantonness and immorality (*kenakalan*), I would not be able to abide by the rules and thus create problems in the neighbourhood. "It's not my opinion," apologised Denny, the neighbour who had helped me find the boarding house, as he broke the news that I could not have any romantic liaisons in my new home, "it's the kampung's. Kampung rules. The kampung isn't a free place (*tempat bebas*) like the marketplace. There are lots of things you can't do."

Despite my assurances that I would obey the kampung rules, this anxiety surfaced again and again while I was moving in. This reflected awareness that if I were to break the rules, it would not only be me who was accountable. Denny would be blamed for introducing me to the kampung. The RT leader, who had to register my residence, was likewise concerned lest the breaking of kampung rules reflect badly on his leadership and damage his prospects of re-election. Khalid, as boarding house supervisor, was further implicated, since it was his responsibility to look out for *zina* next door. The owner of the boarding house, who lived outside the kampung, was worried that his own social standing would be disrupted by any misdeeds that I committed in his building. Responsibility for the moral viability of the neighbourhood did not rest with occupancy alone. By owning land and a building within the kampung, this man bore responsibility towards the network of social relations that existed within it, even though he was not directly involved in that network himself.

Given that the kampung rules were so firmly laid down, Chandra's mistake seems clear. Yet the only evidence that he had committed the prohibited *zina* is that the door was shut and the lighting dimmed when a male guest went into his room. This in itself did not contravene the kampung rules and could have many other possible explanations. The problem, I would therefore suggest, was Chandra's broader failure of neighbourship. Certainly he had been active in communal RT neighbourly events, but he had not complied with the obligations of legibility necessary in a kampung so overtly concerned with monitoring for *zina*. What the women specified as making them feel uncomfortable with Chandra's presence was his illegibility. His closed-off character and the closed door to his bedroom gave rise to distressing imaginings of what was happening behind the literally closed doors of their own kampung, acts that Allah could witness but which they could not see and thereby prevent.

Zina prohibitions mean that "the kampung" as a demarcated cluster of houses becomes a salient entity within which members should get to know one another for the purposes of monitoring and regulation. Though in some ways helping to create a unifying sense of kampung (at least amongst Muslims), such demarcation problematises the status of migrants such as Chandra, whose transient stays and unknown nature disrupt long-term residents' certainty that sins will not happen in their midst. This point seems to echo the fear of the "unknown" migrant likely to revert to criminality at any time. For all that RT ideology emphasises harmony, the potential monstrosity of the unknown neighbour remains the suppressed reality that can resurface uncannily, to draw on Žižek (1994), and make "home" feel anything but homely.

There is, however, a further twist to the tale. After Chandra's departure, my neighbours ceased warning me of the terrible perils that might befall me on night-time journeys home. While residents from elsewhere in the town remained convinced that Kampung Jawa was both undesirable and dangerous, Diyah eventually admitted that she did not consider me to be at substantial risk from thieves, and that the isolated break-in I suffered early in my stay (Chapter 1) had come as a terrible shock to her. Rather, she had warned my neighbours to scare me with tales of crookedness for fear that Chandra might commit a sexual assault:

> Poor Amat [a rickshaw driver staying in the boarding house], Chandra definitely wanted him. And we were all a little bit scared, what about Nick? Chandra definitely wanted you as well. We were scared that if you came back in the middle of the night, maybe Chandra would be sitting, waiting for you, wanting you. Who could help you if it was like that? This is why we gave you and Amat advice, don't come home in the middle of the night, and told you there were pickpockets and thieves. It's actually quite safe here in Kampung Jawa, but we wanted to protect you from Chandra.

The tales Amat and I had been told about Kampung Jawa thus came to take on a new significance. My neighbours had tactically deployed the stereotype of their kampung as unsafe in order to increase its security, a tactic they adopted as good Muslims and citizens, and as figures charged with looking after and supervising the tenants in the boarding house. In this respect, migrants are problematic not only because of their potential to commit crimes but also, through their lack of knowledge of the town and consequent vulnerability, their potential to become victims. In terms of a kampung's moral geography, victimhood is as troubling as criminality, since both attest to the possibility of acts occurring within kampung space that would disrupt the moral and cosmic order for all residents inhabiting it. My neighbours were keen to avoid this, yet for the sake of preserving neighbourhood "harmony", they did not voice their concerns directly (see also Guinness 2009: 137). Rather, they cloaked their warnings in the language of gutter criminals until they felt they had enough evidence against Chandra to remove the threat.

In a Tanjung Pinang neighbourhood, it is important to be known by your neighbours, which in turn involves being *seen*, something that goes well beyond the "intimacies" allegedly fostered through RT activities. Such intensive monitoring of residents is both necessary and desirable to ensure a properly "neighbourly" orientation in the kampung. This applies especially strongly in central areas like Kampung Jawa, which are well known for having become crowded with buildings full of short-term, transient populations, as a consequence of which the stresses and anxieties of living alongside unknown neighbours readily encroach upon the experience of urban life. For all that RT activities bring people together, something more is required to establish a sense of neighbourliness and security within a neighbourhood: this is where discourses of "kampung" that portray the neighbourhood as a morally charged bundle of relations become important. The snag for reclusive individuals such as Chandra is that they can believe the formal structures, institutions and events of the RT are enough for them to integrate into the neighbourhood, only to find that failure to observe the implicit obligations of visibility lead to their being viewed with suspicion and are eventually evicted.

Discos and Churches

Although the moral order of the neighbourhood was seen to be compromised by migrants, Malays were regarded as equally problematic. This may seem counter-intuitive. The idea that responsibility for *zina* might extend across a radius of 40 houses was described as "Islamic culture" (*budaya Islam*), and was therefore common to all pious Muslim townsfolk. Moreover, as noted earlier, Malayness is widely attested to be "synonymous with Islam" and this adage was much cited in interviews to legitimise the enforcement of anti-*zina* social control. Since Tanjung Pinang was "Malay land", action needed to be taken to stop anything that would corrupt the Malay values that were intrinsic to it. However, whilst Malayness worked to legitimise neighbourhood surveillance, it also subverted it. Jamil, a Muslim Batak working in the civil service, related how he had realised this to be the case after moving into a new house in a district in which the majority of the population were Malay, but which had also been the location of a notorious discotheque:

When that disco was still open, there were always lots of girls
hanging around outside late at night. Girls waiting to do
immoral things inside the building, if you know what I mean.
I would often have to go out and tell them to leave the area,
explaining to them they were creating a problem for the local
residents, because of the 40 household principle.

   But my neighbours were angry with me! They were Malays,
and Malays are scared of conflict. They wanted to maintain a
peaceful atmosphere in the kampung. But this is the hypocrisy
and wickedness of Malays. If you ask a Malay about Islam, he
will start to talk self-importantly about what a good Muslim he
is and how Malayness is identical with Islam. I asked my neighbours, 'You practise Islam, but are you Islamic people?' They
were confused! The meaning of the word 'Islam' is that you
should propel yourself forward in religious matters. But Malays
don't want to do that because of the [anti-conflict] values I just
mentioned. Weak-willed! They feel aggrieved because of what is
happening in the discotheque, and they complain about it constantly. But they do not want to do anything about it.

These remarks show very clearly how Jamil's fears and concerns
regarding Malays led to the neighbourhood becoming a space of
unease for him. As a home, the neighbourhood is supposed to feel
safe and secure, including within the Islamic paradigm. Informal surveillance and codes of ethical conduct thereby become an established
norm. But that sense of security is undermined by the suspicion that
weak-willed Malays are eroding the force of any such surveillance,
allowing wicked and immoral acts to provide a direct spiritual threat
to their pious neighbours.

   For long-term Muslim migrants such as Jamil, "Malayness" is
as problematic as "migration" in disrupting the moral order of their
kampung. Such migrants explained to me that because only they
could be trusted to enforce the prohibitions on *zina* that were appropriate to so-called "Malay land", they were being forced to behave
as Malays ought to, on the behalf of their Malay neighbours.[3] This

---

[3] Guinness (2009: 138) notes that neighbourhood and religious authorities in
Yogyakarta also experienced a "paralysis" when it came to confronting disruptive
youth behaviour. For Guinness, this aversion to conflict reflected a deep commitment to values of harmony amongst neighbours. Jamil, however, recast Malay
recalcitrance as an ethnic failing.

sentiment led them to stake distinct claims of belonging, which were predicated neither on Indonesian citizenship (as in the RT) nor on indigeneity (since they were not Malay). Rather, they "belonged" because their actions did a better job of expressing and enforcing the values of the region's Malay culture than did the actions of the native Malays. This conviction was intensified by the increased public attention given to Malayness, regionalist ideologies that paint the islands as "full of Malays", and the ongoing political debates over how to remedy Malay inadequacies (Chapter 4). Indeed, Jamil was far from the only non-Malay Muslim I met to say that "when it came to Malayness, [he was] better than Malay people themselves", or to offer such a claim as grounds for deserving equal standing in the new province. Conversely, when Malays retort that these migrants, who see themselves as making the town a safer home for everyone, are "outsiders", the latter react with disappointment, bitterness and anger.

These tensions had the potential to radically disrupt the harmony, integration and mutual tolerance that both the state and citizens hoped would characterise neighbourhood life. Some differences in outlook and values could be accommodated within RT activities, as argued above. Others, however, became explicit issues of political contention around which an RT leader might be re-elected or deposed. A group of young Bataks belonging to the Riau Islands branch of GMKI (Gerakan Mahasiswa Kristen Indonesia, Indonesian Christian Students' Movement) discovered this to their cost after they attempted to set up an education centre for disadvantaged children in the Pantai Impian district. The centre, which ran for a few months, offered out-of-school support to primary school children wishing to consolidate their studies in Indonesian, English and Mathematics, but whose families could not afford to send them to expensive private tuition centres (*les, bimbel*). Viewing their work as a form of charity, the students were adamant that the GMKI centre should be open to anybody, regardless of religion, and free of charge. In their view, they were helping Tanjung Pinang to become more "advanced" (*maju*). The course soon proved popular with children and parents alike, teaching over 50 pupils every day until, to the volunteers' horror, the RT leader demanded that it be closed down.

To formally register the building as an education centre required a letter of support from the RT leader, something he was not prepared to give. His first objection had been that the building was an illegal church. When the students countered that the "G" in GMKI stood for "*Gerakan*" (Movement) rather than "*Gereja*" (Church), he replied that he found it inconceivable that anyone would open an entirely free education centre unless they had an ulterior motive, such as converting Muslim children to Christianity. The students asked Muslim parents to vouch for the secular credentials of the course and even offered the RT leader the chance to observe as many lessons as he wanted, but he could not be persuaded to support the venture. Several students told me they were convinced this was because he was trying to safeguard his prospects of re-election as RT leader by pandering to those in the neighbourhood who objected to the presence of a Christian institution within what they thought should be Malay, Muslim space.

Whatever the RT leader's real reason, this suspicion was enough to shake these students' confidence that they were really welcome in their hometown. One, who had already lived in several provinces in Indonesia, said that he had never been anywhere with as much discrimination as the Riau Islands. His friend agreed, telling me that the "Malays" here are extraordinarily fanatical. Events such as this, he emphasised, made him feel he should safeguard his interests by joining an *ikatan*. Within a few days, news of the centre's closure had spread, to the immense dismay of Christians throughout the town.

However, in districts with a different demographic balance, similar concerns with re-elections could actually work against the interests of Malays and Muslims. For example, civil-administrative authorities forced a family of Tanjung Pinang Malays to make a cheap sale of ancestral land that they held on the island of Karimun to the Bataks who had illegally settled it, seemingly because those Bataks had already been registered as members of an RT and thus were an important voting bloc in forthcoming local elections (Long 2009). My Malay interlocutors in Tanjung Pinang were painfully aware of such cases and feared that, as numbers of non-Malays and non-Muslims in Tanjung Pinang grew steadily, they might be the next victims. The prospect seemed palpable to many, who were concerned that their ethnic group's "weak will" might let them down if they had to fight for their rights. This heightened their own interest in supporting groups such as Malays United, or lobbying political parties to safeguard Malays' interests. That in turn increased the anxiety of non-Malays over their place in the province. Nobody felt confident that their situation was unassailable. Far from becoming a space of "integration" and "community", life in Tanjung Pinang's neighbourhoods thus remained shot through with a persistent insecurity, a recurrent uncanny feeling of being simultaneously "in place" and "out of place" in one's own home. The perhaps universal anxieties surrounding how to interact with neighbours and new-comers had come to take on a distinctive inflection in the new provincial capital: a consequence of the demographic and political changes the town had recently undergone, but also of the very ways in which neighbourhoods themselves were conceptualised.

6

Hauntings

I had spent the whole afternoon with Pertiwi and her family, and the rain showed no sign of abating. As it drummed down on the corrugated iron roof, we could barely hear ourselves speak, so drew together in the corner of the living room, close enough that there was no need to shout. Joko, Pertiwi's youngest son, pulled out his cameraphone and showed me a series of pictures that he claimed had been photographed in and around Kampung Jawa. The first showed two boys smiling near a food stall. In the background lurked a translucent figure, with long black hair covering its face and spatters of blood on its white nightdress. The next showed a nurse waving as she descended a staircase while to her right, suspended in mid-air, was a similar figure with its head facing down as if it had been hung. "Spooky, huh?" smiled Joko as he tapped at his phone to magnify the image. "Look," he added with a broad grin, "if you zoom in, you can see its face. Look at those eyes, so black!"

"Tanjung Pinang is certainly a very spooky town," added Joko's sister Umi, a housewife in her late thirties. "Do you know what those are, Nick? They're *mak hitam*. They're a kind of vampire. They are always women. Often they have long hair and they wear white clothes, always white. These pictures were taken very near to here." Joko added that the food stall in the first picture was from just across the road, next to a house that had been mysteriously abandoned for several years. "There are a lot of *mak hitam* here," continued Umi, "and I often see them. Usually, if it's raining like this they come close to me, because I have an umbrella. So the *mak hitam* walk alongside me. When the rain becomes less heavy, they fly away — and I can see that too."

"Spooky!" shouted Joko. He was really enjoying himself.

"But I have never been afraid of them," said Umi reassuringly. "They aren't evil. I am much more afraid of human beings than I am of vampires."

Feeling Spooked

When Riau Islanders talk of their province as being "spooky" (*angker*), they do so with reference to the scores of entities known as *makhluk gaib*, which translates literally as "mysterious creature". The category is wide, and includes ghosts, vampires, *jin*, and many more. Although the term *gaib* is drawn from Arabic, islanders of all religious and cultural backgrounds acknowledge the existence of a hidden, mysterious realm (*alam gaib*) which overlays our own realm and in which these creatures dwell. They are usually invisible but sometimes "appear" in the form of possessions, apparitions, or by performing other "mysterious acts", all of which are classified as *kegaiban* (mysterious happenings) and described as being *angker*. An important feature of life in the town, the prevalence of *makhluk gaib* led a number of my respondents to declare, with a tremor in their voices, that Tanjung Pinang was "the spookiest place in the whole world". Yet as my encounter with Joko and Umi revealed, this "spookiness" could be a source of delight and security as much as one of unease or horror. Having encountered such varied reactions to the mysterious creatures that haunted the Riau Islands, I began to wonder exactly what factors determined whether a creature was felt to be frightening or fun. As I researched that question in greater depth, I discovered that the answers revealed an important new perspective on my understanding of the new Riau Islands Province and its multicultural society, but also on the psychology of the uncanny.

Uncanny, unsettled feelings have long been associated with the domain of spooks, spectres and spirits, and "uncanny" is at least one possible translation of the word *angker*. Yet how and why such feelings situations arise in human encounters with "supernatural" or "otherworldly" beings is yet to be fully understood. As outlined in Chapter 1, Freud, the most influential theorist of the uncanny, argued that such feelings were likely to be elicited in contexts marked by the reappearance (or "irruption") of something that was once familiar but which had been repressed (Freud [1919] 2003: 151). Such repression can take several forms. Some of Freud's examples are explicitly linked to psychoanalytic models of consciousness; thus literary or artistic depictions of a severed head seem uncanny because they undo the psychical repression of castration anxiety. Yet he also notes that different species of the uncanny can be found in "real life". Superstitions such as the evil eye, or curses that come true, all seem uncanny for reasons that have little to do with psychoanalysis. Freud suggests their uncanniness derives from their resonance with an animistic view of the universe that individuals are supposed to have surmounted through rational, scientific education — and which societies are supposed to have surmounted through the teleological path of modernity. For the truly modern person, this species of the uncanny can no longer exist (Freud [1919] 2003: 154).

Subsequent theorists have identified further species, notably the "spectral" uncanny that surrounds ideological discourse. For Žižek (1994: 21), any ideology involves the repression of information that contradicts it; and when this suppressed reality resurfaces, it has a haunting, spectral quality. One may thus feel deeply unsettled — "haunted" — by encounters with that which is "secretly familiar" (Willford 2006). Alternatively, the repressed may "return" in the form of an actual spectre, which is perceived by and haunts a human being. Samira Kawash (1999), for example, has argued that colonial rule in Algeria relied upon an ideology that suppressed the fact that Algerians were fellow human beings, just like their French rulers. Following Žižek, she suggests that it was this suppressed sense of Algerians' humanity, subjectivity and suffering that was reflected in the spectres and vampires that haunted French colonisers' dreams. Sophia Harvey (2008) has used a similar approach to interpret the unsettling power of what my informants would recognise as *makhluk gaib* within Singaporean horror films. Suggesting that Singapore's national ideology of temperate, secular modernity is haunted by the repressed realities of tropicality and ethnoracial folk beliefs, she illustrates how those are the very domains represented by ghosts and spectres within Singaporean cinema.

Whilst this attention to the ideological dimensions of "spectres" could enrich the anthropology of Southeast Asian "spirit beliefs", my ethnographic materials also suggest that the frameworks devised by cultural theorists of the uncanny warrant substantial qualification. I therefore advance three arguments in this chapter. First, that careful attention must be given to the cosmologies surrounding a particular *makhluk gaib* to determine whether it is in fact "spectrally" representing the return of the repressed. A more cautious approach allows for a more nuanced analysis, focusing attention on the specific circumstances in which such an interpretation is appropriate, whilst also opening the possibility that there might be very different reasons for invoking the affect of "spookiness" or *angker* in reference to "spirit phenomena". Second, these spectral affects of unsettledness or "horror" should not be taken for granted: examining such sensations in an ethnographic context suggests that what Žižek terms "the spectre[s] of ideology" have only a limited ability to shock, unsettle and disturb.

This leads me to my final argument — that the cases in which *makhluk gaib* proved truly unsettling were associated with a quite separate "species of the uncanny". Hitherto, authors interested in exploring why "spectral" entities evoke uncanny feelings have tended to focus on the character of such spectres and the circumstances in which they appear. However, in the Riau Islands, *makhluk gaib* are social actors with which human beings can have a variety of relations. While everyone that I spoke to had their own ideas as to how to interact with *makhluk gaib*, what proved incredibly unsettling was the thought of how their neighbours might be interacting with the *makhluk gaib* that lived, or were believed to live, in their midst. This feeling did not just lead Riau Islanders to feel uncomfortable in the places they called their home; it convinced them that their lives were at risk. Two main factors led to such fears taking hold. The first was the knowledge that the Riau Islands was home to people of many different backgrounds and belief systems: it was both multicultural and multicosmological. The second was the stereotype of the backward, weak-willed Malay that had become so widespread in, and so central to the identity of, Riau Islands Province (Chapters 4 and 5). The thought of how such Malays might be trying to engage with *makhluk gaib* proved haunting indeed, heightening Riau Islanders' feelings of ambivalence towards the new "Malay province" in which they lived.

Mysterious Taxonomies

The notion of *alam gaib* as an invisible realm which overlays normality, irrupting unexpectedly from time to time, resonates with models that see the uncanny as disconnecting individuals from the self-evident urban realities in which they feel at home. Indeed, in recent years, faced with surging numbers of "mysterious happenings", some government and religious leaders have instigated campaigns to re-educate the population in the ways of *alam gaib,* encouraging citizens to visualise an *alam gaib* all around them and thereby recalibrate their sense of "the normal" (*biasa*). In Freudian terms, they deliberately strive to avoid repressing, suppressing, or superannuating belief in these mysterious creatures in order to promote a happier and more homely mode of belonging in the town. Such endeavours typically draw on reformist Islam to promote a simple and coherent understanding of *alam gaib* in which mysterious creatures are invisible Muslim subjects (*jin*) that should be treated with the same respect as one would show to human neighbours. This deviates from the mysterious and multifaceted conceptions of *alam gaib* that were held by the majority of Riau Islanders I met. For most people, even when they were aware of reformist Islamic interpretations, *makhluk gaib* could not be pinned down definitively to any particular system of cultural interpretation.

The difficulties of producing satisfactory frameworks for analysing *makhluk gaib* are already familiar to anthropologists. Early colonial scholar-administrators such as Walter Skeat (1984 [1900]) and R.J. Wilkinson (1906) simply defaulted to unsystematic lists of gods, spirits, demons and ghosts. Tackling the issue in Java, Clifford Geertz declared it a hopeless task:

> There is no doctrine in these matters ... Spirit beliefs in Modjo-kuto are not part of a consistent, systematic and integrated scheme ... What the carpenter called *lelembuts* ... others might as easily claim are *gendruwos, sétans, demits,* or *djims* ... People are not consistent but tend to use such words as *demit, danjang, lelembut* and *sétan* in both a wide and narrow sense, to indicate spirits in general and to indicate certain fairly definite subtypes of them (Geertz 1960: 17, 19, 24).

Eventually he produced a classification according to what the "spirits" could do, but since most "spirits" could do most of these things, its usefulness is questionable. Worse, he dismissed informants' terminological inconsistency and contestation of categories as noise in the ethnographic system, an obstacle to understanding, rather than the thing to be understood.

A similar imperative to clarify led to several influential studies arguing that a set of core indigenous concepts underpinned the many observable phenotypes of Malay "spirit belief". Thus for Mohd. Taib Osman (1989: 115), "supernatural entities which are traceable to Hindu and Islamic sources are in fact conceived in the same manner as the indigenous spirits. They are also worshipped within the framework of animistic beliefs". In this view, diverse names, concepts and magic words conceal a shared fundamental framework which hinges on "the most ancient survival of the old Indonesian belief system ... the notion of *semangat*" (Osman 1989: 78).

Osman is not alone in positing *semangat* — a term he conceptualised as "vital essence" or "soul substance" — as pivotal to Malay thought. The structuralist re-analysis of colonial ethnological notebooks by Kirk Endicott (1970) also asserts the concept's ubiquity and uses this as a premise to suggest that certain binary oppositions can be identified across the cultures of maritime Southeast Asia:

> *semangat* : 'free spirits'
> the bodied : the bodiless
> the constrained: the free

Humans, animals, plants and non-living objects are all believed to possess *semangat* as their vital essence, leading Endicott to argue that *makhluk gaib,* which he described as "free spirits", must be the "vital essence" of something else. If *semangat* is located within tangible, material beings and objects, then *makhluk gaib* are the vital essence of the non-material environment — for example, the experiences of sickness and death (Endicott 1970: 64). His theory of the centrality of *semangat* and its dichotomous relationship with bodiless "free spirits" has since come to underpin many analyses of Southeast Asian "spirit phenomena".[1]

However, these models are of little assistance in understanding the accounts of *makhluk gaib* that I gathered in the Riau Islands because the "fundamental" concept of *semangat* that was documented in the colonial era has since become obsolete within many regions

---

[1] Examples include the work of Faucher (2002: 158–62), Laderman (1991: 40) and Ong (1988: 30–2).

of Indonesia. By the time of Independence, many Indonesians were rejecting the term *semangat*, with its mystical connotations of vigour, enthusiasm and dynamic flux, in favour of *jiwa*, a more discrete, bounded, notion of the soul. Today, *semangat* conventionally means motivation, zest and drive. It is no longer seen as an overarching cosmic principle but as a quality unique to humans. My informants conceded that "old-fashioned" notions of *semangat* as a vital essence remained in some love spells, as noted elsewhere by Cynthia Chou (2003: 58–63), but they insisted this was a "metaphor", and that their own essence was not *semangat* but *jiwa*.

With *semangat*'s ontological primacy stripped away, little benefit remains from theorising *makhluk gaib* as relationally-conceived "free spirits". Nor can we endorse Osman's suggestion that Islamic, Hindu, or other "non-native" concepts have been integrated into an enduringly indigenous framework. Rather, multiple alternative frameworks — of which there are plenty circulating in Tanjung Pinang — might be used to make sense of these mysterious creatures. Thus *makhluk gaib*'s conflation into an overarching category of "spirits" evokes unhelpfully reductive connotations of disembodied ethereality. Consider the case of *jin*, *makhluk gaib* which Endicott (1970: 53) considered paradigmatic of bodiless "free spirits", but which were theorised by many of my informants to be corporeal. Created by Allah from fire rather than clay (*tanah liat*, the substance of humans), *jin* are invisible to the human eye, but have bodies, eat, sexually reproduce, age and die. These *jin* are mysterious, but are neither "spirits" nor "supernatural". Moreover, when alleged specimens of *makhluk gaib* are recovered, they are frequently subjected to x-rays, DNA testing and display in exhibitions. Such practices see the creatures engaged with as something very different to the disembodied "essences" that they were once thought to be.

Yet not all my interlocutors saw these creatures as "natural" creations that could and should be studied. For example, when a travelling exhibition of captured and mummified *makhluk gaib* came to Tanjung Pinang, friends in the Pentecostal Church warned that the creatures on display were probably "*demons*" (English used) sent by Satan to spread evil in the world, and that even being in the same exhibition hall as them would put one's soul at risk. They were forthright in their admonishments that I must not attend. As Geertz had found, there was little terminological consistency when referring to particular creatures: what the exhibition curators suggested was a *jenglot*[2] or a *gendruwo*[3], the Pentecostals glossed as a "demon". Unlike Geertz, however, I found that whatever label they used, it channelled distinct assumptions, values and judgements, the nuances of which reflected significant differences in worldview and were thus essential to understand.

And there are many labels. Taxonomies of *makhluk gaib* derive from all the main religious and "ethnic" folk traditions, and are supplemented and challenged by new taxonomies circulating in the media. With residents able to watch TV dramas filmed in Java and Bali and Singaporean channels that show horror dramas from China, the USA and Japan, *makhluk gaib* emerges as a category of very little conceptual unity: the only thing members of the category have in common is their hidden and mysterious *gaib* character. This identification brackets them outside a known domain ("the normal") whilst foregrounding their mysterious, unknown — and possibly unknowable — nature. The further character of any *makhluk gaib* is thus highly contextual and contestable, a matter of speculation and interpretation. Hence demonological taxonomies alone cannot equip the anthropologist to analyse mysterious happenings; understanding also rests on an appreciation of the alternative interpretive categories with which any folk explanation must vie.

The significance of this point can be seen in the following encounter with a *makhluk gaib*. In 1998, Eunice, a young woman

---

[2] Only two or three inches tall, and with large, sharp fangs, the *jenglot* is a vampiric creature that is believed to be immortal provided it receives a daily diet of fresh blood. Opinion was divided amongst my informants as to whether *jenglot* were "natural" *makhluk gaib* that could be captured and domesticated by humans skilled in dark arts, or particularly powerful sorcerers who had used their dark arts to change themselves into vampires in a bid for immortality. However, *jenglot* can be killed by capturing them in a bottle and depriving them of blood, and it was such specimens that were displayed in travelling exhibitions.

[3] A *makhluk gaib* particularly associated with the island of Java, *gendruwo* are often described as large hairy creatures that live in wooded areas, behaving aggressively towards those who enter the forest and assuming the form of a handsome young man to seduce any young women wandering alone outside village boundaries. Very hairy humans were sometimes described as the offspring of such liaisons and put on show in travelling exhibitions. For further discussion, see Wessing (2006: 42–47), who advances an interesting case that *gendruwo*'s role in discouraging "immoral" behaviour means they might be best conceived as a form of "spirit guardian".

of Chinese descent, was engaged to Albert, also Chinese, who was studying in Jakarta. This was at the height of the Asian economic crisis, and food shortages and mass unemployment had prompted a lack of confidence in the government. In May 1998, thousands of students gathered in Jakarta to demand Suharto's resignation and the transition to a more democratic system. When four students were shot by security forces, riots broke out across Jakarta. Chinese Indonesians, perceived as illegitimately dominating the country's economy, were particularly targeted (Siegel 1998). This was a difficult time for Albert. He wanted to support the pro-democracy protestors but had to be careful he was not attacked by anti-Chinese rioters. After many sleepless nights, he returned to Tanjung Pinang in a poor condition, thin, tired, with dull eyes. Eunice said he had lost a lot of his "*brightness*" [English used].[4] One dusk, Albert started to shout and scream uncontrollably during the call to prayer. He only became calm once there was no more noise from the mosque. His teeth grew so they looked like "fangs" and if a *dukun* (a practitioner who specialises in resolving "mysterious happenings") visited the house, he would become very angry, "as if he wanted to eat the *dukun*". Eunice was convinced that he was possessed by a *makhluk gaib*, but she was unsure what kind. Eunice and Albert's parents "tried everything": after a Chinese *dukun* had failed to help, they contacted a medical doctor and a Malay *dukun*. This last *dukun* said that Albert had been possessed by two *makhluk gaib*, a man and a woman. Eunice was uncertain what kind of *makhluk gaib* they were supposed to be. Albert got so angry with the mosque and the Malay *dukun* that she thought they could be "Malay" *makhluk gaib*, perhaps *jin* or *pontianak* (a creature said to be the spirit of a woman who died whilst pregnant). Then again, Albert had been so angry with the Chinese *dukun* she still thought it might be a Chinese ghost. Albert was eventually sent to a mental asylum in Singapore from which he returned "with his evil look gone" but shaking uncontrollably. He resumed his studies in Java and shortly afterwards broke off his engagement with Eunice. She still wonders what happened to him, and whether he was really cured.

---

[4] Eunice explained that for the Chinese, every person possesses "brightness" (reflecting the "active" and "masculine" cosmic principle of *yang*), and when this becomes "slow", people are more vulnerable to danger.

This story is typical in showing how multicosmological the interpretation of mysterious happenings can be. Albert's susceptibility to possession lies in a "brightness" cosmology that Eunice explicitly labelled as "Chinese". But in explaining the possession itself, it is less clear what framework should be used. The family "tries everything" and without complete success. Although Eunice is neither Malay nor Muslim, she is prepared to believe that "Malay *makhluk gaib*" inadmissible in Chinese Buddhism might exist in Tanjung Pinang and to hire a Malay *dukun*. In treating the possession, Chinese cosmology is not enough. Presented with the possibility of losing a loved one, the family draws on all the explanatory frameworks at their disposal. Distinct cosmological differences are here surmounted in the face of threat, and yet despite this, *alam gaib* retains an elusive quality, with no answers or closure forthcoming from Albert's treatments.

The case demonstrates how the plurality of discourses about *makhluk gaib* itself constitutes a resource upon which Tanjung Pinang's residents draw to make sense of bewildering and mysterious events that happen to them. This necessitates a very different approach to "Malay magic" from the descriptions of closed cultural systems that have usually been offered by anthropologists. In contrast to Osman's model of "Malay spirit beliefs", in which ideas from diverse sources are integrated into a single framework, Albert and Eunice's experiences show how multiple cosmologies can be recombined through the suspension of disbelief: several cosmologies are then drawn on simultaneously, whilst nevertheless held to be separate. Philosophically irreconcilable differences are thus able to be either surmounted or underscored. This has profound implications for the experience of life in Tanjung Pinang.

The Haunted Town

Hantu, usually translated as "ghosts", have long been theorised as detemporalised and non-personalised beings. Whether deriving from fears of mortality (Endicott 1970: 75), or the malevolence of the dying (Winstedt 1951: 22), ghosts were said to travel indiscriminately and anonymously, representing "the spirit of blinded vengeance" (Wilkinson 1906: 24). While this paradigm is compatible with Endicott's structural oppositions between the material and the non-material, interpretations of ghosts in the Riau Islands are often very different. Far from being indiscriminate, ghosts take on social significance from their apparition to a given person or in a given place. In such cases, haunting often represents details of the past re-emerging and troubling the (perhaps ideological) assumptions that a break with the past has been made, although as Žižek stresses, a returning "spectre" need not be historical but can be anything that is unsymbolised in a dominant discourse. In Tanjung Pinang, localised biographies of ghosts are generated which mark them as returning repressed — or at least suppressed — fragments of the town's past. Yet as well as troubling dominant discourses, the interpretation of ghosts can also serve to entrench them.

One day, after finishing classes, Teddy, a Chinese Indonesian schoolboy whom I got to know well as a member of the Riau Islands vocational school debating team (Chapter 7), went to the public swimming pool. The pool was deserted, and despite being a strong swimmer, Teddy felt uneasy being there alone. There was something *angker* about the pool's atmosphere, though he couldn't say what. He entered the water and began to swim. After several lengths, disaster struck:

> I was about a metre away from the side of the pool. I kept trying to do it, to swim and swim, and yet I couldn't move forward. I felt there was something, a hand, dragging my legs down. For about a minute! It was the ghost in the pool. I thought, 'Oh, I'm definitely going to die here, I'm definitely going to be killed by a ghost! How can this have happened? Why?' But I'm a Buddhist, and I thought I would try praying to the Buddhist God [*Tuhan yang Budha punya*],[5] 'Please don't let me die in this swimming pool, please let me live'. I had never prayed so hard. But after I made the prayer I was able to move forward and climb out of the pool...

---

[5] This may refer to the Adi Buddha, a self-emanating, self-originating Buddha that Indonesian Buddhists worship given the national requirement that all religions posit a "supreme being". Buddhists disagree over the Adi Buddha's capacity for divine intervention. However, other Buddhists stressed that they had a God who was "just like the Christian God, but a Mother, not a Father". Teddy himself was unclear on these details, simply invoking the "Almighty God" (*Tuhan yang Maha Esa*) alluded to in the *Pancasila*, the Indonesian national philosophy.

Another schoolboy told me that a friend of his from primary school had drowned in the swimming pool, an event he too attributed to a ghost. Rumours of the being inhabiting the pool were widespread. In trying to explain it, informants recalled that the site once contained a fish pond, which was used as an execution site and mass grave by Japanese soldiers during the occupation. Discussion of the Japanese Occupation was usually rare (Chapter 3), but could be prompted by the puzzles ghosts presented. The violent wartime past neatly accounted for the particularly malevolent nature of the ghost in the pool. According to Chinese cosmology, violent murder produces a ghost trapped permanently in the living world, unable to access the world of the dead until it has killed a living human to replace it. If that victim is killed by drowning, he or she cannot enter the world of the dead either, and so lies in wait as a vengeful ghost (Emmons 1982: 20–1). Hence Teddy's anxiety that he might become the next ghost:

> I was so lucky I managed to think to pray to God, because if I hadn't, if I'd panicked — only thinking about how I was going to die — then I definitely would have died, and become a ghost myself, waiting for the next victim.

Eddy, a Bugis man who had grown up in the Riau Islands as a child but had since travelled the world, took a less credulous stance. He told me he "[didn't] believe in ghosts or anything else like that. They are figments of people's imaginations". I was therefore surprised when, one day, Eddy said he had heard I often ate dinner at the Melayu Square foodcourt, and was worried for my safety because of the mysterious happenings there. Newly opened in 2005, the foodcourt sits on a piece of land that had been reclaimed from the sea in the 1990s. The possibility of human sacrifices during the reclamation made several informants wary of the foodcourt, thinking it could be haunted. The unreclaimed perimeter also had a troubling past, known as "a forest where people would come to commit suicide". Ghost sightings were regular, damaging the trade of nearby hotels. Eddy, however, explained matters differently:

> The area near Melayu Square has a reputation for being haunted. Actually, it isn't haunted, but it has a strange aura (*aura aneh*). Go there at night — it's very dark. And why is that? There are lamps, but they aren't effective. Many people are killed there,

usually because of motorcycle accidents — it can even happen during the day. They are there, and suddenly they start to think of their boyfriend or girlfriend, and their concentration disappears, and they are killed. It often happens like that. It's because the land there has a negative energy. In the past, many people went there to hang themselves. Normally it was Chinese who had lost gambling games and only wanted to kill themselves. It was like that for many years. Also, when the Japanese came, they arrived in that area. It made an energy that is still in the ground. There were certainly many who were killed at that time.

This formulation of "energy" was a relatively unusual way of describing *angker* locations. Yet although Eddy denied the existence of ghosts as metaphysical beings, he still conceptualised the events of the past as having an eerie agency upon the present, mediated through place and land. Like the malevolent ghost of the swimming pool, past trauma remained in the place where it occurred and served to reproduce itself by inducing trauma in the present.

Public areas such as foodcourts and swimming pools can easily be — and are — avoided by the wary. Matters become more complicated when the *makhluk gaib* exist within one's own home. This happened to a family of Malay migrants from Mainland Riau who had recently purchased a newly built house on the outskirts of town. Their story is typical of many. Shortly after moving into the household, the family's young daughter fell ill with a high fever. Her cousin Yuliza related how a *paranormal* (a practitioner specialising in resolving "mysterious happenings") detected a whole family of ghosts:

> It was a very large family. There were grandparents and lots of small children, all playing in the house and living there as a family. So the *paranormal* gave them an offering of some food. He gave them yellow rice stained with turmeric, and some salt and some limes, and left it for a day. For a whole day we couldn't go in the house … When we went back inside, all the food had been moved about, as if someone had been playing with it. Anyway, the ghosts agreed to leave and after that my cousin instantly got better. It turned out the house used to be on top of a Chinese cemetery, but my uncle didn't know that. He had just arrived in the town.

Yuliza believed these ghosts to be the "*spirits*" [English used] of dead Chinese who were buried underneath the house. Tanjung Pinang was prone to these kinds of hauntings, she explained, because many areas recently cleared to accommodate the surging population had been used as graveyards by Chinese communities in the past. She herself had been able to see ghosts in her youth and still glimpsed horrific sights when driving past the town cemeteries. She was weeping as she recounted the details:

> I have seen ghosts in Teluk Keriting graveyard. They were women, dressed all in white, and with long black hair, but the hair was covering the face so I didn't see what they really looked like. And they were moving around the graveyard! It was so awful. I never want to go past that graveyard again. I will never drive past it on my motorcycle. If my friend is giving me a lift, I will always insist we take a different route.

These examples are typical of ghost narratives throughout the town, and whilst they vary in cosmological details, in each case the potential for unpleasant apparitions shaped informants' engagements with portions of urban space. The public pool, Melayu Square and the road past Teluk Keriting graveyard were all carefully avoided by certain informants because of the *makhluk gaib* that might appear there, whilst domestic haunting required swift *paranormal* intervention. Only Teddy, who had survived by appealing to an interventionist god, felt he could return to the haunted swimming pool again:

> Dendang Ria is the most *angker* swimming pool in the whole town! But I do now have the courage to swim there again. I have been able to defeat the ghost once. The ghost tried to take me and couldn't succeed because I was able to appeal to the Buddhist God. So if I go there again, the ghost will not want to try to take me again. And if it does, then I can defeat it again in the same way.

There are other uniformities to the tales. Rather than locating ghosts in derelict spaces, or "holes in the urban fabric" as typically observed in studies of the urban uncanny (Cohen 1999: 14; Edensor 2005: 837), the haunted sites are popular leisure destinations and family homes. Furthermore, explanations were usually rooted in references to "the Japanese" or "the Chinese" past. The narratives surrounding these haunted places therefore appear to subvert official histories that see the archipelago and town as being "Malay land", downplay the early presence of the Chinese, and stress the lack of conflict during the occupation. As Andrew Willford (2006: 39) comments, "silencing, and the ideological and institutional work that buttresses it, can produce ... certitude, but not without leaving uncanny traces of the surmounted other". It would appear that the certitude that Tanjung Pinang is a Malay town is disturbed by unsymbolised histories resurfacing in the form of troubling spectres.

Public discourses of the Japanese Occupation focus on a limited range of facts: the change in currency, the wartime diet, snatches of remembered Japanese. It is very hard to elicit recollections of what life was like in the islands during the war (Chapter 3). Ghost stories, however, draw on and express the trauma the town's population underwent. People who go to places haunted by wartime events die in violent ways (motorcycle accidents, drowning whilst battling with a ghost, etc.) and their bodies, when recovered, are usually mutilated. Whether the narrative of replication centres on the reproduction of ghosts or of negative energy, today's "mysterious happenings" and tragedies translate the atrocities of the Japanese Occupation into a contemporary context. Though these events are very different to the executions and battles that "mysterious happenings" are said to derive from, their violence and horror act as means by which contemporary townsfolk can access and imagine the degrees of violence that permeated Japanese times but which cannot be readily expressed on their own terms, establishing a clear link between contemporary trauma and the historical landscape.

Writing of the ghost narratives surrounding the Japanese Occupation of Singapore, Faucher (2004: 196) suggests that the questions of memory associated with haunting are always political. I agree. But while she suggests that political action enforces selective "national amnesias", allowing only certain memories to resurface, I would contend that these returning spectres might themselves be ideologically constructed. We need to think twice about psychoanalytic approaches that undertheorise "the repressed" or "unsymbolised" that is apparently "returning". Although sites such as the swimming pool are widely accepted to have been the location of genuine wartime brutality, many claims are more questionable. Possibilities of Japanese mass graves are invoked to explain "mysterious happenings" in areas that maps indicate were thick jungle in the 1940s. The *"angker"* site of the battleground at which the Japanese first arrived is alleged to be in at least four separate locations, while historical evidence suggests no such battle even occurred. Rather, the Japanese sent emissaries to announce in advance that they came in peace, and that they too were Muslims, and were thus welcomed with open arms by the aristocrats and community leaders of the archipelago (Wee 1985: 141). The subsequent collaboration, which saw thousands of Riau Islanders consigned to forced labour or torture by local Malay aristocrats goes unspoken in interpretations of ghosts as residues of exclusively "Japanese" violence. Haunted sites do serve as memorials, articulating traumatic events that informants otherwise feel uncomfortable about narrating. However, such memory narratives do not derive from specific histories of particular locations so much as broader, ideologically constructed notions of the Japanese Occupation that are actively localised when "mysterious happenings" occur. Indeed, the peddlers of these tales were often the descendants of migrants with no first-hand knowledge of the occupation. Their accounts were not based on "historical memory" so much as a "historical imaginary" which they narrated as "historical knowledge" of their town in attempts to show that they belonged to it. In the process, these narratives reconfigured the urban landscape, articulating otherwise inexpressible histories in a purified and acceptable form.

The second dominant ghost story concerns the Chinese. Houses are often considered haunted because they are built on top of a Chinese cemetery or because a Chinese, bankrupt through opium and gambling, committed suicide where the house was to be built. These disruptive intrusions of a past era upon domestic urban space reinstate the widespread distribution of Chinese pre-independence, another point largely unsymbolised in popular historical discourses. They also reinstate the Chinese presence — which is associated with the crimes of gambling and drug addiction — as disruptive, polluting, and, for the Muslim majority, heretical (*kafir*). Despite Islamic discourse stressing the impossibility of ghosts, Muslim informants speculated that perhaps, for "heretical" Chinese, it would be possible to become a ghost. Although this defies the basic Islamic principle that all humans, pious or impious, lie in their graves after death until judgement day, the impious being tortured in their graves by angels (*malaikat*), it reflects the multicosmological dimension of life in Tanjung Pinang. Non-Chinese townsfolk were aware of the important role that ghosts play in Chinese culture: it is performed to them every lunar seventh month when offerings are burnt and pig

Figure 6.1 A Chinese family burns offerings to ghosts in a Tanjung Pinang shopping mall (Source: author)

carcasses are paraded through the town as appeasements to hungry ghosts (Figure 6.1). Hence they reasoned that perhaps Chinese could become ghosts, whereas they could not. Unlike Endicott (1970: 47), for whom "spirit substance" was distributed along lines of biological and material distinction, for my informants, the potential to become or have dealings with any particular *makhluk gaib* was circumscribed by cultural boundaries. In the multicosmological society, the metaphysical implications of "being human" are not shared across humanity but distributed according to ethnocultural categorisations.

It is thus significant that "Chinese ghosts" always afflicted non-Chinese Muslims. Chinese themselves might report the appearance of "angry ghosts", usually of relatives, in their dreams but attributed the appearance of "mysterious figures" in the house to *penunggu* ("inhabitants"), benevolent creatures "something between a ghost and an angel". Most Chinese were surprised to hear that "the Chinese" were widely considered responsible for domestic apparitions. Those most likely to suffer from Chinese domestic hauntings were, like

Yuliza's uncle, migrants who "did not know" there had been a cemetery or burial in that location, or people living in new housing districts. The appearance of a *makhluk gaib* is thus connected not only
with a Chinese past but also with the uncertain knowledge that a
new arrival has regarding their home. Of course, such sites rarely
present firm evidence of a Chinese burial, but the possibility retains
a fearful grip on the imagination: Chinese cemeteries are conventionally a long way out of town, so cemeteries could plausibly have
been located in areas now subject to new housing developments.

Residents expect Tanjung Pinang to be "Malay land" and, because it is a widely asserted local axiom that "Malayness is identical
with Islam", it is expected to be "Islamic land" as well. Such expectations have only been entrenched by the ethnonationalist politicisation
of the Riau Archipelago as "Malay" during the push for provincial
autonomy. "Mysterious happenings" such as domestic apparitions,
or the unexplained sickness of a family member, can provide an
unpleasant revelation that the space one inhabits is actually, in some
senses, "heretical land". However, unlike the *makhluk gaib* of Japanese
execution sites, which can only be liberated through creating another
hostile being to take their place, the domestic Chinese ghosts can
be, and are, "cleansed away" (*dibersihkan*) through the employment
of a *paranormal*. On the one hand, then, ghost stories reinscribe the
significance of the Chinese past, an unsymbolised domain. Yet unlike
Kathleen Brogan's interpretation of "cultural haunting" in American
literature, in which a poorly documented, partially erased cultural
history can be recovered and made use of through narrative (Brogan
1998: 2), there is nothing triumphant about this return. It occurs
only to be thwarted. Tales of Chinese cemetery ghosts are invariably
tales of successful exorcism, the removal of Chinese contamination,
and the re-ascription of the house to the Malay, Muslim space it
was always supposed to be assigned to. As this happens across the
town, so urban space is progressively "purified" of an unruly historic
Chineseness and, despite the continuing residence of many Chinese
Indonesians, security in the town's fundamental identity as Malay
land is re-established.

So the case of apparition, in which historical trauma and
"Chineseness" are used as interpretive frameworks to explain mysterious happenings, involves the conflation of various cosmological
possibilities in establishing "historical" and ideologically charged
narratives that anchor ghosts in, and remove them from, particular

locations. Whilst unsettling, these ghosts possess a homely quality too: in their ability to be removed or to conceal further horrors, they act as a prop as much as a threat to dominant ideologies. A shadow of their uncanny potential recurs in their narration, but this can quickly be shrugged off and consumed as a pleasurable spine-tingling thrill. It takes a different species of the uncanny — one not so easily remedied through recourse to mysticism — to make Riau Islanders feel truly unsettled in their multicosmological home.

The Longest Cable Bridge in the World

In April 2006, Tanjung Pinang was terrorised by a headhunter (*penebuk*) roaming the town in search of human children. Early that month, the headless corpse of a young woman was discovered in the jungle just outside the town's boundaries. Shortly afterwards, several schoolchildren disappeared without a trace. Alongside the usual rumours of kidnappers abducting children to sell to childless Singaporeans, a new possibility emerged: children were being harvested for their heads. Panic set in. Old women braved the midday heat to accompany their grandchildren home from school; frantic parents raced through the alleyways of urban neighbourhoods looking for children who had wandered off. On Dendun Island, the neighbourhood watch ran a constant night-time vigil against headhunters, patrolling the streets with lanterns and knives. A sense of unsettledness and anxiety pervaded the province. On porches, in offices and in restaurants, everyone was talking about who or what the headhunter might be and why it was attacking.

The predominant explanation related the attacks to the impending construction of a bridge between two of the Riau Islands: Batam and Bintan. Proposed to boost manufacturing and tourism, the bridge would also be a substantial tourist attraction in its own right. Almost seven kilometres in length, it would be the longest cable bridge in the world. Yet the official excitement was not shared by the town's population. The bridge cut straight through one of the most mystical areas of the Riau Islands, the Lobam Sea. This was widely considered home to a powerful and evil *makhluk gaib*. Were a bridge to be built in this region, disturbing the *makhluk gaib*'s home, then payment would certainly be required. The *makhluk gaib* would demand an entire headful of human blood for every concrete bridge support post driven into the sea floor. If it did not receive this payment, it would claim the blood in another way; most probably by destroying the bridge and harvesting the blood of all the travellers on it at the time.

Opinions differed regarding the headhunter's identity. Some informants suggested a prospective building contractor, perhaps with government support, had employed a professional headhunter to supply the materials they needed. Several informants believed the headhunter was itself a *makhluk gaib* sent from the Lobam Sea to start collecting heads. Others disbelieved that a *makhluk gaib* would demand human blood. They conceptualised the headhunter as a superstitious Malay living in the vicinity of the bridge development. Scared that his home would not be safe unless heads were collected, he was thought to have begun his own virtuoso harvest. This interpretation was plausible to many. Malays were, after all, extremely backward, or so it was reasoned. Indeed, provincial secession was partly premised on sloughing off the conditions that had rendered Malays so backward (Chapter 2). Hence the figure of the uneducated and primitive indigene, which new forms of political affiliation sought to assist, also haunted the imaginations of urban society as they tried to identify who was responsible for conducting such terrible crimes.

A "lunatic" was eventually arrested for the murder of the headless woman, but with rumours that the police had framed him, the matter was never truly resolved. Yet headhunter scares were not unfamiliar to my informants, any more than they are to regional anthropology (see Hoskins 1996; Wessing and Jordaan 1997). In 2000, a similar scare had surrounded the construction of the Barelang bridge linking Batam, Rempang and Galang, whilst a smaller local bridge had been the focus of a scare in 1986. Informants who lived through these as children recounted being confined to the house for months while headhunters were active in the town. And although architects that I interviewed denied that Riau Islanders had ever offered human blood to *makhluk gaib* in living memory, and although there is no documented evidence of headhunting taking place in the islands' history, even those sceptical of the headhunter scare asserted that such things had indeed happened before Malays had become "civilised". There is, however, no documented evidence of headhunting taking place in the Riau Islands' history.

Islanders' arguments on this front call to mind one of Freud's "species of the uncanny". Writing of Western beliefs in the omnipotence of thoughts and the return of the dead, he suggests that:

> We — or our primitive forebears — once regarded such things as real possibilities; we were convinced that they really happened. Today we no longer believe in them, having *surmounted* such modes of thought. Yet we do not feel entirely secure in these new convictions; the old ones live on in us, on the look out for confirmation ... For anyone who has wholly and definitively rejected these animistic convictions, this species of the uncanny no longer exists (Freud [1919] 2003: 154).

These remarks apply pertinently to headhunting in the Riau Islands. As informants' theories of culpability reveal, two distinct loci of danger and uncanniness are associated with headhunting narratives. In one, the threat is from the *makhluk gaib* itself, which either haunts a constructed bridge with the prospect of collapse, or forces seemingly respectable governments and architects to work with murderers in order to pre-empt its actions. In the other, which considers this conceptualisation of *makhluk gaib* as superstitious or misguided, the danger lies rather in the beliefs of more "primitive" Riau Islanders, and the ways they may act on these — including turning headhunter themselves.

Freud's comment on the "uncanniness" of the secretly unsurmounted thus applies in two senses. Most directly, it declares the feeling of uncanniness felt by informants who try to shrug off headhunters as fairytale bogeymen, not what one would see in a developed, civilised or modern society, yet in their hearts believe the rumours to be true. It also points to a broader "uncanny" located not in the headhunter or the *makhluk gaib* of the Lobam Sea but in the social environment of Tanjung Pinang. This uncanny feeling says, "I thought we *as a society* had surmounted these beliefs, but it seems we have not." While this "urban uncanny" inheres in an urban population, not in particular structures, informants found the town's flagship development projects provided especially visceral connections to the disturbing thoughts of those around them. "I thought of Melayu Square and how big it is," commented one young civil servant who ate at the foodcourt on a regular basis. "There must be hundreds of heads buried underneath it. I wanted to vomit."

For many in the town, construction sacrifice was not just unpleasant but actively wrong. Late in 2005, the suburb of Tanjung Unggat decided to renovate its harbour. A *paranormal* involved in the construction work released the unfortunate news that a *jin* living in the area was demanding the blood of a freshly slaughtered child for the construction work to be allowed to proceed. Local residents and the builders called a public meeting, where fierce debate raged over what should be done. Jeni, a religious studies teacher, led a group of sceptics, protesting that it was very clear in the Qur'an that *jin* and humans inhabited different realms. *Jin* ate filth (*kotoran*) and so the blood of a child would be no use to it. In fact, if the *jin* ate flesh or blood, it would probably fall ill. The group concluded that it was unacceptable to give the blood of a child, this was not an appropriate demand for the *jin* to have made, and the *paranormal* was to renegotiate with the *jin*.

At the next meeting, the *paranormal* reported the *jin* had conceded it would accept a goat. The animal was duly found and brought to the harbour works. Jeni, however, remained outraged. First, he argued, if there really was a *jin* in the sea, it could not be negotiated with in this way. Second, the blood and meat of a goat was as little use to the *jin* as a child. To feed blood to a *jin* was to misunderstand the nature of *jin* as revealed in the Qur'an. His arguments and scriptural evidence convinced the majority of those gathered, but this was only a partial reprieve for the unfortunate goat, which was subsequently sacrificed to Allah and eaten by the local residents.

Jeni insisted that there had been no subsequent problems with the harbour repairs but others, beginning to doubt his theology (and their own), refused to use the harbour for fear the *jin* was waiting to claim human blood. They cited the example of the bridge near the Ramayana department store, which had supposedly been built without a sacrifice. Although it had not suffered any structural collapse, it was said that one day a family had travelled under the bridge in a canoe, and their vessel had then emerged empty on the other side. Subsequent investigations found a set of skeletons in the river bed at the point where they had disappeared.

But we should remember that not all townsfolk admit the existence of *jin*. Chinese Indonesians in particular had little sympathy for this concept in their cosmology. The idea of sacrificing a human or animal to a non-existent *jin* proved troubling for many of them.

They suggested that the trauma of sacrificing a child at a building site would cause the location to be haunted by a vindictive ghost that would revisit the violence upon humans using the building. A small, highly aggressive ghost seemingly suspended in mid-air was said to haunt the Ramayana department store and Chinese informants confided they were convinced this was the ghost of a four-year-old boy whose head was said to be in the foundations. Meanwhile, non-Chinese informants suggested the ghost was the product of the store being built over an unmarked Chinese burial, each group locating the uncanniness, danger and disorder symbolised by the ghost within the cosmologies of the other.

The construction sacrifice issue is so powerful because of a fundamental paradox that cripples the viability of a multicosmological society. Headhunting is beyond the limits of civilisation, development and modernity, since it requires the murder of an innocent human being, and yet also fundamental to these, at least for those who believe that *jin* and other *makhluk gaib* live in and own areas of empty land. For them, unless there is headhunting, the "developed society" that finds its symbolic expression in construction projects, urban expansion and high-rise skylines will literally topple. Whether it uses human heads or not, a construction project will be, for some people, a space of fear, disquiet and distress. In this light, we can hardly say that discourses of *makhluk gaib* are turned to as a means of grappling with the ambivalences of global modernity, a logic frequently offered to explain their apparent proliferation (Bubandt 2006; Geschiere 1998). Rather, the cosmologies and ecologies of Tanjung Pinang's already-present *makhluk gaib* intersect to generate precisely such an ambivalence. As the new Riau Islands Province unveils ambitious building projects to "put itself on the map", singles out the ambiguous figure of "the Malay" as distinctly regional, and continues to attract migrants with highly diverse cosmologies, the sites in which these problematic intersections occur themselves proliferate. These sites are not haunted merely because of the startling numbers of *makhluk gaib* documented in Tanjung Pinang. It is at the moments when divergent discourses of *makhluk gaib* fail to either reconcile or transcend their points of difference that such creatures become most threatening. On those occasions, a sense of uncanny alienation is experienced not only in the locations and moments at which the creatures become apparent. It pervades life in the society that seemingly allows them to flourish unchecked.

Spectres of Malayness

The study of "spirit beliefs" has enjoyed a lengthy and distinguished history within the anthropology of Southeast Asia. Ghosts, demons and other denizens of a spooky and mysterious realm have long provided fodder for travellers and ethnologists, which is hardly surprising given the prominence of these themes in everyday social interaction. Yet as I have shown in this chapter, classic models for the study of such beliefs, and the urge to derive a coherent classificatory system that underpinned them, are of little help in understanding how Riau Islanders think and feel about *makhluk gaib*.

Rather than forming a bounded field of "Malay magic" (cf. Endicott 1970; Skeat 1984 [1900]), "spirit beliefs" in Tanjung Pinang fall into many streams that intertwine and oppose. Moreover, those dynamics of intertwining and opposition are central to the affective experience of managing "mysterious happenings". At times they might be combined in ways that provide a source of comfort, as in the case of Albert's possession. In other cases, such as that of construction sacrifice, cosmological diversity became iconic of alienation, difference and threat. Thus, for all the provincial government's attempts to smooth relations between various groups, ideas about what people might believe and how they might act upon those beliefs work to configure the town's population itself as something which can render home "unhomely". These suspicions and fears help to explain the unease that informants attach to particular categories: "orthodox Muslim", "Riau Island Malay" and "Chinese". They make Tanjung Pinang a home with hidden dangers, a town in which invisible elements that are widely acknowledged, but frequently overlooked in the bustle of everyday life, stand primed to irrupt, uncannily, at any time.

Yet while *makhluk gaib* might be widely described as *angker*, and resonate closely with the spectres and spooks of the classic Western "uncanny", there are, as Freud himself anticipated, multiple species of uncanniness at play in the Riau Islands. For while entities such as ghosts appear to resurrect disturbing repressed fragments of the past, resurfacing as Žižekian spectres that quite literally haunt the ideology of regional Malayness, closer scrutiny suggests this "uncanniness" is itself implicated in processes of ideological mystification. The activities that it spurs, such as rituals to "cleanse" formerly Chinese land or narrations of the Japanese Occupation that leave out the complicity of local aristocrats, conceal marginal and potentially subversive histories of the Riau Islands: dominant ideologies of Malayness are left intact. Thus feeling unsettled in one's hometown, paradoxically, becomes part of one's mastery of it.

The other species of the uncanny that I have set out in this chapter is a much more unhomely beast. Deriving from the unsuccessful or incomplete suppression of "superstitions" and "cultural beliefs" within a population, it breeds unsettledness both in acute moments of panic and in the brooding fear of what beliefs might lurk in the minds of one's neighbours. Malays, under such circumstances, are not merely seen as "backward" but also as a source of considerable danger. Moreover, unlike Malays in the neighbourhood, who can be monitored, controlled or circumvented, this threat stems from Malays "out there", somewhere in the province. The fear of such Malays quickly rips through both the comfort of everyday life and the political rhetoric that a Malay province is a place where any Indonesian could feel at home. While such a stereotype of "the Malay" persists, Umi will not be the only person in the Riau Islands to believe that she has more to fear from humans than she does from vampires.

7

The Human Resources Crisis

I was ordering some noodles at a food stall one evening when a scruffy looking man on a motorcycle parked beside me and asked me where I was from and why I had come to Indonesia. Was I, for example, looking for a wife? I replied somewhat curtly that I was a social scientist who was there to do research, whereupon he grabbed my hand and shook it warmly. "Have you come here to solve the human resources crisis?" he asked, breaking into a joyful grin. "That's the research this province needs!"

Others were inclined to agree. Riau Islanders often complained that their province was "backward" and "economically stagnant", placing the blame squarely at the foot of the region's undisciplined, unmotivated and poor quality "human resources" (*sumber daya manusia*, SDM). The Riau Islands' alleged "human resources crisis" had even been a lynchpin of arguments against their becoming a new province, with Saleh Djasit, the governor of Riau, arguing that "the Riau Archipelago's human resources are neither ready nor capable of accepting or setting into motion the wheels of a Riau Islands provincial government" (Sumanti Ardi 2002: 65). When the separation went ahead, it therefore became a priority for the new administration to demonstrate that the archipelago's human resources could be nationally and globally competitive.

Assertions of low "human resource quality" intersect closely with local perceptions of the Riau Islands as home to an indolent Malay culture (Chapter 4) and as having suffered decades of neglect (Chapter 2), but the vocabulary through which these concerns are expressed represents an intriguing reconfiguration of development

173

discourse and what it means to be human. Indonesians first began discussing "human resources" in the context of management and recruitment, but by the 1990s, there had arisen a new political imperative: the crafting of *high quality* human resources who would be able to contribute to national development. It seems likely that this was triggered by growing interest in concepts of "human development", "human capital" and "capabilities" amongst international agencies such as the United Nations Development Programme (Srinavasan 1994). Whatever its origins, however, the vocabulary of "human resource quality" has proliferated across Indonesia ever since and is now pervasive in politics, corporate training and the public sphere. It has also generated new ways of understanding and experiencing oneself, and of evaluating oneself in relation to others. Singapore, for example, was widely celebrated in the Riau Islands for having become a "global city" despite having few natural resources of its own, a feat my informants attributed to its excellent human resources. When Riau Islanders looked at Singapore, they saw what their homeland, which enjoyed an equally strategic location, could have become. It saddened them to know that Singaporean visitors felt the islands were just like Singapore had been in the 1960s (Lindquist 2009: 109). It was almost as if the Riau Islands had been held back in time: held back by their human resources.

An ethnography of Tanjung Pinang would thus be incomplete without recognising anxieties over human resources as a critical dimension of contemporary Riau Islands life and policy. This is not, however, to suggest that the rhetoric of a "human resources crisis" should be accepted at face value. Quite aside from the many problems inherent in reducing human beings to the status of "resources", the discourse of a "human resources crisis" suggests it is individuals, and their capacities, motivation and skill sets that are to blame for problems that might better be understood from a structural and political economic perspective. High levels of unemployment, educational underachievement, and difficulties experienced by Riau Islanders in securing jobs within the flagship projects of the Indonesia-Malaysia-Singapore Growth Triangle are all frequently cited by islanders as evidence of the region's poor human capital. Yet these can all be explained in other ways: the tremendous surge in the archipelago's population has far outstripped the availability of jobs in the formal sector, while the associated poverty means that many children must either forego education altogether or spend time after school working, rather than studying. A dearth of universities and colleges in the archipelago meant that islanders seeking higher education were forced to relocate to other regions of Indonesia. While this was manageable in the years when the islands still used the Straits dollar, many people found it prohibitively expensive once the rupiah became the standard currency. Since the late 1990s, higher education has become more accessible in the region itself, but predominantly in private institutions with high tuition fees — there was no state university in the Riau Islands until Universitas Maritim Raja Ali Haji was granted such a status in December 2011. In the case of the Growth Triangle, islanders have been disadvantaged by recruitment practices which source labour preferentially from Java and Mainland Sumatra (Ford and Lyons 2006: 264). Furthermore, whilst Riau Islanders often imagine Growth Triangle projects to employ huge numbers of workers, the number of job opportunities has steadily diminished as companies have relocated to areas with lower land and administration costs, such as South China and Vietnam.

From this perspective, it is hard to conclude that the region's human resource quality is really the principal factor hindering its development. However, my focus in this chapter is not the validity of such a diagnosis but rather, given its prevalence in Tanjung Pinang, the effects it has on people's lives. Analysing the ways in which Riau Islanders and their administrators believed that someone could become a "high quality human resource", and the policies they put in place to achieve this, illuminates how personhood, agency and capacity are experienced within the Riau Islands in ways that have important implications for understanding regional citizenship, governance and transnational relations. Theoretically, the investigation reveals the extent to which studies of "governmentality" — defined by Michel Foucault (1991) as an art of government which seeks to "improve" the entire population by encouraging them to conduct and regulate themselves in specific ways — might benefit from paying attention to the reflexivity, doubt and affective states that citizens experience when they follow governmental edicts (see also Conclusion). Most significantly, I will argue, the "bad faith" that citizens and officials alike had towards the government's attempts to improve human resource quality in the Riau Islands served not only to undermine their efforts, but even to drive some of the very best human resources away.

The Motivated Human Resource

My interlocutors in Tanjung Pinang used the term "human resources" in several different ways. For some, it seemed to denote a region's overall manpower, as in one schoolgirl's explanation that "human resources are all the people in one area that can use their minds, power and energy to develop and make prosperous the society around them". Others thought it referred to the "resources" — such as skills, gifts, talents and knowledge — that humans in any given region had. A secondary school teacher defined "human resources" as "the skills that we have in our lives and that we use for our livelihoods. They give an advantage to us". However, whether the term itself was used to refer to people or to their skills, there was consensus on the defining features of the Riau Islands' "human resources crisis": the region's labour force, whilst large, was of "low quality" and lacked the necessary skills and mindsets to be "globally competitive".

So what makes a human resource stand out as being of "high quality"? As elsewhere in Indonesia, officials in the Riau Islands have been strongly influenced by ideas originating from Western social psychology. These ideas, however, have not been imported wholesale. They exist in a form that is at once vernacularised and held in awkward juxtaposition with local intuitions about what makes somebody an efficacious person. Indeed, it is the dynamic interaction between different understandings of efficacy that gives human resource development initiatives their unexpected and precarious character.

In the 1950s and 1960s, during the heyday of modernisation theory, social psychologists in the United States instigated an ambitious attempt to explore the psychological origins of economic development. This research programme culminated in the publication of David McClelland's *The Achieving Society* (1961), in which the author argued that a country is more likely to develop economically when its population exhibits a high degree of a psychological drive, which he termed "the need for Achievement", often abbreviated to "*n* Achievement" or simply "*n Ach*". McClelland argued that the average levels of this trait, which was associated with values of entrepreneurship, competitiveness and a strong motivation to succeed, varied starkly across different populations. Rejecting genetic or climatically deterministic explanations, he argued that such differences could be traced to cultural factors. Of these, a high need for achievement was most likely to be associated with individualistic forms of religious practice, frequent exposure to achievement imagery, and childrearing practices that placed "a stress on meeting certain achievement standards" (McClelland 1961: 345).

The Achieving Society was soon on the reading lists of countless university courses at a time when ambitious young technocrats from newly independent postcolonies were travelling to Europe and the USA to study economics, development and social planning (Nandy 1987: 51–2). These students were exposed to and excited by McClelland's ideas and the individualistic psychologism of modernisation theory, hoping to draw on this to improve economic growth in their own countries. Although subsequent studies showed McClelland's arguments to be both flawed and deeply ethnocentric (Long and Moore 2013), it was too late: by then, his ideas had become a staple of technocratic governments around the world.

Indonesia was no exception. As Arief Budiman (1979: 213–4) has noted, McClelland's thesis proved popular with the New Order government as it tried to instil "development-mindedness" in the citizenry. A particular champion of McClelland's ideas was the Indonesian anthropologist Koentjaraningrat, who drew heavily on them in his analyses of how the Indonesian mentality should be adapted to better suit development. Explicitly invoking studies by achievement psychologists, Koentjaraningrat (1969: 61–2) argued that Indonesia "needs the achievement motive in a large number of citizens, [but] the number of Indonesians with that cultural value is still extremely low". "To build the mindset and spirit of development," he suggested in a subsequent work, "our children must be reared with deliberate awareness so that fifteen years later they will have a high achievement orientation" (Koentjaraningrat 1974: 76).

30 years later, McClelland's ideas still held currency with intellectuals and officials in both Mainland and Archipelagic Riau. The stereotypes of the weak-willed unambitious Malay or Riau Islander resonated with McClelland's portrait of someone lacking in *n* Achievement. The short story "Riouw ANNO 2204" (Fakhrunnas 2004), for instance, tells the story of Durna, a researcher in the year 2204 who travels to Riau (the author's use of the term encompasses the islands and the mainland) to research Malay history. By this time, Riau has become completely overrun with migrants and only a handful of Malays survive. Durna meets an academic, Professor Hayba, who asks her for her opinion as to why the secessionist Riau

Merdeka movement failed. She suggests that the participants lacked solidarity.

> 'But most of them were Malays, weren't they?' interrupted the Professor suddenly, quite startling Durna.
>
> 'I don't know for sure whether McLeland [*sic*] ever researched what the level of *n* Achievement was for Malays,' commented Durna reflectively (Fakhrunnas 2004: 106).

The implication is stark: even when they were just steps away from obtaining a republic of their own, Malays' low need for achievement let them down. Moreover, the dystopian picture that the story paints of a Riau without Malays is a clarion call to increase this need for achievement and for Malays to reassert themselves while they still have the chance. Indeed, one of the most important aspects of achievement thinking in the Riau Islands is the notion that human resource quality is always malleable and capable of being improved. Thus, although some residents of Tanjung Pinang do ascribe particular achievements or successes to the "innate" attributes of the achiever, such as "talent" or "intelligence", these attributes are rarely seen as limiting factors. In the words of Anna Gade (2002: 360), who researched young women's efforts to become skilled at Qur'anic recitation in South Sulawesi, "one makes up for lack of talent through being motivated and inspired which ... is better than talent".

To contribute to such a process of "motivation" and "inspiration", newspapers in the Riau Islands often profile high-achieving children (*anak berprestasi*), presenting them as exemplars for readers, or their children, to emulate: "Amanda, who caused a stir because her Final Exam marks were almost perfect, can be an example for you to reach for achievement (*prestasi*)" (*Tribun Batam* 2008). Profiles of this kind are amongst the most popular articles to be featured in the local media, and are frequently discussed over the family dinner table or between parents anxious about their children's future prospects. Their text typically plays down any notion of innate ability, rather stressing how, through motivation, diligence, religiosity and discipline, students rose from average to reach levels of high attainment. A profile of Yaya explains how, after a year of studying "lazily", she scored only 50% in her Mathematics exam. The shame of this gave her motivation to study Maths harder. Now not only has algebra become her hobby, but she has gained the highest Maths score in the school and was the second-ranked student in her year group overall (*Tribun Batam* 2007b). Yaya's story shows how indolence conceals the potential for achievement which can be reactivated through motivated diligence. In another profile (*Tribun Batam* 2006), Siti, a schoolgirl whose exam results were the best in Batam, attributes her success to "studying non-stop". Siti describes that she was "often ranked first in the school" once she had adopted a routine of studying for five hours every day outside of school. Moreover, before her final exams (*UN*), she would wake up at 3 am to study before the dawn prayer, and then frequently pray alongside studying because she "wanted to get good marks".

The challenge, then, is how to best inculcate a diligent work ethic. M.S. Suwardi, a historian and prominent public intellectual, answers this question in an article reflecting on how to surmount Malays' inadequacy at trading. "It was suggested by McClelland that if the mental virus "*n* Achievement" was disseminated, businesses would grow," he writes. "It goes without saying we should foster this in the younger generation from an early age" (2002: 68). Suwardi's remarks echo McClelland's argument that social planning could lead to subjects developing a stronger degree of achievement orientation. In *The Achieving Society*, McClelland (1961: 418) had suggested that "the simplest and most effective way of increasing *n* Achievement" was to encourage people to "produce achievement-related fantasies" that might then "instigate activities aimed at producing achievement". In a previous publication, he had suggested that the achievement motive was strengthened by the pleasure of meeting "standards of excellence" that had been "impressed" upon someone by their culture — or by the shame of failing to do so (McClelland *et al.* 1953: 275). Both of these ideas influenced Indonesian policy. The 1970s and 1980s saw a proliferation of state-sponsored tournaments and contests (*lomba*) as well as references to "achievement" (*prestasi*). While the latter term had been little used in 1950s and 1960s Indonesia, it subsequently began to saturate public discourse across the nation, to the extent that the 2004 citizenship curriculum stressed students' duty to "identify opportunities for *prestasi* and approach these with due preparation and enthusiasm", whilst the desirability of *prestasi* led to advertisers insinuating that consuming their products would turn shoppers into high-achievers.

The importance of the concept of "*prestasi*" in contemporary Indonesia is shown clearly in Tom Boellstorff's account of *gay* and *lesbi* Indonesians who attempt to present their homoerotic love as "the ultimate *prestasi*" such that "through *prestasi* [they] express a desire to overcome separation and be reunited with the nation" (2004: 393–4). This analysis, however, draws on a rather idiosyncratic notion of *prestasi*, which equates it to "any good deed", notably those that foster "social connectivity" such as adopting a child or caring for a sick relative (Boellstorff 2004: 390–1). This is not common usage in the Riau Islands or, my informants suggested, elsewhere. Indeed, the West Sumatran writer Muhibbullah Azfa Manik (2005) asks in an article on his website why Indonesians are so *dis*inclined to think of acts of compassion and assistance as *prestasi*. Rather, the term is usually equated with the forms of attainment and rankings in competitive situations such as contests, tournaments, exams, or business: situations which also predominate in the magazine stories analysed by Boellstorff. When entering a contest, enrolling in a course, or applying for a job, the application form typically includes a box where one should document one's previous *prestasi*: the Riau Islanders I knew never listed worthwhile deeds, but rather awards and rankings — especially those acquired in formal competitive settings.

Competitions have long been popular in Southeast Asia. Reid (1988b: 193–4) argues that in the precolonial period, contests were staged so as to demonstrate a ruler's ability to organise, and this still holds true. Indeed, it is particularly pertinent to a young provincial administration attempting to prove its credentials. However, this in itself does not explain the nationwide enthusiasm for competitive events, a phenomenon that one anthropologist has dubbed the "culture of contests" (Strassler 2006: 59). The appetite for such events is particularly strong in the Riau Islands, such that visitors to Tanjung Pinang from other parts of Indonesia are frequently taken aback at the sheer number of competitions being staged in such a small town. Scores of tournaments are held every week, testing everything from colouring and public speaking to robot-building and minibus-driving, and they are all anchored in the rhetoric of human resource improvement. Billboards advertising contests often do so using slogans peppered with human resource-related terminology (Figure 7.1). Similarly, an official from the Education Department in Batam explained his hopes for a national contest for vocational school students in the following terms:

Figure 7.1 A billboard advertising the 2006 MTQ (Qur'an recitation contest). The slogan reads: "Kepulauan Riau's first provincial-level MTQ: a means of increasing the quality of human resources that are of good moral character." (Source: author)

> Via this contest, the quality of education can be augmented such that, in the future, the human resources of the Riau Islands Province will have the power to compete globally and to meet the recruitment requirements of the worlds of business and industry (*Media Guru* 2010).

So just how does a contest improve the quality of human resources? One possibility, advanced by Karen Strassler (2006: 60), is that the contest obliges people to conform to official expectations and judgements of value in ways that might lead to them appearing to be a "high quality human resource" in the eyes of the government, but which may actually stifle innovation and creativity. This finds some support in the answers that contestants in Tanjung Pinang gave when tournament application forms asked them to describe their reasons for entering. For example, at one tourism ambassador-cum-beauty contest, an event open to both men and women (Chapter 8), every participant had described their motivation as either being to increase their awareness of local history and culture, or to promote it to others. To me, however, they spoke of rather different reasons. Although they felt the officials running the contest would want to think they were interested in boosting their knowledge, they were actually entering in pursuit of *prestasi*:

> **Yudith:** I love to compete in contests (*berlomba-lomba*). That's my hobby! I'm always looking for ways to increase my *prestasi*.

> **Hendra:** This beauty contest is quite boring for me, and I don't think I'm very good at it. I would prefer to be doing a speech or debate competition. I actually enjoy that. But at the minute, the only competitions running are modelling and beauty contests [...] The way I see it, the judges are all corrupt or incompetent anyway — it's because they're Indonesian judges — so who wins is really quite random. If that's the case, I should enter as many competitions as possible and sooner or later I'm bound to win. The more I enter, the more *prestasi* I get.

Every competition, by definition, generates *prestasi*, because every contest has a winner. In this sense, the proliferation of contests actualises many of McClelland's recommendations, creating situations where "standards of excellence" are enforced (with affective consequences surrounding both victory and defeat), and inculcating daydreams and fantasies of becoming a champion that might in themselves stimulate "*n* Achievement". For my informants, achieving was not only understood as a civic duty, but experienced as a pleasurable, even compulsive activity.

Teddy, who at the time I met him was already accustomed to entering several competitions a month, explained a little of the thrill of *prestasi*. He recounted the day he had been announced as top of the school in his final year of junior high school. As he went up to the stage to collect the trophy he found that he was:

> ... dizzy and could hardly walk. I was crying, but because I was so happy. And then when I took the trophy and I heard the applause ... It was the most perfect moment of my life. After that I knew I had to enter a lot of competitions so I could experience that again.

These remarks underscore how the emotional and sensory dimensions of *prestasi* make it appealing: the swimming legs, tears clouding his eyes, the sound of the applause — a uniquely intense pleasure that prompted him to search elsewhere for a repeat experience. Many of these physical sensations are dependent on social factors in developing an atmosphere of suspense and grandiosity. Having gone through a ritual of *prestasi* from which one emerges as a winner, the fact monumentalised in a large, shiny trophy, social relations are also transformed, at least within the spheres in which the competition is meaningful. Teddy recounted that competition success made his life "a lot better" — now, whenever he passed by teachers who didn't know him, they would smile and say hello, something they had never done before. Likewise, Esther reported her pride that, amongst her friends, she alone was personally known to the mayor "because I am always representing my school, and always winning!"

The pleasures of achievement were sometimes more closely linked to specific aspirations, appearing to offer an economic and social pathway to much-desired futures. Yanto, a young Javanese man who was studying governance at one of Tanjung Pinang's private universities, dreamt of working for the Department of Tourism, playing a role in bringing foreigners into the Riau Islands. When not studying, he busied himself volunteering at tourism-related events in the hope of acquiring both experience and connections that would help in his future career. He was adamant that success in a beauty or modelling contest — especially if he became champion — would result in his being "noticed" and further incorporated into departmental programmes. In this way, *prestasi* became a source of social capital to help him realise his aspirations. Suhardi, a Riau Islander studying medicine in Jakarta, also found *prestasi* to be a source of capital, specifically, prize money. Though not guaranteed to win every time, his success rate in modelling and tourism ambassador contests allowed him to subsidise the costs of his medical course with winnings. He used the remainder to cover the costs of flights to attend even more such competitions.

It was not just competitors who were excited by the competition format. Local policy makers liked it too. Pak Irwanto, an official from the Department of Tourism explained that

> When other children see champions, they become envious and want to be just like them. The champions will become a model

for their classmates. The classmates will see that they have won the prize, and that will give them motivation to be more disciplined so that they can win a prize in the competition next year. It is an excellent socialisation strategy.

In this case, what is being socialised is *not* primarily a particular body of content, but rather the motivated and disciplined disposition that will turn a Riau Islander into a "high quality human resource". Through aspiration and envy, it is believed that children will both increase their standards of attainment and adopt the competitive character that is required of them in the global era. This is an attractive prospect for most people in the islands. Nevertheless, the ability of the contest to deliver such outcomes is complicated by a second way in which Riau Islanders conceptualise and experience human resource quality: as the outcome of a process of regional creation.

The Relational Human Resource

Visiting Slamet in his coffee shop usually involved in-depth discussion of the articles in that day's edition of one of the local newspapers. On one occasion, though, Slamet was much more interested in talking about what was *not* in the paper. There had been no profiles of achieving children for almost three weeks. "How," he asked, "can I be expected to motivate my daughter when I don't have profiles to inspire her?" This question caught my attention, not only because it showed the importance of "achievement" within Slamet's family but also because of the causal logic to which it pointed. Whilst newspaper profiles present discipline and diligence as individual traits, Slamet was acutely aware that he was responsible for motivating his daughter, and that he was reliant on local journalists to help him do so. Motivation, and the achievement that it brought, was understood to be a relational phenomenon.

Relational, sociocentric models of personhood have long been associated with Indonesian societies, although as Douglas Hollan (1992) rightly cautions, they should not be taken as an exotic, Orientalising, alternative to "egocentric" Western selves. The question is not one of radical difference in the way people from different cultures exist in the world, but rather which of two (or more) parallel models of the self is emphasised in any given context — and to what degree. The fact that human resource quality could differ so sharply across a nearby state border or, in Pertiwi's words, amongst people of "the same race" who "live so close", was enough to convince most Riau Islanders that achievement motivation was an outcome of the relations in which one was embedded. To the extent that it was intrinsic to the person, it was not an inevitable outcome of genetics, climatic, or evolutionary factors. Instead, laziness and lack of discipline were the potentially rectifiable outcomes of how that person had been formed by manipulable aspects of their social and material environments. Just as the "marine environment" explained the low achievement orientation of coastal Malays (Chapter 4), so the urban and educational environments were scrutinised and blamed for making children lazy.

The first point raised when informants discussed the quality of a school was usually its "facilities" (*fasilitas*). Facilities were seen as important not only because of the educational opportunities they provided but also because of their subtle psychological influence on motivating students to achieve. One pupil explained that "if the people of the Riau Islands want to improve our human resources, we need to improve the local public schools by, for example, renovating broken and damaged buildings, buying new chairs, tables, and many other things that are needed for the teaching and learning process. This will automatically increase the competency of students because they will be motivated to study harder". Markus, a journalist, attested to this, citing how outraged he had been by a trip to a primary school on the island of Pangkil. "Its roof is very bad and has holes in it. If it rains, water sometimes drips into the classroom." He then started to mime somebody creeping around very carefully: "The children have to walk around like this because they don't have shoes and there are sharp nails in the floor. How are children who study in a building like that going to become better human resources?" In the imaginations of parents and students, the Riau Archipelago fared worse than other regions in Indonesia because its schools were dirtier, with uncomfortable furniture and stained unpainted walls. Hence staff at an expensive new private school were adamant their classrooms would maximise educational potential. "Look at these facilities," boasted a teacher as she showed me round, "I think we are the only school in Tanjung Pinang to have air conditioning and blue walls. Students will love studying here."

This logic applied not just to the material environment; it also applied to the teaching staff. Beladona, a Javanese pupil in junior high school, used one of her homework exercises to fantasise that she herself had once studied in Britain, where the more comfortable and sympathetic environment had increased her ability to learn. "I don't really like my new school [in Tanjung Pinang] because the teachers are not understanding and the rules are strict," she wrote, "The school here is not clean. It's muddy. I liked my school in England where I learnt a lot of new things. I really enjoyed studying there." A Chinese boy, Tommy, undertaking the same assignment remarked that "the school [in Tanjung Pinang] is not as good as the UK because the school here is dusty and very hot. No air conditioner, only fan, and the teacher is very bad. Not as good as the UK, where the teacher is kind."

Such views were widely shared, and echoed the broader provincial concern over human resources. Informants remarked that most local teachers and education officials had been born on small and outlying islands and had learnt how to teach in the years when the Riau Islands were "not yet aware of modern educational standards". Wealthier private schools explained they had tried to circumvent this problem by recruiting directly from Jakarta, only to find that no teacher was willing to make the move to the islands on the salary they were offering. This is the paradox faced by the Riau Archipelago's residents. They need to improve their human resources but the people who are in positions to help them do this are themselves human resources of low quality. This situation was contrasted sharply with towns and provinces elsewhere. Beladona and Tommy, of course, imagined that the problems of dirtiness, strict rules and fierce teachers would not affect schools in Britain. Even within Indonesia, however, there were telling comparisons to be drawn. Fatimah had taken part in a teaching exchange with a school in the city of Ambon (Maluku Province) and was shocked by what she found: "I had thought Maluku would be the worst province in Indonesia," she explained, referencing Eastern Indonesia's reputation for backwardness, "but it was better than here. I think this Riau Islands Province must be the worst in the whole country!"

Framing the problem of achievement in this way constructs an important and deterministic relationship between a citizen's performance and their hometown or region, which, through its administrative policies, facilities and human resources, delimits their capacity for achievement. I see here a productive parallel with recent Melanesian ethnography that has stressed the creative potential of land (Leach 2003). Creations, which may include pigs, crops, trees and people, are extensions not of labour but of the land itself, and their mobility and detachability render them "land that moves", always associated with that originatory land until and unless they form new relations and become attached elsewhere (Strathern 2009). But one can be created badly. In the Riau Islands, the sense of having been created "regionally" involves many undesirable factors — "Malayness", "marine-orientation", the political topography of neglect under internal colonialism, all of which casts a shadow over attempts to boost the province's human resource quality and competitiveness. Indeed, whenever such a cross-regional comparison is made, the implicit association between human resources and the places from which they come brings the flawed process of regional creation painfully to mind, inflecting Riau Islanders' optimistic hopes for their province with affects of hopelessness and despair.

Geographies of Achievement

Amongst the many competitions staged in the Riau Islands every week, one particular category stands out in importance: the prestigious national competitions in which competitors from the Riau Islands will be ranked relative to participants from every other province in Indonesia. Respectable rankings are desperately longed for by provincial officials, as "proof" that, following political devolution, the new province can create competitive, high-achieving and forward-looking citizens, not the backwater inhabitants its detractors predicted. This is as much a strategy of self-legitimation to the province's own citizenry as it is a defiant declaration to the rest of Indonesia that the new Riau Islands Province is a force to be reckoned with.

This drive was evident in the government's tremendous support of the national Qur'an recitation contest (Musabaqah Tilawatil Qur'an, MTQ). When the province was eventually ranked joint eighth out of all 33 provinces, the head of the Department of Religion was unequivocal in his delight. Announcing the result to a packed stadium who had gathered to celebrate the ascension of the Prophet Muhammad, his words met with rapturous applause. "We are in the top ten provinces in Indonesia," he declared. "Extraordinary! Now all the other provinces in Indonesia must acknowledge that we are high-achieving and they must take us seriously as rivals."

When five vocational high school students (four Chinese and one Malay) were selected to represent Tanjung Pinang at English-language debating in the provincial branch of the LKS (Lomba Kompetensi Siswa, Students' Competency Competition), they were hoping their efforts, if successful, might meet with similar levels of delight. The LKS is a prestigious competition incorporating over 50 different contests in areas ranging from cookery and traditional dance to cabinet making. It is the focal point of a vocational school teacher's year. Yet the debating team's experience illustrated a more general feature of achievement thinking in the islands: the government's campaign to produce high achievers of "global" competitiveness foundered in the face of a human resources logic that saw them as having been imperfectly created by the region from which they came, exposing the widespread bad faith in narratives of provincial development.

The team had been selected amidst ambitious aspirations that students from Tanjung Pinang might make it into the top five teams in Indonesia. Teddy, the second-placed debater told me that he did not mind if the team was ranked lower, provided the Riau Islands team beat Mainland Riau, their former "coloniser". Although the call for provincial autonomy had been fuelled by the rhetoric of Malay ethnonationalism, Chinese Teddy said that he felt a non-ethnic loyalty to his new province. He rejected the argument that the Riau Islands Province should be for Malays only and hoped that success in the contest would do two things: show the rest of Indonesia that the islands' independence had been successful in allowing their human resources to flourish, and send a strong message to the Riau Archipelago's population that Chinese and other non-Malays were committed to their province and able to bring it glory and *prestasi*.

A similar principle underpinned the involvement of Pak Ginting, the Batak teacher who coordinated team selections. He explained that he wanted to do this not only because he valued debating as an important educational tool, but because it was an area in which he could show that he had managed to make a contribution to the development of the Riau Islands:

> People here see me as a Batak, and they think I am an outsider, that I don't care about this province. If I was a Malay, or even a Muslim, then I would be a headmaster by now. As it is, I am just a deputy head. I can't say this to other Indonesians, they

will deny it, but you are a researcher and you can see the discrimination for yourself. Developing debating is a way I can prove that I am committed to this province, even though I am a Batak and a Protestant. And hopefully, if the province does well, people will see that and reward me for it.

On paper, the team looked strong enough to carry out these hopes. Both Teddy and Martina had been school champions, while Bella, Adana and Clarissa were top of their classes in English and ranked highly in other disciplines. Nor was there a problem of motivation. When they were selected, the children had been delighted, grinning broadly and, in Teddy's words, "almost crying with excitement". But different tears had been shed in the first training session. Fadli, their coach, described how Martina had trailed off crying only 20 seconds into a five-minute speech, whilst Clarissa had arrived at the session with her father, demanding to be withdrawn. Indeed, the reason I met the team at all was that one of my neighbours in Kampung Jawa worked at the same school as Fadli and Pak Ginting, and hoped that bringing a Westerner to their final training session might motivate them to do better. As it happened, I had already been heavily involved in school and university debating for many years, so was also able to give them some practical tips on how to deliver an effective speech. Fadli was very grateful, saying that, compared to how discouraged they had seemed in the previous three days' training, the pupils were now motivated, excited and smiling. They still looked sullen and nervous to me. Some time later, they would confess that, although they found the session interesting, their overwhelming sense as they left it remained one of dread. Their anxiety had been that however well they might understand the rules of debating, their English would never manage to stand up against the students from Batam, and they would suffer a humiliating defeat.

The pupils' attitude towards teams from Batam exemplifies the power of understanding oneself and one's capacity to achieve as the outcome of regional creation. Amongst the Riau Islands, Batam occupies an ambiguous status, for it was spared the process of internal colonisation by Pekanbaru at the expense of direct control via Jakarta. While the rhetoric supporting provincial independence still considered this to be an exploitative and denigratory relationship, there was little doubt in the minds of the people I met in Tanjung Pinang that Batam had a distinct advantage when it came to the question of human resource quality. This was not attributed to the Jakarta administration per se but rather to the foreign direct investment secured by the Batam Authority. The island was frequently spoken of as a "big city" or an "industrial city" that was "full of foreigners". In other words, it conformed to Riau Islanders' paradigm of a successful, developed town, premised closely on the role model of Singapore. With their neighbouring city-state proving increasingly expensive to visit, many people in Tanjung Pinang regularly travelled to Batam to experience a "developed atmosphere", and what they told me were "Western activities" such as shopping in malls or visiting the Ocarina Water Park. These experiences led them to believe that Batam must also be developed in other ways — such as its human resource base — drawing on an associative, rather than a causal, logic of achievement.

These concerns were in evidence at the opening ceremony of the provincial-level LKS. While the presiding official was explaining how the tournament would improve provincial human resource quality by providing opportunities to compete "at the highest level", and exhorting pupils to "do your best and be a winner!", members of the audience were furtively talking amongst themselves, predicting which teams would triumph. A journalist from *Tribun Batam* approached the Tanjung Pinang squad, enquiring what their expectations were for the event. Fadli, dutifully echoing the opening speech, said that the pupils would try their best and hopefully win. The journalist raised his eyebrows incredulously. "Surely it's not likely that Tanjung Pinang will stand a chance at the English debate competition," he remarked, "After all, Batam is an industrial city with close links to Singapore. It has so many international schools!" This reactivated the pupils' anxieties, and the next day they reported they had barely slept, kept awake by the fear they would be beaten.

This was a common story amongst the members and coaches of Riau Island teams. It could have particularly dire consequences in the field of sport. Hery, who had grown up in Pekanbaru but was now was a coach for the Indonesian martial art of *pencak silat* at both municipal and provincial level in the Riau Islands, told me that children in the region were particularly challenging to coach. The immediate difficulty was the lack of facilities. He noted bitterly that, while most provinces trained their *pencak silat* squads in "international standard facilities", the Riau Islands team was forced to

Figure 7.2 The Riau Islands *pencak silat* team training by the roadside (Source: author)

train on a patch of sand by the side of the road (Figure 7.2). A deeper problem was that children in the Riau Islands were brought up in ways that fostered a counterproductive mindset. "The kids here are too weak-willed," he explained, "they don't have the maturity to compete with other provinces. Here in Tanjung Pinang, they're champions. So they don't bother training hard. Then suddenly at the national level they realise they've been drawn against a team like West Java, or a kid who's been national champion. They worry about it so much they can't sleep. Well, if you don't sleep the night before a match then automatically, that's you out of the running..."

For the LKS debaters, their anxieties were prompted less by their opponents' previous track records, than by other factors that seemed to point to their superior human resource quality, in particular their appearance:

> **Teddy:** I thought, 'There's no chance we can win if we go to Batam, they'll all be much better than us' ... But I thought that it was still nice to be able to go travelling to Batam, we could go

to the malls and see what Batam was like for free. But then I also thought, 'Well, going to Jakarta would be nice too. I've never been to Jakarta...' But I still didn't think we would win ... The ones that scared me were Batam Business School, because they came in, and that fat boy, he was so scary, he had really good English and I know that he really wanted to win, and they were wearing those waistcoats, and really smart stylish clothes, and we were just in our uniform, and I thought, 'Oh no, we will lose...'

Fadli: Yes, and SMK Kartini [an expensive private school in Batam] wore clothes that were extremely fashionable, and yet I was surprised it was their speeches that were the worst of all.

As these remarks show, the associations that Riau Islanders drew between developed lifestyles — as evidenced in smart and fashionable clothing — and the prospect of achievement had a tremendous influence upon their expectations of who would actually triumph in a competitive situation.

Yet to the great surprise of everybody, not least themselves, the Tanjung Pinang team was eventually declared the undefeated champion of the provincial event. Over the months that followed, I got to know the team much better; Fadli had asked me to help him open an informal "debating club" that would meet every Sunday morning at his house. I was also asked to run some more formal training sessions by a teacher from Martina, Clarissa, Teddy and Adana's school, who had usurped Fadli as coach (in what many believed to be an attempt to secure a free trip to Jakarta) but who admitted she knew nothing about debating. Since the LKS organisers had invited me to help judge the debating competition, I was also given the opportunity to accompany the team to the national finals in Jakarta.

The "geographies of achievement" that had been so clearly in evidence during the contest in Batam were equally apparent in the national finals of the LKS. Every day, the tournament issued a free internal newsletter which from the outset identified the "Big Four" provinces that the organisers expected to dominate the competition: Jakarta, Yogyakarta, West Java and Bali (although in a politically incorrect aside, the editors tipped post-tsunami Aceh to win the prize for brick-laying). The prime factor that differentiated the Big Four from the other 29 participating provinces was the quality of their human resources. "Other regions are considered worse not because of their limited opportunities for practical work, but because of a poor understanding of the material that will be contested", an article in the newsletter explained. "This is an important factor in the com-petition, to the extent that a shortfall in the human resources in the schools of various provinces should become a point of reflection, so they will do better in every contest to come" (*Jurnal LKS SMK* 2006). Meanwhile, one tournament convenor that I spoke to con-fided his expectation that that new provinces such as the Riau Islands would perform very badly. "Their new governments are not good at allocating appropriate funding and training," he said. "They are still learning how to be a province."

Expectations for the Riau Islands team were therefore set low. The team engaged with the situation in a complex way, simul-taneously telling me that they were "optimistic" they could get into the top ten provinces and possibly even the top five, whilst also expressing terror at the thought of being drawn against teams from almost anywhere in the country. As it happened, they were placed highly, getting through to the quarter-finals and eventually ranked sixth in Indonesia. This attests to the true power of tournaments — their unpredictable capacity to overturn established hierarchies of provincial quality, as well as to re-entrench them. "Sixth rank! Wow!" shouted Teddy as he heard the news, "I was hoping we'd be able to get in the top five. But sixth is almost fifth!" Reflecting on the tournament when we returned home, however, he admitted that he had "thought at the national level we would definitely lose, because these were the best students from all over the country from pro-vinces like West Java and Jakarta and everywhere and they'd defi-nitely be really good but it turns out we were pretty good too. I was very surprised!"

These results placed the Riau Islands well ahead of the 19th-placed Mainland Riau, whose speakers were reputed throughout the tournament as being angry about how well their archipelagic counterparts had done. Martina told me that these participants had joined forces with speakers from other disappointed provinces (South Sumatra, Lampung and Bali) to create an "anti-Riau Islands league", boycotting the team and spreading rumours that they were secretly transvestites (*waria*). Of these ungracious losers, the Bali team had been particularly inconsolable when their Big Four expectations foundered in the face of an elimination during the octo-finals. Knowing I had filmed the debate, the Bali coach approached me

asked for a copy of the recording. Without watching it
~~ained~~, he had no idea how he might possibly explain
...s defeat by the "backward" province of West Sumatra to his
headmaster and provincial education office. Such events demonstrate
how high the stakes in national competition really are: there is the
sense of an order of how things should be, and incredible shame,
anger and tears if that order is upset and an alternative hierarchy of
achievement is revealed.

The Riau Islands students, however, were content to bask in
the glow of their accomplishments, especially once individual speaker
rankings were announced: Martina had been the tenth best speaker
of the tournament, and Teddy the sixth. They could return to
Tanjung Pinang happy with their *prestasi* and the name they had
built for the Riau Islands, where Pak Ginting would champion them
as an educational success story and simultaneously boost his own
reputation. Tanjung Pinang, it seemed, had done well. But while this
story seems to exemplify McClelland's logic of achievement orientation leading to hard-earned results, even in the face of regional
prejudice, the debaters received nothing of the public celebration that
had been granted to the eighth-ranked participants in the Qur'an
recitation contest. Instead, just a few months after they returned from
Jakarta, the Riau Islands government cut all funding for English-
language debating activities in the province.

Achievement in Bad Faith

Why would a province seeking to improve its human resource quality
suddenly cut off the lifeblood of an activity in which it had established this degree of achievement? Education department officials
justified their decision as a simple matter of cashflow: their budget
was limited and sending students to competitions in other parts of
Indonesia was very expensive. Difficult choices had to be made and
they had to prioritise activities that were in keeping with the province's identity, such as "cultural" contests centred around traditional
dance, drama and poetry, or at which it was likely to succeed.
Hearing this, Fadli asked me to accompany him to the provincial
education office, hoping he could persuade the officials that the
previous year's *prestasi* augured well for the future, especially since
four of the students in the team would still be at school the next
year. Mardiana, the official we spoke to, was unconvinced:

This province is not yet good at English language. It has never won anything for English language, and maybe we should invest the money in things we are good at and can win. Your vocational school kids aren't that good. When have our vocational schools ever been champions in English debate? I've never heard of such a thing, and if it had happened, I would definitely have heard of it. Sixth rank is not champion. Sixth rank doesn't earn prize money for the province, it doesn't get eight million rupiah, or twelve million rupiah or anything like that, does it? So what is the use? Our vocational schools are still extremely ordinary (*sangat biasa aja*)!

As we returned home, Fadli glossed the situation with a single phrase: "I feel so sorry for this province..." When the schoolchildren heard, they were disappointed, but also angry. Yusuf, an active member of our debating club, declared himself shocked by the bureaucrats' attitude: "It's as if they don't even care!"

However, whilst the government attributed their decision to spending squeezes, and the schoolchildren blamed it on governmental incompetence or apathy, I suggest that this case offers a window into a broader cultural phenomenon that affected both the administration and the schoolchildren themselves: a disposition of bad faith towards the new province's attainments whereby, as explained in Chapter 1, subjects might believe passionately in a concept whilst simultaneously perceiving it to be at odds with their notion of an authentic self. Moreover, the evanescence inherent to the notion of bad faith can also account for those blissful moments of good faith in which one fully believes one's conceit (I am an achiever, I am a credit to my province, my province has the ability to create me as a high quality human resource), and the anguish of cynicism when one admits the deception (I am not really an achiever, I am a flawed regional creation of a bad province and I do not trust the judges who gave me that title).

The bad faith of the high-achieving Tanjung Pinang debaters was clear as they gloried in their selection and even expressed optimism that they might be in the top five teams in Indonesia, whilst simultaneously being wracked by anxiety that they would be utterly defeated by teams from Batam and other provinces. Local discourses of themselves as remarkable were trumped by a discourse of associative logic that viewed human resources as the outcome of various structural qualities discernible in a region. This led to a fundamental alienation from, and disappointment in, the authentic regionality that these achievers believed would hamper their performance. Cruelly, this can sometimes be a self-fulfilling prophecy. In the national LKS quarter-finals, the Riau Islands team panicked, jettisoning their own ideas and techniques to imitate the style and densely forensic vocabulary of the speakers from Jakarta in a repetitive and incoherent fashion — a strategy that led to their defeat by a big margin. The confidence that they had spoken of after a strong performance in the preliminaries and octo-finals had dissipated. Of course, everyone knew that Jakarta had received a lot of coaching from expert trainers at Universitas Indonesia and were favoured to win the competition. But by this associative logic of achievement — that differentials in opportunity necessarily translate into differential outcomes — the Jakarta team had come to set the standard to which the Riau Island speakers had to hurriedly and inadequately conform, and thereby inadvertently secured their own victory.

Tracing the debaters' attitudes towards their own prospects and attainments, we see precisely the evanescence between good faith and bad faith that Sartre's model anticipates. Excellent results in the preliminary rounds allowed them to feel that they were "really good too", a confidence which foundered in the face of meeting teams from the Big Four, only to be restored when final team and speaker standings were announced. Thus successful outcomes allowed for good faith — albeit a transient and unstable good faith — in their achiever identities and human resource quality as ratified through the "objective" and nationally-endorsed measures of results and scores. They expressed pride in being in the Riau Islands team and delight in outranking Mainland Riau, the province that held them back for so long. Through their bodies and minds, created by the Riau Archipelago (and more specifically Tanjung Pinang), the province and town became newly equated with the capacity to achieve. The fact that the province had committed to improving human resource quality made this flexibility in outlook all the more understandable for it opened up wide possibilities as to how good the regional processes of human resource creation really were. Nevertheless, entrenched ideas about the flaws in the creation process would not disappear, especially when they were reiterated both at home, through the vocabulary of a "human resources crisis", and in the denigratory attitudes of those coming from places unambiguously associated with achievement. The terrible irony is that the political rhetoric surrounding the creation of the Riau Islands Province, namely that it represented an opportunity to foster a globally competitive population of human resources in what was currently a backwater, led Riau Islanders to orient themselves towards the category of achievement whilst undermining their ability to become confident, motivated citizens who could hold their own in the global marketplace.

A similar disposition of bad faith was evident in the attitudes of officials towards their citizens' achievements. While the Department of Education was quick to publicise the achievements of the debating team, Mardiana's remarks made it clear that the office did not have sufficient faith in the quality of those human resources to gamble the costs of funding them a second time. As funding cuts loomed, Mardiana was all too willing to suspend the vision of a high-achieving province in favour of one filled with low quality human resources who were unable to cope with English language and would be better off sticking to Malay dance and other cultural activities more in keeping with their presumed skill sets. For all that the students battled with and tried to throw off the shackles of a hampering regionalism, provincial administrators ultimately viewed their achievements with cynicism, still modelling the teenagers' capacities as over-determined by a conceptualisation of the province that their own *prestasi* was supposed to have overturned. The discourse of the human resources crisis, it seemed, had proved so resilient that it withstood its own solution.

The very fact that the government would take such a stance has had its own impact upon the ways in which Riau Islanders view their own human resource capacity and the significance of their own individual achievements. Over time, islanders who had been excited about the government's pro-achievement policies came to view politicians' claims about the province's human resource quality as "empty talk". For the school debaters and their friends, who felt the impact of administrative bad faith very directly, there were more personal consequences. Martina, for instance, decided to give up debating as soon as she returned home from Jakarta. She explained that because people knew she had done well in Jakarta, they would expect her to be very good if they saw her in a debate. She felt embarrassed at the prospect that people might see how bad she really was. The government's conclusion that she was "very average" did little to convince her otherwise. Preferring to use the achievement she had acquired to her advantage rather than risk exposing herself as a fraud, Martina turned away further opportunities to showcase and improve her own human resource quality in the field of debating. Teddy, by contrast, received Mardiana's news with outrage. He had returned from Jakarta proud of his accomplishments and confident that he and the Riau Islands Province would win a prize next year — provided that Batam were not better than him, which he still rather suspected they might be. The provincial government's lack of enthusiasm was no reflection on him but rather on its own poor human resources. "I used to think I liked living in Tanjung Pinang," he told Fadli and me over lunch a few weeks after the funding cuts were announced, "but not now. The government is so bad, they don't know how to organise things well. I didn't realise that before, but now I can see it. When I'm older, I would like to help my province to improve, but I don't want to just be stuck here if it's like this. I think I would rather live in Java or abroad."

Indeed, this did represent a turning point for Teddy. Whereas once he had thought that he would spend his life studying and working in Tanjung Pinang, instead he moved to Batam, where he took a job in a bank to fund future studies in Singapore. "It is something that I have to do," he explained when I met him there in 2009, "I have to stay here until I can make enough money to leave. But once I've gone, I will not come back to the Riau Islands." This stance can hardly be attributed solely to the saga of the LKS. But it was in Teddy's fall from grace as a champion debater that he began to perceive and relate to the province in a completely new way, thereby stripping the Riau Islands of one of the high quality human resources that their administrators were so desperate to create and retain. A year after our meeting, in May 2010, he sent me an email to say that he was studying accountancy in Singapore: "It's like a dream come true, finally I can study overseas," he wrote. "Just hoping for the best ..." He has not yet come home.

Transnational Creations

Given the emphasis that Riau Islanders place on regional creation as a means of ensuring human resource quality, and their doubts regarding their province's ability to do this effectively, it is only logical that Tanjung Pinang's residents should turn their attention and their hopes to the creative influence of more "developed" locations. Indonesian cities such as Jakarta, Yogyakarta, Pekanbaru and

Padang all offer Riau Islanders important opportunities for education, training and human resource development, as do locations
in Malaysia and, for those wealthy enough, Australia, America and
Europe. Yet one location stands out as the preferred personal development destination to which most Riau Islanders feel they can
realistically aspire: Singapore.

Even a stay in Singapore was thought to transform one for
the better. Raja Jaffar, as we saw in Chapter 4, described his time
in the city-state as formative in ways that drew heavily on the logic
of regional creation: "I was sort of altered by the environment". Yet
as Teddy discovered, realising this aspiration took time, effort and
money: getting someone into a school or college in Singapore remained an expensive and difficult process that excluded all but the
richest or most determined Riau Islanders and relied heavily on the
skills of brokers. At worst, these middlemen were charlatans, securing
"registration fees" for applications that never proved successful. At
best they were careful professionals who used in-depth knowledge of
the Singaporean education system to maximise their clients' chances
of getting a place. One broker, Agustina, explained that the Malay
language exam in school placement tests was much easier than
the paper in Mandarin. Even though many of her applicants were
Chinese Indonesians who were enthusiastic about their children
sitting for a Mandarin exam, she always advised them to choose
Malay. "It's practically the same as Indonesian," she asserted, "so they
can do very well at it." Nevertheless, Agustina described her job as
frustrating, principally because too many of her clients expected too
much. "I can understand why parents want to send their children
to Singapore, because the quality of schooling here is so poor," she
explained, "but this is the thing I always say, 'If you want to study
in Singapore, you need to be very serious. It's not like Indonesia
where you can get away with anything, you need to work hard to
get in and keep working hard to take advantage of the opportunity'."
These criteria, she explained, ruled out the majority of applicants.
"I think it's suitable only for a handful. But there are lots of them
that want to go. Today a boy came with his mother, but when I
looked at him he doesn't have the quality. Maybe he could have, but
he's lazy. He wants to go, he really wants to go, but he doesn't want
to work for it." Indeed, brokers were quick to relate tales of students
they had sent to Singapore only to later receive reports that the

students had lost interest in their studies or been thrown out of job placements because of a bad attitude. Such students were, as one broker explained to me, "already damaged; too influenced by Indonesian ways of thinking". Thus, while studying in Singapore was a way to increase human resource quality, applicants had to pass a high threshold in terms of disposable income, human resource quality they had already attained, and malleability in their patterns of thought. As Agustina lamented, this was more than most Riau Islanders could do.

In consequence, there was a consensus amongst my informants that "Singaporean" methods and facilities needed to be brought to the Riau Islands to tackle the root causes of the problem. In some cases, this was done by specific individuals, such as Veronica, the owner of an extra-curricular English course. She had previously run a "*bimbel*" (*bimbingan belajar*), an intensive private study centre that admitted children from the age of three, but her assumptions about how to educate a child were shattered when she went to Singapore and met an employee of its Ministry of Education. "A lot of the parents here don't want to spend time with their children helping them prepare," she said, in another damning indictment of Indonesia's "instant culture". "They want their children to be able to read and write straight away. Almost all of them, from all kinds of backgrounds. So they send them to a course, a *bimbel*, like I used to run. Well, a few years ago I met Mrs Chang in Singapore, and she explained the Singapore kindergarten system. After hearing that, I didn't want to run my course anymore. I realised it was damaging the students because they were learning these skills too early and they did not know how to socialise, how to speak to an audience or anything like that. So I closed the course. Better for those children to go a kindergarten." The parents had been upset because in Tanjung Pinang, kindergartens are associated with singing songs, eating cakes and playing together, rather than activities that ambitious parents think might foster human resource quality. Veronica agreed these kindergartens were suboptimal, but still thought they were better than her course had been. "I am trying to develop something more like the Singaporean system," she explained, "I began in my English course, for older pupils, and soon I will open a kindergarten myself." Though her businesses attracted a lively custom, Veronica still experienced difficulties. "The parents, they don't really understand what I am trying to do. And it is hard to get staff who know how to teach in a good way." I asked her what she thought the problem was. She answered bluntly: "Human resources."

Yet the harnessing of Singaporean expertise was not restricted to individual endeavours. One of the most widely repeated mantras within administrative discussions of the Riau Islands Province is its "strategic location", something that islanders hope can be exploited to the benefit of the population as a whole. The Indonesia-Malaysia-Singapore Growth Triangle had proved a disappointment because the knowledge and skills development opportunities that flowed across the border were predominantly restricted to the employees of specific Singaporean businesses. Moreover, the standard of English required to get even a menial job such as a cleaner in the Bintan Resorts was considerably more advanced than that of most Riau Islanders, leading to the recruitment of large numbers of staff from elsewhere. To the horror of Tanjung Pinang's residents, many of these workers were not even Indonesian but Filipino. Discussing this situation with several of my neighbours over hot tea, Fatimah told me that this only served to demonstrate the "arrogance" of Singaporeans, their unrealistic expectations, and the unequal basis of the "partnership" they had sought to forge.

As noted in Chapter 2, it was the centralised administrative structures associated with the Growth Triangle that were blamed for ignoring local needs; regional autonomy and the creation of a new province offered new hope that the islands' location close to Singapore might be exploited more strategically than had been the case in the past. While the news headlines about cross-border relations centred on the economic prospects and opportunities of creating a Special Economic Zone (SEZ) or Free Trade Zone (FTZ), bureaucrats in the provincial and regency governments were working hard to harness human resource development through these schemes, often doing so in ways that were concerned not just with population-scale levels of human capital, but with their own quality as human resources as well.

Selma was a high-ranking Malay within the provincial government's payroll office. Inviting me to lunch with her colleagues from several departments, she told me that she had reservations about the SEZ, including the lack of clear plans for how it would be used to benefit the Riau Islands and the constant delays in issuing the necessary regulations for it to be operative and effective. Nonetheless, she was very hopeful that it might lead to "a group of Singaporeans coming over to the governor's office and training us all". She particularly hoped they would be able to train the staff to speak better English. "That kind of training is a necessity," one of her colleagues added. "We need to be able to speak English if we want to communicate with other countries for the good of the province, and of Indonesia." She imagined this was likely, since the removal of legislative obstacles to fast and efficient investment would allow foreign businesses to move to the Riau Islands on a larger scale than had ever been the case previously — meaning the non-Indonesian partners had a vested interest in ensuring the bureaucrats they worked with were as well-trained as possible. It would also be a potent symbol of cooperation.

In the municipal education department, similar reasoning had led officials to invite over Singaporean trainers to improve the quality of Tanjung Pinang's high school teachers. From Singapore's point of view, this was an opportunity to invest in better human resources and gain political capital, thereby ensuring the future prospects of their transnational cooperation. However, matters were less clear-cut in practice. One widely publicised programme was devoted to training English-language teachers and was staged in the school where Fadli used to work. It was not long before Fadli was receiving detailed reports of what was happening from his former colleagues:

> It has been a big failure. When it began, there were almost 50 teachers enrolled for the class. But now there are only 12. They say they don't like the way the Singaporean teaches them. Any time they make a small mistake, he stops them and corrects them and makes them say it correctly. It destroys their motivation. Finally, they protested and now they are going to get a new teacher.

The next week, the class (which had now swelled to 23) did indeed have a new teacher, Mr Tan, although he retained the same habit of correcting small errors. "Whenever I hear you, I will stop you," he warned benevolently, before guiding them through a listening comprehension exercise on horse riding for the disabled. In the ten-minute coffee break, and again after the class, teachers admitted that Mr Tan was much better than his predecessor, but still an inadequate choice. He had made several gaffes in the course of the class, from admonishing the teachers not to talk to one another "in

Malay" (rather than in Indonesian) through to errors in his English, such as his mispronunciation of "dressage", which was duly exposed by the tape. They grumbled that they disliked the way he pronounced his words — it felt too "Asian" and not like the pronunciation of a "native speaker". They also resented his manner of handling the class. All of these problems were seen as indicative of a more fundamental problem: the "arrogance" of Singaporeans.

Yet one of the most notable aspects of such encounters with Singapore is their ambivalence. Singaporeans are seen as excellent human resources compared to Indonesians but also as inauthentically excellent, not quite the paragons of modernity that Riau Islanders believe they believe themselves to be. The reaction of one teacher, a middle-aged man named Hansel, showed this poignantly:

> We were promised a native speaker, but when we arrived, it was a Singaporean. There are lots of native speakers in Singapore. A lot of tourists, a lot of businessmen, and a lot of teachers. It's easy for them to get native speakers. But here it's very hard. Why couldn't they send us a native speaker? That's what we need, and that's what we asked for!

Firman, a secondary school teacher, underscored this when he told me that Riau Islanders were "not allowed to speak like Singaporeans, they don't have proper English. They have Singlish. It's like a Creole language, and we can't have our children speaking that." For him, Singapore was not something to be emulated but rather a resource to be exploited, a conduit for native speakers that ought not to be engaged with too deeply on its own terms. Elsewhere, I have argued that such ambivalence can partly be attributed to the moral and ethical complexities associated with drawing a national border across what had historically been an undifferentiated space and the expansionist, colonial overtones associated with Singapore's cross-border activities when the Growth Triangle first began (Long 2011). Riau Islanders responded to these perceived injustices by condemning Singaporeans on both ethical and intellectual registers, denouncing them as wicked or arrogant, and arguing that the differences between the two populations had been overstated. Hansel's complaint that Singapore knew the Tanjung Pinang teacher wanted native speakers but cruelly sent a Chinese person instead contains elements of both.

When Singapore sends "assistance", whether that be in the form of monetary investment, a factory, infrastructure, or specific skills training, these latent hostilities and ambivalences colour the ways in which people in the islands perceive and engage with it. Riau Islander recipients of Singaporean beneficence are thus caught on the horns of a tricky dilemma, torn between their own complex resentment of Singapore and their desires for self-improvement. Such ambivalence proves especially problematic when the assistance has been sent to contribute to their own processes of human development and self-formation because, as in the above case, it has the capacity to stymie, subvert, or indeed entirely thwart the aims of the exercise. Yet, ironically, it is these same islanders who will lobby hard for human resource development schemes and protest vociferously that they are being neglected by their government (and by Singapore) if such measures do not take place. Shot through with a simultaneous desire for Singapore and an impulse to reject it, and presenting themselves as motivated opportunity-seeking citizens when they know they will find accepting help from Singapore intolerable, these people's efforts to participate in building a successful and high-achieving province can also be seen to be conducted in a counter-productive disposition of bad faith.

An Achieving Archipelago

Human resources are a hot topic in the Riau Islands and will doubtless continue to be so for many years to come, a consequence of the archipelago's geopolitical location, national discourses of *prestasi*, and an ever-growing appetite for the "global" lifestyles associated with good human capital. Given that political parties, NGOs and lobby groups in the islands have all put heavy emphasis on the archipelago's history of neglect under the Pekanbaru administration and the backwardness of its indigenous population of Malays, human resource development has become a central feature of provincial policy in the era of regional autonomy. Yet by emphasising a notion of regional creation within political rhetoric, the new provincial government has undermined trust in its own capacity to deliver what it promises, fomenting resentment and disillusionment towards the Riau Islands Province. Some people are driven away; others speak of nostalgia for the days of Suharto and a Unified Riau. Most simply carry on despondently, seeing the Riau Islands as the latest addition to what Cindi Katz (2005: 24) has termed "the archipelago of marooned places".

Appreciating the complexities of the human resources crisis therefore requires close ethnographic attention to the emotionally charged lifeworlds that arise in the wake of regional autonomy. To trace the structural changes that have taken place — the increased staging of contests, the allocation of resources to achievement and motivation-oriented events, and the incoming flow of Singaporean expertise — would tell only half the story. As has been seen throughout this chapter, it is precisely the slippage between these dominant figurations of Riau Islanders' lives and their lived existential reality, fraught with doubts, anxieties, bad faith, ethical dilemmas, resentments and frustrations, that frustrates structural arrangements' ability to deliver their objectives. Yet that does not mean that the region's human development programmes have been unproductive. It is simply that what has been produced are not "high quality human resources" so much as distinctive new conceptions of what it means to be an Indonesian and a Riau Islander, opening up new ways of conceptualising the self, citizenship and, as I shall argue in the next chapter, Malayness.

8

Achieving Malayness

Khaidir looked great in his costume. He at least thought so, and I was inclined to agree. An 18-year-old who had recently graduated from senior high school, he was about to take part in a cultural parade (*pawai*) with a group of his old school friends. To make sure they looked the part, they had all rented luxurious Malay clothes from an expensive local salon. Before taking to the streets, however, he wanted to give his grandparents, aunts and uncles a sneak preview. Speaking from behind the curtain that covered the doorway to his changing room, he asked us if we were ready and then stepped forward, his head held high and his hands in the position associated with traditional Malay gait: his right hand in front of his stomach, fingers closed, and thumb pointing upwards, and his left hand in a similar position behind his back. Not usually someone to show his emotions, the faint smile on his face spoke volumes of his confidence and happiness. He walked forwards, gave a gentle bow, and began a dignified catwalk-like turn. He was barely halfway through when his grandfather interrupted. "Idiot!" the old man spluttered. "What are you wearing?!"

Combining lustrous chocolate satin with a few sparkly silver trimmings and a stylish silver and maroon silk waistcloth (*songket*), Khaidir's costume suited him very well. For his grandfather, however, it exemplified everything that he loathed about the current taste for wearing "modified" versions of traditional clothes (*baju Melayu*). "Do you call that Malay dress?" continued his grandfather relentlessly, very upset. "There's nothing Malay about it! It's all modifications. You don't even know how to wear the waistcloth properly."

Khaidir never finished his catwalk turn. His confident posture turned into a deferential hunch, his eyes fixed on the ground, as he explained that he needed to get going: the parade would soon be starting, it would be awful if the others were kept waiting. After hurriedly bidding us all farewell, he slunk out the door. His grandfather discussed the matter no further but remained agitated and distracted for the rest of the evening.

This episode stuck in my memory because Khaidir's initial confidence, his grandfather's anger, and the awkwardness with which their difference of opinion went unresolved shows just how much affective charge can surround the performance and display of Malay culture. This is not a trivial concern. Countless dances, parades and "traditional" theatre performances are staged every year in the Riau Islands and at considerable expense. They are important events in people's lives, and a principal means by which the Riau Islands administration presents its vision of Malay culture to citizens. They are therefore events with high affective and political stakes, which may ostracise, exclude or unsettle some audience members, but also generate new recombinant expressions of what Malayness is or can be. The stakes are heightened still further by the fact that most instances of cultural performance are not mere "displays" but contests. Even Khaidir's parade pitted participating groups against one another for the titles of best costumes, and best contribution to the parade — and this was one of the least competitive cultural events I observed in Tanjung Pinang. Malay culture thus became intertwined with the imperative to improve "human resources" and the pleasures and pains of achieving (Chapter 7). At the heart of this chapter is the question of how these two aspects of cultural performance interact.

Certain combinations of achievement thinking and cultural performance can prove thoroughly "unsettling", with the visions of Malayness and achieving citizenship that they articulate being both troubling for and troubled by the alternative notions subscribed to by competitors, audience and judges. Yet other cases have a rather different effect. Building on the observation of Renée Bergland's (2000: 12) that "the uncanny" may, in certain circumstances, serve as a source of pleasure, I propose that emerging forms of cultural performance, which emphasise entertainment, strategy and achievement at the expense of adherence to codified "traditional culture", unsettle categories of region and ethnicity in ways that actually offer their audiences new opportunities to feel "at home".

Creating Regional Culture

The children's book *Loving the Land and Sea: Getting to Know the Cultures of the Indonesian People* (Rahimsyah 2005) is widely available in bookshops throughout Indonesia. So are many others like it. Costing only 4,000 rupiah (US$0.42), each page gives an illustrated list of the "traditions" of a particular province: its foods, costumes, weapons, houses, dances and songs. Though every province has a slightly different design for each of these, the same types of traditions can be found in every province's "culture": unity, as it were, in diversity.

Rahimsyah's book epitomises the Indonesian concept of "regional cultures" (*budaya daerah*), one of the most striking legacies of New Order cultural policy. Devised in an attempt to give substance to national cultural identity and defuse the potential for regional factionalism, these invented and codificatory catalogues of culture appeared to pay homage to "authentic" regional cultural identities, whilst actually propagating a highly simplified vision of Indonesia's multicultural landscape and delegitimising alternative or minority ethnocultural symbols within each region (Guinness 1994). In the process, many aspects of Indonesian social life were extracted from the unselfconscious domains of customary practice and turned into something to be displayed and be self-conscious about (Erb *et al.* 2005: 153). This process, described by Gregory Acciaioli (1985) as one of "aesthetification", has been heavily criticised by anthropologists for stripping cultural forms of their rich and complex meanings and reducing them to the comparatively banal domains of "art" or "clothes" (Parker 1992; Yampolsky 1995).

A related criticism concerns the ways in which regional cultures were standardised, turning the performance of dance and music into a matter of conforming to (invented) tradition rather than of innovation or creativity (Bakan 1999). One of the means by which this was accomplished was the staging of "cultural contests", which remain a popular format in the Riau Islands to this day. Anderson Sutton's (1991) incisive analysis of *gamelan*[1] contests in Central Java

---

[1] A Javanese or Balinese musical ensemble featuring gongs, xylophones, plucked strings and other instruments.

and Yogyakarta reveals how regional government offices pre-circulated cassette recordings of *gamelan* performance to ensure that entrants conformed to the official definition of "Yogya style". The closer a performance was to that given on the tape, the higher the score would be. Although many performers resented this arbitrary delimitation of technique and style, it was one to which they were forced to conform if they wished to obtain *prestasi*. Official versions of "culture" were therefore both publicly performed and valorised through their associations with victory, naturalising official definitions of regional culture in the eyes of the audience.

In the post-Suharto era, "regional culture" continues to play an important role in social life and local politics. "Cultural performances" are still widely held, the contest format remains a popular vehicle for showcasing talent, and "regional culture" continues to be seen as a means by which notions of ethnic identity can be balanced with notions of provincial and national citizenship. This is particularly evident in the Riau Islands, where the promotion of local Malay culture represented, for many, the best chance of integrating and uniting the population of the new province. Malay culture served, in the words of one journalist, as an "umbrella symbol" for the whole province, uniting Riau Islanders of diverse ethnicities and religions in a shared love of the aesthetics and values associated with Malay performance traditions. The deputy governor at the time, H.M. Sani, attested to this position in an interview with the media, explaining that "Tanjung Pinang should be viewed as collective property (*milik bersama*) ... We in Tanjung Pinang derive from various hybridities and cultures. But remember that pluralism is a symbol of togetherness — especially with Malay culture, which is able to unify us" (*Media Kepri* 2007).

Thus government-sponsored "cultural performance" contests cast Malayness as inherently integrationist. Enacting and mastering Malay culture is a process that was hoped would actively strengthen citizens' ties with the region, regardless of their background. Indeed, as noted earlier, making oneself "more Malay" is often seen as a duty incumbent upon migrants to the province. Such integrationism draws added strength from the premise that the Riau Islands' "Malayness" is a hitherto untapped resource for the province's tourism industry, a pressing concern since stronger enforcement of anti-gambling and anti-prostitution laws under regional autonomy have closed down many lucrative streams of tourism income (Ford and Lyons 2008).

While these integrationist concerns show continuity with the New Order's efforts to defuse the fissiparous potential of ethno-cultural diversity, the power dynamics associated with cultural performances have shifted considerably. Whereas the authoritarian New Order regime facilitated the top-down codification of culture, subsequent democratisation has allowed multiple formulations to coexist and compete for the support of the electorate, prompting a greater degree of public discussion and reflection on what regional culture should actually be. Coupled with the hotly contested nature of Malayness and the competitive dynamics of state-sponsored contests, this leads to cultural performances often falling short of their aim to entrench and consolidate a notion of being at home.

An Ambassador for the Islands

In July 2006, the Riau Islands Province held its first ever *bujang dara* competition, a form of beauty contest for young, unmarried men (*bujang*) and women (*dara*). When one of the judging panel dropped out at the last minute, I was asked to stand in as a "guest judge" by one of the contest organisers. This opportunity offered me a privileged insight into how "Malay culture" was both performed and assessed in an event which was to have considerable bearing upon the ways in which the Riau Islands would be defined for and presented to an international audience.

Although informants would regularly describe it as a beauty contest (*kontes kecantikan*), the aims of a *bujang dara* competition are wider reaching, the winners being appointed as provincial "tourism ambassadors" (*duta wisata*):

> **Compere** [*talking with me informally*]: The first placed contestant gets a contract for a year with the Department of Tourism to be the face of Riau Islands tourism. So they enter in the brochures, and they get to stand at the harbour to greet tourists, and to attend special events and so forth. And they get given money. Maybe five million rupiah! So to win, they need to be assessed on beauty, and they have to dance a Malay dance, they need to have good English, and they need to be able to answer the questions well. I think they have to answer questions about tourism, but it can be all sorts of questions.

Whilst *bujang dara* contests — a phrase that Suryadi (2005: 147) has described as being "full of local [Riau] nuances" — are only found in Mainland and Archipelagic Riau and some regions of Kalimantan, equivalent "tourism ambassador" contests are widespread in Indonesia. Since the contest does not merely examine beauty, but also tests and displays the contestants' knowledge of local tourist attractions and their ability to convey this in English, it is considered an event that "promotes and improves human resource quality". One newspaper explained that:

> The competition's aim is to find the talent and potential of our high-achieving teenagers ... As a result we will be able to improve our human resource quality and preserve Malay arts and culture for our younger generation ... May it succeed in improving our teenagers' human resources and also manage to increase [our] tourism and locally generated revenue! Hopefully! (*Surat Kabar Senior* 2006)

As this commentary shows, the contest aimed to combine the preservation of regional culture with economic and human development. Such diverse aims, however, do not always mesh together straightforwardly.

Following scholars who have traced the ways beauty pageants inscribe ideas about nationhood and normative identity upon women's (or in this case, young people's) bodies, by "choosing an individual whose deportment, appearance and style embodies the values and goals of a nation, locality or group" (Cohen and Wilk 1996: 2), I suggest that this *bujang dara* contest can be read as a normative argument in favour of integrationist Malayness. Yet it was also about dramatising hierarchical relationships between the Riau Islands' youngsters as measured in terms of *prestasi*. When these divergent bases for assessing "performance" could not be reconciled, the entire contest lost legitimacy, and the Malayness in which the entrants were competing became severely compromised.

The Beautiful Malay

> I once read in the newspaper that a black woman won Miss World! I was very surprised — how could the judges think a black woman was beautiful? But if a black woman can win Miss World, then we Indonesians shouldn't be ashamed of being *hitam manis* [lit. 'black and sweet', referring to the attractive dark complexion of some Indonesians]. Mind you, the winner

of this competition can't just be beautiful. All our contestants
will be marked on the '*Three Bs*': *Brains, Beauty, and Behaviour*!

— Tourism official in his opening speech

The *bujang dara* contest had four judges, each allocated a different area of expertise on which to score the contestants. A mid-
ranking tourism official was in charge of studying entrants' portfolios
of modelling photographs to select the "photogenic champion" (*juara
fotogenik*). This was a task separate from the main competition,
which the other three of us had responsibility for adjudicating.

The first judge, Hajjah Dewi, was the owner of a very successful wedding salon. Her task was to evaluate the contestants' "cultural
arts" (*seni budaya*). It was this category of "cultural arts" that spectators, the contest entrants and the opening speech referred to as
"beauty" (*kecantikan*), with clear implications of attractiveness. Dewi
was to mark two aspects of the performance: a Malay dance and the
contestants' appearance when on parade, though as events transpired,
trouble with the power supply interrupted the dance performances
so much that they could not be formally scored. The inclusion of
dancing was nevertheless an important aspect of the event. Specifying
proficiency in Malay dance demanded the embodiment of Malay
dancing rhythms, movements and steps, obliging contestants to be
made "more Malay". Even should they wish to maintain an alternative conception of themselves, be that ethnic, or couched in terms
of multiethnic citizenship, they were expected to draw upon a canon
of knowledge embodying Malayness in order to qualify as an ambassador, and therefore as a symbol of the province.

The second aspect of Dewi's task was to mark the parade. In
this section, contestants came on stage in male-female pairs, dressed
in "traditional Malay" clothes, walked downstage with a "traditional
Malay" gait, and bowed to the audience with a "traditional Malay"
greeting. As they did so, the comperes read out information from
the contestants' entry forms, underscoring how the contestants exemplified the values of *prestasi* and moral restraint. "Alisha was born on
13th August, and once won a speech contest! Suhardi, who often
wins *bujang dara* competitions, says that he hates all kinds of immorality, especially *free seks* [promiscuous or pre-marital sex]!" These
statements were greeted with cheers and applause from the audience
and approving nods from the judges.

Although the parade required the internalisation of "Malay"
comportment, everyone talked about it as assessing "beauty". This

raises the question of why it should be scored under "cultural arts" and whether being beautiful could itself be taken as a cultural art. It thus becomes important to distinguish between the two ways in which beauty was assessed in the competition. The first, a more Euro-American notion of determining whether an entrant is physically attractive, was located within the bracketed-off photogenic champion selection. In the main competition, conceptions and scores of beauty were mediated through Malay clothes.

The clothes in question, variously described as "palace clothes" (*baju istana*) or "Malay costume" (*busana Melayu*) represented a contemporary re-imagining of sultanic opulence, featuring swathes of padded satin laced with gold and silver thread, often in vibrant colours and adorned with sequins. Ironically, in the sultanic period, wearing yellow (the royal colour) had been an insult to the ruler (Liaw 1976: 76), whilst more contemporary Indonesian formulations of Malay clothing stress the inherent modesty of its design (Tarigan *et al.* 1996: 25); the *bujang dara* contest disrupted both these models. The compere notwithstanding, female participants did not wear the Islamic headscarf, while many contestants both wore yellow and masqueraded as rajas. The clothes were not expected to express values of restraint or hierarchy, but rather to provide a spectacle, a visually arresting dramatisation of ethnocultural identity. Such clothes had become an essential component of formal and public events, and sometimes contest organisers asked judges to mark the quality of competitors' clothes in an effort to make sure that no expense was spared in renting the most sumptuous outfits possible.

To do well in the *bujang dara* required entrants to successfully appropriate "palace clothes". Dewi explained the process of formulating her scores as follows:

> I have to ask myself: how do they wear the clothes? Do they look good in the clothes? Can they move well in the clothes? Because these are Malay clothes, not everyone can wear them well. Number Nine ... he might be good-looking to a Westerner but for me he can never be the winner. He is too thin for the clothes. Perhaps there [Britain] people should be thin. But a Malay needs to be a little bit fat, he needs to fill his clothes, to look healthy. Then when he moves, the clothes stay close to him — like Number Seven. But when Number Nine walks, it's like he's loose in his clothes.

Figure 8.1 An "attractively plump" male beauty contest participant, alongside the female compere (Source: author)

Dewi's assessment of beauty was less about cultural perceptions of attractiveness than about cultural politics. In assessing the "beauty" of these clothed men and women, it was the Malay clothes that set the bar: Number Nine might be very handsome, but he did not suit the clothes. The palace costume is a powerful symbol that is both ethnic and regional, since the sultanic era, as noted earlier, is remembered as the Riau Archipelago's "golden age". Yet the costume is no mere form of reductively "objectified" culture — its very materiality as an object gives it a generative agency. The loose cut of the costume, combined with the stiff inflexibility of the padding and *songket* waistcloth, demands to be filled in a particular way in order to make a convincing Malay who can move in the smooth and dignified way that evokes the idealised sense of how sultanic life must have been — and how Malay life should continue to be today (Figure 8.1).

　　　Umberto Eco (1986: 192) has written of how certain clothes, by their very design, can impose an identity and "demeanour" upon the consumer, citing his own experience of a pair of jeans that forced him to adopt a new style of walking. Although a set of "palace clothes" might promote a Malay demeanour, its agency is less that of Eco's jeans than that of Cinderella's glass slipper: it is an article "made for Malays" that through interaction with the human body in performance can identify "convincing Malays" in a way that over-shadows alternative definitions of Malayness. It is not so much an example of how Malay culture has been circumscribed and codified as an artefact that works to identify and generate Malayness. Thus in order to master "cultural arts" and win the competition, the contestants must also be mastered *by* the material cultural markers of this knowledge. Through this "acid test", which can be passed or failed by any ethnic group, the *bujang dara* competition tries to "promote and preserve Malay culture" whilst also maintaining openness (*keterbukaan*) in the face of multiculturalist accusations of ethnic exclusivity.

The Logics of Tourism

> **Compere:** A question for Number Six. If you are chosen, what contribution will you make to the Department of Tourism?
>
> **Number Six:** If I win in this contest, for our nation and to solve the problem that is faced in our tourism, I'm going to help our government to promote to abroad! I'm going to help our government to promote to investors! And the last, I will help the government with trying to improve human resources so they can be professional workers to work well in the tourism sector!

Once all 12 contestants had completed their parade, they were called back on stage for the question-and-answer session, marked by the chair of the judging panel, Raja Adnan — an aristocrat originally from the island of Lingga but now working in the history section of the provincial tourism office. The questions, already leaked to contestants several days beforehand to help boost their performance, were designed to test their "knowledge of tourism". To this effect, each participant was either asked to provide information that a tourist might want to know — such as descriptions of the principal attractions in the Riau Islands, the purpose of *bujang dara* contests, or the administrative structures of the province — or to tackle issues in the theory of tourism, such as what makes an attraction popular, or whether the Riau Islands would always have to rely on the sex industry to attract visitors. High-scoring answers typically drew on formulas present in policy rhetoric such as the high potential of tourist sites, the need for good human resources, or the historic significance of the sites described.

Amin Sweeney (1987: 98–100) has argued that postcolonial Malaysian and Indonesian languages have become characterised by "formulas ... carefully calculated to evoke an emotion in those who hear them". This argument certainly seemed to hold true for Adnan who was impressed by formula-laden answers even when they bore little relation to the question:

> **Compere:** A question for Number Twelve. Name the tourist attractions in Kabupaten Lingga.

> **Number Twelve:** Good evening. Lingga is a very high-potential island. It has a high value because of the historical places. And why don't people know Lingga very well? Because it is not well promoted! And that's why I'm here to tell you that we should promote and preserve our historical sites, not only in Lingga but also in all of Riau Islands Province.

Although her answer completely failed to identify the tourist attractions about which she had specifically been asked, this contestant still received Adnan's highest mark. In referring to Lingga's high potential, its historic value, the need to promote it, and its place in the provincial tourism strategy, she drew on formulas that were familiar and convincing to the judges and audience.

Since these formulas were highly normative visions of local tourism, it is worth considering the assumptions and principles underpinning them. The starting premise was that the Riau Islands and Tanjung Pinang were "high-potential" and thus inherently attractive to tourists. One question, for instance, asked: "Why are many tourists attracted to Penyengat Island?" — a formulation that presumed Penyengat really was an attractive tourist destination. Given this, the factors that prevented tourists from visiting were categorised in two ways. First, there were powerful external factors that deterred tourists such as unreasonable fears of terrorism or disease, hostility to Islam, or cheaper prices elsewhere. Second, there were problems with the tourist industry's human resources and thus the promotion of local attractions. The assumption persisted that the tourist attractions themselves were of high quality and would be popular with tourists "if only they knew".

In practice, many of the Riau Islanders I knew considered this idea laughable. "Where are the extraordinary tourist attractions?" joked one shopkeeper. "There aren't any! Not unless you count Batu-24! [a prostitution complex]." For many in Tanjung Pinang, especially those who came from areas near the tourist centres of Lake Toba, Bukittinggi or Central Java, it was impossible not to make an unfavourable comparison between the Riau Archipelago and their place of origin. One Minangkabau motorcycle taxi driver explained that he had been so disappointed with his visit to Penyengat that it was "impossible for him to consider Tanjung Pinang as anything other than a place to work". He then suggested that, if I hoped to get a PhD from researching culture, I would be well advised to relocate to West Sumatra as quickly as possible! For these people, other things came to symbolise the ultimate tourist experience: the culturally meaningful sites in their home province, famous sites that had become national symbols, such as Borobudur temple, and the retail tourism of Singapore. By contrast, the cultural tourism on offer in the Riau Archipelago involved small, unimpressive buildings related to a historical background that they felt was "overrated".

Nevertheless, the government's model should not just be dismissed as overambitious propaganda. Rather, its claims were grounded in normative associations between Malayness, government policy and tourism practices: a set of relationships that were internalised and socialised by the *bujang dara* contestants. While officials and townsfolk alike were quick to point out that several of the islands' beaches were "better than Bali", the provincial tourism strategy centred on cultural tourism. This decision reflected the need to develop jobs in the tourism sector, primarily in urban centres, as well as the more general government policy to fulfil perceived obligations towards Malay culture as the "indigenous" culture of the region. Under this model, which took "traditional Malay culture" as something to be cherished and preserved, historical sites and cultural forms were assumed to be inherently interesting because of their ability to connect people with their Malay selves.

The difficulty this encountered in practice was that many Riau Islanders, especially those self-identifying as non-Malay, did not like the tourist attractions because they meant very little to them. Such attitudes, of course, stood at odds with the belief that the province's multiethnic society could be united and unified through the promotion of Malay culture and Malay history. From the point of view of the Department of Tourism and Culture, anyone living on "Malay soil" has a right to claim and enact a certain Malayness. The challenge was in encouraging them to exercise that right. The "socialisation" in evidence in the *bujang dara* contest can thus be seen as an attempt to inculcate a Malay "orientation" in both competitors and audience. Certainly it was in no way attempting to legitimise the provincial government's efforts to date: entrants were unrestrained in their criticism of the poor human resource quality, poor marketing strategy and lack of experience that shackled the provincial Department of Tourism, remarks which the audience readily applauded and which Raja Adnan listened to with sad nods.

If the performance and adjudication of the "parade" section of the *bujang dara* contest enacted the "ideal Malayness" of the clothed body, performative dimensions of Malayness were also being tested in the question-and-answer session. An "ideal Malay" and "an ideal Riau Islander" should feel affinity with a Malay cultural and historical site and its associated narratives. Their Malayness inheres in the interactivity between place, history and person. Proving this interactivity through recounting details of the places accurately and enthusiastically — and remember here that the answers were believed by all viewing to be spontaneous — shows them to have become Malay, at least within one particular dimension of their social person. By entering the competition in search of *prestasi*, contestants from a variety of ethnic backgrounds exposed themselves to these narratives and underwent such transformations in order to win, thereby presenting themselves as exemplars for other *prestasi*-hungry youths. Of course, somebody working as tourism ambassador should also understand the administrative structure of the province and have a sensible approach to theories of tourism, and so several questions on such topics were included as well.

How to Win a Bujang Dara Contest

I was the final judge. Having a genuine "native speaker" was not only prestigious; it also allowed more accurate scoring since I would know "for real" what was correct and incorrect English. With no guidelines on how to score, except the specified 50 to 100 point range, I worked out my own criteria based on how readily I imagined a tourist would be able to understand competitors' answers. Just before the competition began, I was approached by the judge charged with assessing the photographs and given a sombre warning:

> We must be responsible. *You* must be responsible. Do not give
> scores that are very high. Just imagine — you see someone who

is great and you give them 90 or 100. Then the next person is
even better — what happens then?! Score responsibly. I hope you
understand.

Far from convinced that I would be giving any scores in the nineties,
I assured him that I had understood, though it quickly transpired that
I had not.

Since all three judges had been marking separately, our first task
was to hand the score sheets to Adnan who, as the chair judge, was
in charge of totalling the scores. The female contestants' marks had
been so widely distributed that it was clear who the winners were.
Furthermore, all three judges were agreed on the rankings. There was
nevertheless a brief difficulty because Adnan had "never heard of"
Welly, the first-placed female. This was especially problematic because
the comperes had announced that several of the other contestants
had previously won other competitions, and it would create a stir if
these high achievers were knocked out by a newcomer. Adnan therefore announced that the result needed to be "checked". Each judge
had been given a photocopy of the contestants' entry forms in a
folder alongside scoring sheets and it was to these photocopies that
Adnan and Dewi now turned. When they got to Welly's sheet, they
breathed a sigh of relief. "She was placed first in an English language
speech contest! And she has come second in a town debate contest,"
revealed Adnan. "It turns out she is quite an achiever after all."

The male section proved more problematic. Adit, the top contestant, had a score of 229. Hasan had a score of 227. Two contestants, one of whom was Suhardi — the man who had won many
competitions before — had 226. Had there not been a mark for
English language, Suhardi would have just snatched overall victory
but, because I had found his question-and-answer session inarticulate,
my English mark had tipped the balance and put him in danger of
elimination. Adnan looked at me anxiously and explained that there
was a serious problem: "Suhardi is the most *berprestasi*. His dancing
and his knowledge of tourism were really good. He is the man who
ought to win, but now he might not even get third place." As a
result, the marks — which had already been signed as definite and
final — needed to be changed. We finally agreed, after a vote on
the tiebreak, that Suhardi should take third place. Dewi remained
dissatisfied, arguing that because Suhardi's "cultural arts" were very
good and because he "looked very handsome in Malay clothes", he

should get at least second rank. I replied that she had already given him a high score and that in terms of English, which was equally important in the structure of the competition, the advantage lay with Hasan — their scores for "knowledge of tourism" were identical. As a result, I was deeply opposed to changing the totals.

The dispute centred on a disjunction between different technologies of counting and quantifying persons. As I understood matters, the scores were meant to be a measure, on a calibrated scale, of the performances we had seen. The scores thus generated the champion and, by announcing the scores along with the positions, we could make it clear this was a close-run thing. The other two argued that, if one looked at Hasan's entry form, his *prestasi* was very poor — he had once been runner-up in a modelling competition, but nothing else. Suhardi, by contrast, had listed high rankings in ten competitions, including one at the national level, and was studying to be a doctor. It was clear from this previous *prestasi*, Adnan argued, that Suhardi deserved the *prestasi* associated with winning the *bujang dara* contest more than Hasan did, and our marks collectively must have been wrong. Although Adnan and Dewi gave scores reflecting how they measured the performance, such numbers were never intended to be definitive, but rather guidelines that would hopefully corroborate a previously existing hierarchy based on biography and track record of *prestasi* as declared in the entry form.

This difference in viewing the role of numbers became still more evident in the subsequent proposed compromise. Dewi suggested that we allow Hasan to keep his higher score but promote Suhardi, still with a lower score, to second rank. "It's honest if it's like this," she explained, "because we show we prefer Suhardi, but also that Hasan got a higher score." But at this point, Adnan started to have his doubts, since it was far from clear that such an announcement would be well received by the audience. Ultimately it was announced that Hasan would take second place and Suhardi third.

Achieving Citizenship

Colleen Cohen and Richard Wilk (1996: 9) suggest that "slips" in the conduct of a beauty contest "expose the multiple cultural systems and structures of power in which contestants and audiences are enmeshed in their daily lives". Their argument certainly applies to the material at hand. On the one hand, the contest was designed to showcase a series of images with powerful political implications. Young people, consistently represented as the future of the nation in Indonesian rhetoric, were seen to be honouring and revitalising their province's cultural traditions, preserving them for the future. Moreover, since they were wearing Malay dress to answer questions about the tourism industry in English, Malayness could become equated with progress, business acumen, educational performance and good human resource quality: the very things that stereotypes portray as incompatible with Malayness. While contestants' ability to generate such a performance was scored and rewarded, this evaluation was trumped by another type of ranking: that of their previous *prestasi* as declared on the application form. There was a problem when Suhardi lost because he had more *prestasi* to his name than those who had beaten him. Likewise, Welly's victory was not legitimated until the result had been "checked" by seeing her previous *prestasi*. Such dilemmas occur in many types of competitions and are regularly reported by disillusioned judges and event organisers.

The events at the *bujang dara* contest show that for Riau Islanders, "achievement" is not just a momentary event but rather a human quality, a revelation of character and capability that can be accumulated over time to increase one's agency in the social world. Measurable and comparable, the longer one's list of *prestasi*, no matter how many defeats one has endured whilst developing it, the more of an achiever one is considered to be. Yet previous *prestasi* is not an automatic mystification of ability. When the outcome of competitions engenders debate over whether someone really deserves their reputation as an exceptional, high-achieving human resource, it is clear that many still expect such matters to be decided on merit. Yet when someone known as having *prestasi* fails to achieve, rumours can circulate that the competition was rigged or the judges bribed. A "successful" competition is therefore one in which the quality of what is displayed on stage correlates with previous *prestasi*. When unexpected results occur, judges face a predicament. They can privilege the rankings generated by their scores and risk the accusation of having rigged the competition; alternatively, they can privilege the rankings of previous *prestasi* as a "safe" choice which they hope the audience and contestants will accept. That many judges, by their own admission, choose the latter attests to the self-replicating character of *prestasi*, which is part of its allure. Yet when *prestasi* replicates itself within particular individuals' biographies at the expense of others, this actually subverts the government's intentions in supporting so many contests in the first place, namely to raise levels of "achievement" amongst the population as a whole.

Nonetheless, while the adjudication process ultimately centred on the correct allocation of *prestasi*, and many of the entrants had reported that increasing their *prestasi* was an important reason for entering the contest, most spectators still considered this to be an event about Malayness. When the winners were announced, a ripple of shock went through the audience. The controversy was not over Suhardi's third place, which had been the big issue for the judges. Rather it was that Welly had been chosen as the winning female. In assessing her ability to wear Malay clothes, her knowledge of tourism theory and her ability to speak English, and in checking her *prestasi*, the judges had overlooked one other crucial factor: she was Chinese.

The next day, the LAM (Institute of Malay Customs) protested that that a Chinese girl had even been allowed to participate in the competition. They objected on the grounds that the Riau Islands was a Malay province, and so needed to be represented in promotional material by a Malay, or at least someone who could pass as Malay. They suggested that the runner-up, an Ambonese Protestant, would have been a wiser choice. Townspeople were broadly in agreement. "Welly is not of Indonesian descent (*keturunan nusantara*)," grumbled one Minangkabau man, "yet she, as a Chinese person, is going to be the face of the Riau Islands in every brochure and pamphlet? Wah!" Even those who sympathised with Welly's position blamed the event organisers for allowing Chinese to enter in the first place. Others justified a proposed exclusion because Chinese were richer than "indigenous Indonesians" (*pribumi*), could afford English lessons, make-up and even cosmetic surgery, and so were at an unfair advantage during the competition.

Meanwhile, many Chinese in the town had interpreted the protracted discussion between the judges — in reality about where to place Hasan and Suhardi — as being about whether Welly should be allowed to win despite her Chineseness. The conviction spread that she had won only because there was a Western judge who had been able to see what other Indonesians were blinded to by racism. This claim prompted debate over whether it was appropriate or necessary to have English featuring in the competition. Many argued that *bujang dara* contests should assess only beauty, cultural arts and knowledge of tourism; English language, no matter how useful for increasing human resource quality, was better reserved for English-language contests. Subsequently, new *bujang dara* events proliferated. These had an increased emphasis on Malayness, encouraged contestants to recite Malay literature and use Malay rather than Indonesian, and only rarely awarded extra marks to those fluent in foreign languages. Three weeks later, such a contest was set up in Batam and this time, Welly was excluded by a minimum age parameter of 18. The winner of this contest, a student from Karimun, became the *de facto* face of the Riau Islands and Welly, although invited to help welcome guests to the mayor's office for important public events such as Idul Fitri, received far fewer such invitations than the non-Chinese finalists she had beaten.

If the *bujang dara* contest had intended to promote Malayness as accessible to all, and to valorise its celebration by the youth of the Riau Islands, its aftermath revealed the extent to which such integrationist endeavours had their limits. While a wide ethnic participation may have been acceptable to many of Tanjung Pinang's residents, the racial cleavage between Chinese and others was too deep to allow them to accept and endorse the eventual result. What made this particular contest so controversial was not that a Chinese took part but that she scored better in, and won, a competition which was — from the use of the locally nuanced words, *bujang* and *dara*, in the title, through to the scoring of dress and dancing, and the pro-Malayness position implied in the questions and demanded in answers — all about being Malay. The logic of integrationism was then trumped by a Malaysian-style "multicultural" model that demanded extra rights and greater protection for Malays, both in ethnic and (especially) racial terms. For contestants, the competition brought the bitter realisation that the "meritocratic" logic of *prestasi* was still answerable to classifications on the basis of race.

Promoted as a form of public entertainment, the *bujang dara* contest also aimed to promote and naturalise two frameworks of citizenship. The first was a citizenship that managed to be multi-ethnic while respecting and maintaining Malay culture; the other was a citizenship that inculcated values of *prestasi* to develop human resources and the economy. What the contest actually put on show, in Malay costume, was how complicated and precarious both these citizenships can be. Welly admitted to me after the event that she had never really expected to win because her face did not look Malay enough. Her participation in the integrationist event thus exhibited another form of bad faith towards the new province's goals: she believed that Malayness could be a vehicle for bringing people together whilst simultaneously feeling that the racial and cultural diversity of the province's population would overwhelm any attempt to encompass it. Her victory allowed her at last to believe in integrationism and the possibility of belonging in blissful good faith, but only until the crushing moment at which her participation was queried and her victory attributed to the presence of a foreign judge. Welly found the experience devastating. However, for all that the tensions between different understandings of Malayness and its role in the new province often haunted cultural performances, they did not always give rise to the feelings of outrage and disappointment that emerged in the aftermath of the *bujang dara* contest. As revealed by the burgeoning phenomenon of public poetry competitions, cultural performances also offered a vibrant set of opportunities to turn parallel notions of Malayness to very different ends.

Riddle Me a Malay

Pergi ke kenduri di rumah Cik Dolah,	Go to the feast at Dolah's house,
Pergi bersama dengan Cik Atun.	Go there together with Atun.
Sebut mahirut, mahirutlah!	They say you are clever; so be clever!
Yang penting, pandai berpantun.	What matters is that you are good at *pantun*.

— *Pantun* delivered by team Tanjung Pinang B
at the 2006 International Festival of Malay Culture.

The *pantun* is a type of Malay quatrain which, in its idealised form, conforms to strict rules of prosody. The lines of the verse, each of four words, and eight, nine, or eleven syllables, form an *abab* rhyme scheme, and may also exhibit extensive repetition of vocabulary and assonance (Anon 1958; Thomas 1984). In the Riau Islands, this four-line verse is now one of the most actively promoted elements of regional culture. *Pantun* contests (*peraduan berbalas pantun*) were one of the most hotly attended and eagerly anticipated forms of cultural performance. At a political level, the municipality of Tanjung Pinang has tried to define itself as "the land of *pantun*" (*negeri pantun*), and Mayor Suryatati has publicly declared her vision of "a historic town full of cultural heritage" in which "every schoolchild is skilled at *pantun* and dancing" (Putten 2011: 226–9; *Tribun Batam* 2007a). This vision has been internalised by townsfolk to the extent that one primary school pupil admitted in a newspaper interview that she "would feel ashamed if she couldn't write good *pantun*" (*Kompas* 2008). But what makes the *pantun* so relevant to the themes of this book is that these various commitments to the genre were all under-pinned by a shared precept that the *pantun* acts as a "perfect mirror of the Malay soul" (Daillie 1988: 3).

This contention, much like the suppositions that Malays are idle fishermen or superstitious spirit-worshippers, can be traced back directly to colonial discourse emanating from British Malaya and the Straits Settlements. Colonial scholar-administrators working in this region quickly found themselves entranced by the "simplicity" and "romance" of the *pantun*, an attitude which Sweeney (1987: 39) argues was spurred by the Romanticist valorisation of "rustic simpli-city" in the England they had left behind. Believing that "no one can estimate the mental scope of the Malay without an understanding of the *pantun*, the love verse and lampoon of his race" (Wilkinson and Winstedt 1923: 3), scholars compiled vast compendia of *pantun* that were then subject to debate and analysis within the emerging field of "Malay literature".[2]

In doing so, however, they exhibited a series of biases that continue to overshadow the literary analysis of *pantun* through to the present day. The *pantun* was theorised as a poetic medium that provided the Malay with "a relief for his feelings, especially for his sense of melancholy longing" (Wilkinson, 1924: 43) and as a result, those *pantun* which were not "moody" or "melancholy" escaped docu-mentation and commentary. This in itself reflects European predi-lections: "melancholy" and other emotional extremes had become highly prized artistic qualities amongst Romanticists reacting to the disappointments of industrialisation (Henderson 2008). Moreover, because the collectors were concerned with placing the *pantun* within a Eurocentrically-defined field of "high literature", preference was given to verses exhibiting Occidental literary merit. The *pantun*'s fundamentally oral character was downplayed and those examples that disrupted the prevailing notion were given no place in the

---

[2] The most notable collections being Hamilton's *Malay Pantun* (1959) and Wilkinson and Winstedt's *Pantun Melayu* (1923).

collections. Thus A.W. Hamilton (1959: ii), in the introduction to his *pantun* compendium, declared that "public and bawdy limericks" were "almost unknown" within the genre despite the fact that, as we shall see, they were and are a vibrant and important part of *pantun* performance.

Having conceived of the *pantun* as an indigenous form of "high art", analysts of Malay literature were then confronted with the puzzle that has remained at the heart of debates in *pantun* scholarship: how to theorise the relationship between the quatrain's two couplets, and the extent to which the second is foreshadowed by the first. An early commentator on the *pantun*, Charles Adriaan van Ophuijsen (1904), had suggested that there was in fact no connection beyond establishing a rhyme scheme. This explanation proved unsatisfactory to Wilkinson (1924: 46), who asked why, if this was the case, "so crude a poetry [was] found charming by the Indonesians". This question marked the beginning of a decades-long quest by scholars to prove that the *pantun* was not in fact as crude as it appeared, and that the relation between the two couplets was one of foreshadowing, allusion and subtle anticipation, "like the polite cough of a visitor about to step up into a house" (Anon. 1958: 113).

Two trends emerged in consequence of this debate. First, many Malays themselves began to write *pantun* that demonstrated the literary, romantic quality that colonial scholars claimed to have discerned in the poems they collected. Second, the notion that the *pantun* reflected the deep stirrings of the Malay soul led to its subtlety, indirection and apparent "elusive and elfin spirit" (Sheppard 1982: 9) informing broader theories of Malayness. Thus, for Henri Fauconnier (1990: 82), "it is the [*pantun*'s] play of words, the equivocations, the tenuous allusions, that constitute its special charm for Malays", whilst Clifford Goddard (1997: 193) stresses that the *pantun*'s indirectness makes it a "very serviceable resource for alluding to potentially sensitive matters". Such analyses entrench and apparently confirm the stereotype of the bashful Malay who eschews crude bluntness in favour of indirectness, suggestion and propriety.

These ideas have persisted into the postcolonial period and circulate widely in the Malay regions of contemporary Indonesia. Indeed, one reason that the Riau Islands government has found the *pantun* such a compelling form of "regional culture" is because they believe the genre forces authors to express themselves, and hopefully come to understand themselves, in ways concordant with "Malay

values". Just as the presence of Malays in Tanjung Pinang was believed to have a calming effect on the frictions between other ethnic
groups, so participation in this brand of Malay culture was supposed
to bring calm and peacefulness to one's life and relations. It can thus
be seen as a technology for disciplining and governing the self, as
the preface to a *pantun* handbook makes clear:

> The rapid advancement of the age has brought changes around
> us, the likes of which we have never experienced before. Our
> values have been desacralised; our lifestyles and appetites are
> happy to follow the trends of popular culture … Such a situation
> can easily distance school-age youngsters from their sociocultural
> roots. They also lose interest in and appreciation of cultural and
> literary products that in fact contain noble values.
>
> The function of literature that is not only for consumption
> by the brain but also for consumption by the heart (*hati*) is
> extremely useful in sublimating our individual personalities to be
> more gentle and polite. This will allow us to notice the beauty
> of the world which has been described as undergoing a process
> of disenchantment. In accordance with these aims, this book
> [about *pantun*] shows characteristic beauty and utility (Indra
> 2006: i).

In practice, however, the capacity of the *pantun* to enact Malay
values is complicated by three factors. The first is that people in
Tanjung Pinang define and understand Malayness in many ways,
not all of which fit comfortably with the received notion of "Malay
propriety" that informs political notions of the *pantun*. The second is
the *pantun's* oral nature. Unlike those documented in Malaya, which
were studied as written, literary texts, *pantun* in the Riau Islands are
spoken. They are often designed to have a specific effect upon their
audience, and are unlikely to be listened to in ways that allow for a
close and detailed consideration of subtle textual foreshadowing. This
is particularly true in the case of *pantun* contests, where the quatrains
are written spontaneously, with a time limit of 60 seconds, such that
the poet is expected to focus on establishing the correct meter and
rhyme scheme, rather than complex metaphorical constructions. As a
consequence, the "bawdy limericks" that were systematically excluded
from the colonial field of "Malay literature" actually predominate in
Riau Islanders' performances of "the Malay soul".

The final complicating factor is the competitive nature of
pantun contests, which remain the most popular means of socialising

the genre. Although the competition context serves to preclude the indirectness that led to the *pantun* becoming a classic symbol of "Malayness", the notion that the genre exemplifies "Malay culture" continues to be felt very avidly by competitors and judges. Indeed, a crucial dimension of winning the contest is to perform oneself as being "more Malay" than one's competitors through the verses. Examining how and why poets do this, and the audience's reaction as they do so, offers us a new approach for the analysis of *pantun* — one which emphasises strategy over imagery and explores its capacity to simultaneously assert and deconstruct claims to Malayness. It thereby reveals that the government's strategy of promoting the *pantun* and its Malayness, as a unifying symbol of the province and town has dramatised the multiple horizons of Malayness in ways that may simultaneously connect and divide.

The Pantun in Contest

In September 2006, the International Festival of Malay Culture, hosted by Tanjung Pinang, staged a prestigious *pantun* contest which spanned three evenings and attracted teams from across the Riau Islands, as well as from Mainland Riau, North Sumatra, East Nusa Tenggara and West Kalimantan. Although generally considered to have been a very successful event, the debates and dialogues surrounding the contest as it unfolded illuminated the horizons of Malayness with which participants and audience have to engage on a regular basis.

The premise of a *pantun* competition is simple. Two teams of three members come onto the stage and introduce themselves. Each of the teams will be dressed in sumptuous sultanic clothes, similar to those worn in the *bujang dara* contest, and should appear to be the epitome of Malayness. Participants also ham up a strong Malay accent, the quality of which is noted in the "acting" category on the score-sheet, and may even style their hair and make-up in ways that are "traditionally Malay". A member of the first team then delivers a *pantun* containing a question, a process known as "selling" the *pantun* (*menjual pantun*). This question should be related to the overall theme of the contest, which in the case at hand was "Malay culture". The second team is given 60 seconds in which to confer, after which a member must "buy" this *pantun* (*membeli pantun*) by creating a spontaneous *pantun* which answers the question. They

Table 8.1 A judging grid for a *pantun* competition (after Tusiran Suseno 2006: 149)

Material Scored	SELLING			BUYING			TOTAL
	1	2	3	1	2	3	
Completeness of the *pantun*							
1. Overall rhyme scheme							
2. Number of words and syllables							
3. Rhyming between couplets							
Content of the *pantun*							
1. Relevance to the theme							
2. Effectiveness as a question/answer							
3. Speed of response (buying only)							
Performance							
1. Acting							
2. Costume							
GRAND TOTAL							

then sell a *pantun* back to the first team. The process is repeated until each team has bought and sold three *pantun*, these competitive rhymes being framed with many other *pantun* that represent friendly banter between the teams. A panel of three judges score each *pantun* in the selling-buying exchanges according to the criteria detailed in Table 8.1. Each of the three main elements (completeness, content and performance) is scored by a different judge. Because it cannot be prepared in advance, and so is a more spontaneous display of individual skill, the "buying" *pantun* receives additional weighting when factoring the final score. It also receives a score for speed of response. However, despite the scoring sheet's apparent simplicity, how these elements of the *pantun* should be assessed is not at all straightforward.

Particular difficulties surrounded the judging criteria of "relevance to the theme" and "effectiveness as a question or answer".

Since the theme was "Malay culture", the criterion of "relevance" raised immediate questions about the boundaries of what should be considered as "Malay culture". This was most evident in definitional *pantun*, where the buying team was asked to define or clarify a term related to "Malay culture". Questions about history or local places had been explicitly barred, as it was not considered reasonable to expect teams to know about highly localised phenomena. A *pantun* such as the following, however, would be considered appropriate:

Tanjung Pinang B Selling to West Kalimantan:

Pergi ke hutan mencari kayu,	Go to the forest in search of wood,
Pergi bersama dengan Cik Nonya.	Travelling with Cik Nonya.
Kalau Tuan dan Puan orang Melayu,	If you are Malays,
Bubur pusat apa maknanya?	What is the meaning of '*bubur pusat*'?

Bubur pusat is a well-known variety of sticky-rice porridge, and the West Kalimantan team was easily able to reply. More ambitious teams exploited the theme's parameters to obtain a strategic advantage. Older teams chose to ask questions concerning "*bahasa lama*" ("old language"), obsolete vocabulary for types of fishing net, musical instrument and ritual rarely encountered today. In several cases, the judging panel were themselves uncertain of the object at stake in the *pantun*, and the questioning team was obliged to give an explanation. Despite being obscure, this vocabulary's presence within the Malay language — a fundamental tenet of Malay identity — put it above question as a legitimate *pantun* topic. As the competition progressed and the stakes became higher, definitional *pantun* became ever more frequent. Teams of schoolchildren fought back against "*bahasa lama*" by asking for definitions of what they termed "modern Malay culture" such as "skaters" and "punk", with which they imagined their adult opposition to be unfamiliar.

Confronted with such questions, responding teams often panicked and had to confess their ignorance, resulting in a very low score. Yet definitional tactics were not welcomed by the judging panel, who felt it encouraged the participants to ask questions about cultural technologies that were not really part of a living Malay tradition and made the contest too much like a trivia quiz. Emphasis was put on knowledge rather than the art of formulating an intelligent, entertaining *pantun*. Any teams with the presence of mind to dismiss such questions, through responses such as "go and look it up in a dictionary" were consequently rewarded very highly. Against this, selling teams protested that traditional heritage and contemporary lifestyles *were* both part of "Malay culture". Whilst it is difficult to assess to what extent such claims were heartfelt, or simply opportunistic tactics to win the competition, they reflected the extent to which *pantun* performances can turn into unexpected battles over what is properly considered Malay culture.

Another common strategy exploited the criterion of "effectiveness as a question or answer". This is more complex than it first seems because of the ways in which "Malay" theories of communication inform the assessment of the exchange. The judge should not just be evaluating whether a *pantun*'s content was clear or correctly answered. She should also assess whether the question or answer has been phrased in a sufficiently "Malay" way, and indeed whether it is even appropriate for a Malay to utter in the first place. Tusiran Suseno (2006: 72–3) illustrates this particularly well. He gives the example of a fictional contestant who poses the following puzzle:

Melur tumbuh di dalam taman,	The jasmine grows in the park,
Petik sekuntum dikerat-kerat.	Its flowers plucked and its buds cut off.
Heranlah sungguh melihat zaman,	It's truly astonishing to see this era;
Kenapa perempuan berpakaian ketat?	Why do the women wear tight clothes?

This, he cautions, is a trick question (*pertanyaan yang menjebak*):

> It seems very easy to reply to [this] *pantun* — but you must be careful! If the answer is that women are following the trends of the times, it means that Malay women have no opinion of their own and are easily swallowed up by the tide of history.

The answer offered by the buyer must therefore preserve the values and integrity of Malayness, even at the expense of directly answering the question. Tusiran Suseno therefore offers the following *pantun* as a model reply:

Terbang berkawan si burung merbah,	The shrike flies with its friends,
Hinggap di pokok membuat sangkar.	Settles on the tree and makes a nest.
Jike berpakaian sudahpun berubah,	If the styles of clothing have changed,
Mari membahasnya dalam seminar.	Let's discuss it in a seminar.

The invocation of "a seminar" is an especially good answer because it has allowed the poet to respond whilst not saying anything that might betray the name of Malay women or Malay culture. Further-more, the indirect response preserves a particular formulation of normative Malayness.

Trick questions of this kind are effective strategically because they threaten to expose one's opponent as "not Malay enough" to notice the trap and put pressure on the respondent to find a suitably "Malay" response in a very short time frame. Poets must therefore keep a sense of a reified "Malay cultural practice" uppermost in their minds when thinking through questions and answers. Paradoxically, whilst the *pantun* contest manifests itself as a spectacle in which "Malays" — or those who have been enculturated into Malayness — display "Malay culture", the strategic navigation of the contest rests on an implicit understanding (acknowledged when questions are labelled "trick") that this "Malayness" is highly affected. *Pantun* sellers look smug, and the audience crows appreciatively, after trick *pantun* are sold, because they all see the predicament that the flus-tered buyer is in: he knows what he wants to say, but cannot say it because he has to answer in a way that performs himself as a norma-tive Malay. The restrictions of "Malayness" in the context are satis-fying and entertaining to watch because it is recognised that such normativity exceeds the restrictions on speech that would characterise ordinary life. Malayness here is not an identity being straightfor-wardly displayed but the rules of a game explicitly bracketed off from the realm of the everyday.

In the contest, a team from Batam (Figure 8.2) comprising three young women wearing colourful headscarves and Malay clothes offered a trick question to the team from Indragiri Hulu, in Main-land Riau (Figure 8.3). This team comprised two men and a woman dressed in elaborate sultanic gold costume and sporting a traditional Malay topknot crafted by one of Tanjung Pinang's most respected traditional hairstylists. Her choice of hairstyle attracted a mischievous attention from the Batam team.

Batam Selling to Indragiri Hulu:

The *pantun* I have composed is specifically for *Bu Ustadah* [lit. the female Muslim religious teacher]. Don't not answer, will you? Listen!

Dayung perahu ke Pulau Asam,	Paddle a boat to Asam Island,
Perahu kecil tidak beratap.	The boat is small, without a roof.
Katanyapun Melayu itu identik	They say that Malayness is identical
dengan Islam,	with Islam,
Kenapa Cik itu tak pakai jilbab?	Why aren't you wearing a headscarf?

Figure 8.2 The Batam team
(Source: author)

Figure 8.3 The Indragiri Hulu team
(Source: author)

Indragiri Hulu buying from Batam:

I am going to try and answer. As to whether or not the answer is good enough … I'll leave that up to the adjudicators.

Jalan-jalan ke Indragiri Hulu	Go travelling to Indragiri Hulu,
Dapat oleh-oleh ikan sepat	Get a gurami fish as a souvenir.
Kami memang orang Melayu …	We are indeed Malay people …

[… she looks to her team in desperation before uttering the final line]

| *Tadi lupa memakai jilbab.* | I forgot to put on my headscarf earlier. |

This answer was met with unenthusiastic applause and a couple of jeers. Yet as the Indragiri Hulu team commented afterwards, there was little else that they could say because they were caught between too many mainstream formulations of Malayness. To point out that the topknot was itself a symbol of "Malay tradition" would have been unacceptable, as that would have implied that it was not necessary to wear the headscarf, contravening an important aspect of reformist doctrine. To observe that Islam was itself a relatively late incursion into "Malay" culture would have been even worse, violating the orthodoxy that Islamic religiosity was fundamental to the Malay identity. All that could be done was to concede the questioner's framework ("we are *indeed* Malay people") and make a feeble excuse.

This example not only signals how an attempt to safeguard certain normative "Malay values" lies at the core of *pantun* performance; it also highlights how, in a competitive context in which one gains *prestasi* through "being Malay", alternative formulations of Malayness — here exemplified by the headscarf and the topknot — are put into direct competition with each other to the audience's delight. What appears to be banter over a question of costume is in fact a thinly veiled battle over the nature of Malayness itself. Incompatible "Malaynesses" rub against and defeat each other, all within the purview of an activity that is supposedly quintessentially "Malay". In this regard, the *pantun* contest echoes the tensions that pervaded the *bujang dara* contest. But there were crucial differences. While the beauty contest prompted outrage when an "integrationist" model of Malayness won out over a more multicultural alternative due to the arbitrary decree of the judging panel, in the *pantun* contest the two approaches were put in dialogue with each other. One wins and the other loses because of differentials in skill, wit and showmanship, factors that the audience can both witness and appreciate. In such a context, there is something deeply satisfying about watching teams negotiate competing formulations of Malayness and seeing the category being actively unsettled. The audience laughs, and claps appreciatively at Batam's question not only because they admire the virtuosity of the performers but also because the wrangling on stage echoes their own difficulty in grappling with the vicissitudes of being Malay. The way that the *pantun* unsettles Malayness is both heartening and familiar, bringing an affect of comfort to their shared predicament, as well as a cathartic comic release to audience members' harrowed lives.

Laughter and Tears

The competitive process of teams buying and selling each other's quatrains is framed by a much longer and more elaborate sequence in which teams offer and exchange *pantun* for the entertainment of the crowd. These poems sometimes have the function of introducing a particular speaker, but they may also comprise a spontaneous exchange. In such circumstances, the formal and strategic strictures of a competitive *pantun* are slackened, allowing more experimental and eye-catching poems to be formulated. While these are never scored, they help to garner audience support and are widely enjoyed. Humour plays an important — if sometimes controversial — role.

There are many ways in which one can make the exchange of *pantun* funny, all of which are augmented by the driving rhythms and crescendos in the genre's iambic meter (Gil 1993: 75). The opening couplet offers particular scope for a display of wit, wordplay and showmanship because its primary role is to establish the rhyme scheme rather than impart content. Younger teams were especially keen to use it as an opportunity for entertaining the crowd with surreal or comic imagery:

Makan es, mulut berasap.	Eat ice and your mouth smokes.
Berasap mulut, makan es!	If your mouth is smoking, eat some ice!
Bukan saya tak nak jawab ...	It's not that I was not going to answer ...
Yang bunga ancam lewat SMS.	[But] this young woman is threatening me by text message.

This example also illustrates the prevaricatory *pantun* that teams strive to offer when it is their turn to buy. Though some prefer to sit and confer for 60 seconds, many use the minute to offer comic *pantun*, filling the time while their compatriots think up an effective answer. The poem above, for instance, provided a segue into the female member of the team formally buying the opposing team's *pantun*. Audiences particularly enjoy these when, while the "buyer" is still composing their answer, this gives rise to banter between teams, filled with good-natured ripostes and witty remarks. Consider, for example, the following exchange, initiated when Tanjung Pinang was putting off answering a *pantun* offered by Batam:

Tanjung Pinang "Buying" from Batam:

Dari Arab pergi ke Arab,	From Arabia I went to Arabia,
Sampai di Arab membeli helm ...	Once in Arabia, I bought a crash helmet ...

Batam [interrupting]: That's a long way! Why are you going to Arabia to buy a crash helmet? Because Tanjung Pinang doesn't have any, right?!

Tanjung Pinang:

Dari Arab pergi ke Arab,	From Arabia I went to Arabia.
Sampai di Arab kehilangan helm.	Once in Arabia, my crash helmet disappeared.
Bukan Abang nanti tak jawab,	It's not that I am not going to answer,
Abang seorang yang paling handsome.	[But] I am the most *handsome* person here.

Compere: '*Handsome*'? Did you learn that word in Arabia? Or maybe you've been somewhere even further away?

Tanjung Pinang:

Tinggi sungguh pokok kelapa,	The coconut palm is really tall,
Air dibuat sambilan es.	Water was made to become ice.
Adik yang kiri itu cantik jelita,	You on the left are pretty and charming,
Minta nomor HP, Abang SMS.	Give me your mobile number and I'll send you a text message.

This flirtatious banter and Batam's jokes about Tanjung Pinang not having any crash helmets — a play on Tanjung Pinang's reputation as backward and parochial in contrast to the modern and industrial-ised Batam — drew far more attention and sustained applause than the eventual "buying" *pantun*. Another popular type of prevaricatory *pantun* is that used to taunt the opposing team, usually through a reference to their body shape or skin colour, whilst toilet humour was popular in *pantun* of any kind.

Sometimes, however, a humorous approach could prove divisive.

Tanjung Pinang A Selling to Karimun:

Jikalau gulai sedap dimakan,	When the curry is good to eat,
Burung murai hingga di batu.	The magpie-robin will be at the rock.
Kalau 'capcai', nama masakan,	'Capcai' is the name of a food,
Kalau 'Po Chai' — apa benda itu?	As for 'Po Chai' — what is that?

This puzzle garnered over a minute of uninterrupted laughter from the spectators. Po Chai pills are a Chinese remedy for diarrhoea and associated digestive complaints. The spectators' laughter derived from toilet humour coupled with gleeful anticipation of how the Karimun speakers might struggle to explain this in *pantun* form. The eventual answer was an anticlimax as the Karimun team incorrectly guessed that "Po Chai" was a kind of griping pain.

For some, however, the Karimun team should never have been put in such a position. Adi, a Malay who had moved to the Riau Islands from North Sumatra in the 1980s, was particularly angry that the clowning Tanjung Pinang A team were declared victors, claiming it represented a degradation of all that *pantun* should be. For him, a *pantun* should always be very refined (*halus*). He linked this to his own experience of using and receiving *pantun* when courting his wife, a courtship technique which was once widespread across the Malay-speaking world (Karim 1990: 29–32) but which is increasingly rare in the Riau Islands. He strongly disapproved of the predilection for funny quatrains, professing that he would only ever adjudicate them on three specific points: the quality of the Malay language used, whether the *pantun* used "healthy words" (*kata-kata sehat*) to express "suitable values", and the effective use of metaphor. By Adi's reasoning, Tanjung Pinang's flamboyance, self-indulgent jokes and impudent questions should have received heavy penalties; he felt their *pantun* were too coarse and unrefined (*kasar*), and dismissed them as "joke *pantun* (*pantun gurau*) of the kind popular with little children". The eventual victory, he speculated, was probably due to local chauvinism and politics.

Nurul disagreed. She appreciated the Tanjung Pinang team's sense of humour. If people found the contest entertaining and memorable, she commented, they would return to watch it again, and the format would flourish. For her, preserving "'Malay culture" meant rebranding it to suit the appetites of the masses, even if this necessitated humour that some might find coarse. On this point, Nurul appears to have spoken for the bulk of the audience. After the formal competition had ended, a "special *pantun* exhibition" was put on to entertain the crowd. This featured a selection of competitors from the main event, who exchanged ribald and humorous *pantun*, much to the crowd's delight. The weak link emerged when the speakers from Karimun offered their *pantun*. These were not humorous, but plaintive exhortations to preserve the *pantun* as a means of safeguarding Malay culture. In contrast to their respectfully appreciative reception when they had been competing formally, the Karimun speakers now found themselves booed. A middle-aged lady standing behind me cat-called mockingly into the darkness. "Look at that old man! Does he want to sell a funny *pantun*?! He doesn't know how!" Her friends all burst into giggles. The Karimun speaker finished his *pantun* and, with a dark look on his face, stood aside, giving way to a speaker from Lingga, who entertained the crowd with jokes about how his team-mate was "as dark as a Keling".

The popularity of bawdy humour sits awkwardly alongside the piety, indirectness and restraint with which many of the teams sought to boost their scores and chances of winning. In practice, the characteristically "Malay" restraint with which the *pantun* was associated was only activated in relation to topics marked as particularly culturally sensitive, such as religion and female sexuality. Jokes on other themes usually passed without censure. By appealing to broadly shared humour, "Malayness" as embodied in the *pantun* could become relevant and popular. Thus, while audience members such as Adi sat and watched their long-cherished and deeply meaningful *adat* be reduced to a spectacle of "art", others such as Nurul and her non-Malay friends sat and laughed, deciding amongst themselves that traditional Malay culture was worth preserving after all.

However, one form of humour stood out for its popularity: self-referential jokes about Malayness and identity. Just as audiences are satisfied by teams strategically exploiting the incompatibilities of multiple formulations of "Malayness", the ironies and paradoxes of enacting "Malay culture" in such a multiethnic context as the Riau Islands offers poets a particularly rich vein of comic potential. A deft illustration came in a pair of introductory *pantun* offered by a rather short poet of Javanese and Florinese descent, but who lived in Tanjung Pinang:

Ramai sungguh si anak monyet,	The baby monkeys are truly thronging,
Sekalian mekik suara bertempa.	When they all scream, their voices roar.
Saya bergelar Hang Penyet,	My title is 'Hang Penyet,'
Bisa disingkat dengan HP.	It can be shortened to 'HP'.

"HP" is the Indonesian abbreviation for a mobile phone, a specimen of which was then whisked out of the poet's costume amid much laughter and applause. The name has other connotations, however. "Hang" is the prefix given to heroes in Malay epics, whilst Penyet means "flattened" and is typically associated with a popular form of Javanese fried chicken. The poet had thus adopted a playful "Malay" name which was clearly an assumed persona. Any such suspicion was confirmed when "HP" followed his introductory *pantun* with a second poem. The first couplet of this was in Javanese, and the second in Indonesian, delivered with the hard "*a*"s and trilled "*r*"s of a Javanese speaker, a far cry from the Malay accent he had just affected. In the second couplet, "HP" revealed that this was only his "nickname" and that his real name was Raden Johan, Raden being the title of a Javanese aristocrat.

To the extent that a false Malay persona was created and introduced, Johan took seriously the obligation to self-present as a Malay. Yet in the playfulness of the "Hang Penyet" persona, and by revealing his "true" Javanese identity in his second poem, he also reveals the ambiguities of "being Malay" in a province where "Malayness" is at once a distinct ethnocultural identity and a constructed category of provincial membership. The audience laugh, being in on the joke because they themselves negotiate these ambiguities on a daily basis. *Pantun* performance offers a means by which audiences can laugh at and even embrace the absurdity of Malayness through a quintessential medium of Malayness. In this sense, the *pantun* really does have the capacity to serve as both a symbol and a technology of provincial unification.

Coda: Nationalising the *Pantun*?

Joining poets and judges for coffee and snacks after their evening's performances had finished always gave rise to lively conversation. On the final night, a judge named Ismail told me that he considered humour to be something that made the *pantun* a distinctly Indonesian brand of "Malay culture":

> In Malaysia, the *pantun* are more decorative, more metaphorical. That's a normal thing in Malaysian life, though. If someone asks them 'Where are you going?' they won't reply, 'I'm going to the market'. Instead they'll say, 'I want to buy something' or something similar — using allusory language (*bahasa kias*). But they mean 'to the market'! So the big difference with our *pantun* is that Indonesian *pantun* are often very funny (*lucu*). Which is great! But in Malaysia and Singapore, no. Always extremely serious.

Ismail's reflection sparked the enthusiastic suggestion that the group should try to popularise the *pantun* across Indonesia by auditioning selected contestants on a televised talent show. Ilham, a poet from Pekanbaru but now living in Jakarta, had concerns. He relayed the case of a *pantun* he had seen performed using Indonesian in a poetry club in Jakarta. The poem had ended with the line "*harus mencuci kucing dulu*" (you must wash the cat beforehand), but Ilham explained the "cat" was actually a reference to a woman's vagina. There were shocked gasps. Ilham nodded and said that he had been very upset to hear such a phrase in a *pantun*. The problem, he explained, was that Indonesian was too permissive in its scope for such concepts to be uttered. Malay (*bahasa Melayu*), by contrast, was suffused with *adat* notions of respect and restraint, especially towards women, avoiding the problem altogether.

Significantly, however, it was not just this stereotype of the "reserved Malay" that underpinned poets' ambivalence towards the use of Indonesian. A female poet, Arifah, argued that nationalising the *pantun* was doomed to failure because "*pantun* are not funny anymore if they are offered in Indonesian". The group deflated and nodded their heads. "The nature of the Malay dialect and accent make a *pantun* much funnier," Ilham elaborated. "If we used Indonesian that would all be lost." The poet who had first vaunted the idea of a talent contest speculated that it might be possible to use a translator such that *pantun* were performed in both Malay and Indonesian. Although it seemed like a promising idea, it received a lukewarm reception. As Arifah put it, "the humour would not translate".

These remarks point to a curious puzzle. Indonesian is based on, and linguistically very similar to, Malay. Moreover, *pantun* find a receptive audience within the Riau Islands, including amongst people who are not Malay and cannot speak the Malay language. So why should they "fail to translate" to a broader national audience? The answer might lie not in the concept of language but that of regionality. Many aspects of what made *pantun* enjoyable could be transposed to a national context: the display of an opulent vision of sultanic Malayness, the spontaneity of the performance, and the sheer entertainment presented by the clowning and wordplay of the Riau Islands' strongest performers. What would not translate so easily was the way *pantun* contests could subvert the prescriptive and codifying, but often conflicting, notions of "regional culture" that were circulating in the Riau Islands and thereby allow a more dynamic and self-conscious exploration of being Malay in Indonesia. Contest performances could celebrate and affirm the importance of Malayness, while at the same time highlighting and satirising the contradictions, difficulties and absurdities that arise from the commitment to make the multiethnic Riau Islands a "Malay province". Whether through parody or strategic manoeuvring, they highlight the way that audiences engage with and are shackled by conflicting formulations of Malayness, and this makes them very funny to watch.

Yet these moments of humour may also represent something more significant. As Riau Islanders continued to wrangle with the question of what it meant to live in a Malay province, the performances at the *pantun* contest afforded them an opportunity to acknowledge that there was widespread confusion over the scope, limits and character of "Malayness", and to see that the predicaments inherent to being Malay were shared by others in the audience. Such moments temporarily unsettle spectators' attachments to particular formulations of "Malayness", counterbalancing them with a more detached and reflexive perspective in which they recognise its multiplicity, and see it not as an "ethnicity", nor as a code of behaviour, let alone a statement of allegiance to a sultan, but as a paradox, an absurdity, a challenge. Of course, within Southeast Asian Studies, it was a similar conceptual slipperiness that ultimately led scholars to stress the virtues of a genealogical approach to the history of the Malayness concept (Chapter 1); it thus seems duly fitting that the most recent stage in the genealogy that I have traced within this book should be one where Riau Islanders themselves are beginning to recognise the concept's indeterminacy.

What consequences does that have in practice? On the one hand, the growing suspicion that perhaps "Malayness" is not really a thing at all, but just a set of malleable claims, might mean that Riau Islanders' participation within cultural activities and engagements with provincial injunctions to "be Malay" are increasingly to be conducted in bad faith, and pervaded by affective dynamics of the sort discussed in the previous chapter. On the other hand, as the *pantun* contest itself demonstrates, the common experience of engaging with the predicament of "Malayness" offers citizens a new potential basis for shared identifications. Whether this more self-reflexive formulation will go on to have significant implications for social and political life in the islands or simply give way to yet another form of recombinant Malayness, however, still remains to be seen.

Conclusion

In January 2012, as I was finalising the manuscript of this book, I received a phone call from Tirto, a high-ranking civil servant in Jakarta. He wanted my advice on how to conduct a good research interview. Tirto explained that he was about to participate in an official audit of Indonesia's regional autonomy, a project that would evaluate whether or not decentralisation had been a success, attempt to detect instances of best practice that could be held up as exemplary, and make recommendations as to how to adjust laws and policies so that Indonesia could become as well-governed and as democratic as possible. Several issues were causing him particular concern: high levels of corruption in local government; the prevalent practice of buying votes; the rise of regional leaders who ran their regencies and towns as "little fiefdoms" (*kerajaan kecil*); disappointing levels of investment and human resource development in newly autonomous regencies; and the apparent hardening of regionalist, ethnic and fundamentalist religious sentiments that stood sharply at odds with the national ethic of "unity in diversity".

These were familiar concerns. Questions of the kind Tirto was asking have saturated public discourse since the end of the New Order and have strongly influenced the ways Indonesia's decentralisation and democratisation have been assessed by figures ranging from Jakartan bureaucrats and Indonesian media pundits to Riau Islanders sitting in coffee shops and international academics gathering at conferences. They provoke a series of intriguing reflections. How widespread are these unintended effects of regional autonomy? Why do they seem to occur in some areas more than others? Are they necessarily as undesirable as many accounts would make them seem? Would their presence mean that regional autonomy has "failed"? Such questions are understandably compelling to people who care about Indonesia. Yet, even as I gave Tirto what advice I could on research methodology, I was struck by how much this all-too-familiar list of questions seemed to neglect.

Although issues such as corruption, "money politics", or foreign direct investment have obvious ramifications for people's day-to-day existence, Tirto's research agenda did little to acknowledge the many other impacts that decentralisation has had upon the ways in which Indonesians understand themselves, relate to others and inhabit the world around them. Decentralisation has not just influenced the material and political conditions in which people live; it has also transformed the character of their everyday lives, prompting them to ask new questions about who they are and their place within the nation, province, town and neighbourhood. Tirto's own questioning of decentralisation's consequences is itself evidence of this trend: a form of critical public citizenship quite distinct from civic identity under the New Order. In his case, the new questions were mainly procedural, inviting reflection upon regional autonomy as a political process. Such questioning is by no means absent from the Riau Archipelago. However, the very tangible consequence of regional autonomy in the Riau Islands, namely the creation of a new province, made different questions stand out as especially urgent. These were concerned less with "regional autonomy" in the abstract and more with the specificities of the new Riau Islands Province and what it would mean to be living within its borders.

Some questions were entirely novel. Issues such as whether local government officials were capable of running a province, or how the Riau Islands would rank alongside other provinces in national indices of development, were pressing concerns which had not previously needed to be thought about. Other questions were more familiar but took on a new relevance in the context of the nascent province. The matter of how the Riau Archipelago's population could be made more competitive, for example, had always been of concern to inhabitants of the islands. However, since the region's "backwardness" was blamed on underinvestment and neglect at the hands of a "colonial" Pekanbaru administration, breaking the islands away from Mainland Riau had always been a necessary first step towards resolving this problem. Once autonomy had been achieved, the question of how to increase competitiveness re-emerged as a central issue in public discourse. Likewise, while the definition of Malayness had long been a question of academic interest in the islands, it took on an immense political significance once a province had been created "for Malays". Riau Islanders were forced to think hard about whether they were Malay, whether those around them were Malay, what that meant, and what rights being Malay — or non-Malay — could or should entitle them to within the new province.

Such questions have not been simple to answer, not least because an answer that seems to be clear and straightforward one day can prove unsatisfactory the next. Nevertheless, as Riau Islanders have continued to grapple with the questions that decentralisation has presented them with, they have found new frameworks for understanding both themselves and those around them, changed their ways of interacting with relatives, neighbours, colleagues and government, and experienced life in ways that were affectively and emotionally distinct from the experiences they had before. Investigating such transformations does not only enrich our understanding of the changes underway in post-Suharto Indonesia. Putting ethnographic materials from the Riau Islands in dialogue with existing theories of how and why people come to feel "at home" in the world or adopt dispositions of "bad faith" opens up new perspectives on the relations between the affective and the political, suggesting fruitful avenues for the study of decentralisation elsewhere.

Questions of Malayness

From the moment that the activists campaigning for a new province claimed that they were doing so in the name of the Riau Archipelago's "indigenous" Malays and that their movement would give rise to a "Malay province", it was inevitable that Riau Islanders would start to reflect in new ways on the criteria that defined a person, place, or object as "Malay", and what the implications of possessing such "Malayness" might be. As the previous chapters have shown, such reflections can have many consequences, prompting fears amongst non-Malay Muslims that the moral order of their neighbourhoods and towns are being threatened by their "backward" Malay counterparts, causing successful Malay entrepreneurs to feel either relieved or outraged that their achievements go unrecognised, leading Christian minorities to feel that they are unwelcome and surrounded by fanatics, and creating new forms of humour and popular culture that can be shared by Riau Islanders of all backgrounds. In each of these instances, the actors involved have reached their own distinct understandings of "Malayness", reflecting the fact that, despite the public preoccupation with being "Malay", there remains no widely accepted understanding of what that term denotes.

When I chat to Riau Islanders about my research, they often ask me to share "my" definition of Malayness. Sometimes they do so with an earnestness that suggests they are hoping I might be able to offer them a definitive answer to a puzzle that they have been contemplating for some time. In other cases, the request is accompanied by a mischievous smile, suggesting that my interlocutor is gearing up for an intellectual debate. Indeed, were I to offer a definition of Malayness, such a debate would be very easy to stage for there would be no shortage of alternative definitions that could be put forward as superior. Instead, however, I tell them that my interest as a social scientist lies in studying the origins and consequences of people's attempts to advance particular formulations of "Malayness" given that there is not and never has been an agreed definition of the term.

While a few of my interlocutors have responded by explaining what they think Malayness *really* is, many have agreed with my analysis. "It's true, these days the question of what Malayness means is all about politics and self-interest," commented a small-time construction entrepreneur that I met in a Tanjung Pinang coffee shop, while Nazir, a retired university academic, nodded vigorously at my remarks before shouting triumphantly to his friends, "You see! I *told* you there was no such thing as a Malay!"

That, of course, was not quite the argument I was making. While there may be no fixed essence of "Malayness", that does not mean that there is "no such thing as a Malay". Rather there are multiple Malaynesses, each of them emerging through a process of recombination in which fragments of knowledge are pieced together in a way that seems appropriate to contemporary concerns. The recombination of Malayness has been taking place for centuries, as histories of Southeast Asia make clear, but in the context of the new Riau Islands Province it was notable for both its ubiquity and its powerful affective consequences as diverse formulations of Malayness interacted with and unsettled each other.

It was common for Riau Islanders to find that their own understanding of Malayness was not shared by those with whom they interacted. Such discoveries destabilised their sense of being "at home" within their province, their neighbourhoods and even their own selves, infusing everyday life with affects of the "un-homely". In some cases, this situation precipitated new forms of social and political activism (Chapters 3 and 5); in others it led to depression and disengagement, spurring Riau Islanders such as Welly (Chapter 8) to leave the province entirely. Yet the affects engendered by the unsettling of Malayness could also prompt Riau Islanders to reinterrogate and reformulate what Malayness meant to them, as evident in Ali's reconceptualisation of Malays as "evil-hearted" (Chapter 4) or the *pantun* contest (Chapter 8), in which Malayness ceased to be a fixed identity and instead became a predicament that townsfolk could gather to laugh at, pointing to new possibilities for the years ahead.

The case of Malayness in the Riau Islands therefore offers an intriguing challenge to the way that ethnic politics in post-Suharto Indonesia has often been portrayed by scholars. The indeterminacy and fluidity of Malayness subverts such analytic categories as "ethnic chauvinism" (Baidhawy 2007; Davidson 2005: 183; Zurbuchen 2005: 4) or "ethnic loyalties" dating back to the days of Dutch colonialism (Schulte Nordholt 2003: 579), both of which have often been used to make sense of Indonesian decentralisation, but reify ethnic identifications in ways that are quite inappropriate for the Riau Islands. But is Malayness in the Riau Islands just a special case, or are there lessons for the analysis of decentralisation and regional autonomy elsewhere?

The ways in which ideas about Malayness are cast in creative new combinations undoubtedly reflect the unique history of the Riau Archipelago as a cockpit of the Malay World. Home to a precolonial "Malay polity" which was nevertheless multiethnic and diarchic, the archipelago later came to straddle two imperial systems and three postcolonial states, each of which propagated its own formulations of "Malayness". Thus nowadays scores of ideas about Malayness circulate in the Riau Islands, making it all the more difficult to reach any coherent definition. Yet this does not mean that other categories of identity should be presumed to be any more stable or coherent. Indeed, as Brubaker and Cooper (2000: 31) note in a review of recent interdisciplinary research into "identity", "if the real contribution of constructivist social analysis — that affinities, categories and subjectivities develop and change over time — is to be taken seriously, and not reduced to a presentist, teleological account of the construction of currently existing 'groups', then bounded groupness must be understood as a contingent, emergent property, not an axiomatic given."

In cases of decentralisation or regionalism, it is especially likely that movements campaigning for autonomy will try to obtain the greatest number of backers and thereby strengthen their mandate by deploying categories that are wide-reaching, ambiguous and that gloss over tensions or contradictions that might emerge upon closer inspection. However, whilst such categories may be help to galvanise support during the campaign for a new province, state or republic, the case of the Riau Islands reveals how, upon achieving such a goal, those very same terms and ideas can stand out as problematic, becoming subject to intense public scrutiny and laden with affective charge. The question of how diverse formulations of ethnicity and region interact with each other, and to what effect, thus stand to be of significance in many, if not all, cases of separatism and local autonomy.

A Politics of Bad Faith and an Anthropology of Affect

The government of the Riau Islands is by no means exceptional in having set up a series of campaigns and programmes in order to rectify the problems it has identified within its population. These range from campaigns encouraging people to wear crash helmets, drive safely and pay their taxes to efforts to increase citizens' levels of achievement motivation or inculcate a deep love of Malay culture amongst them. These are all enterprises of what Foucault (1991: 100) termed "governmentality", in which a government seeks to address problems of population "either directly through large-scale campaigns, or indirectly ... without the full awareness of the people". This idea has been influential amongst social scientists because it reveals how seemingly spontaneous acts on the part of citizens (such as recycling or voting) in fact represent the ways in which a government has been "educating desires and configuring habits, aspirations and beliefs" such that "people, following only their own self-interest, *will do as they ought*" (Li 2007: 275; Scott 1999: 38).

Governmental campaigns in the Riau Islands have had mixed results. Most Riau Islanders now do wear crash helmets (at least when they think the police might be looking) and believe themselves to drive safely. Taxes are usually paid, albeit grudgingly. In these regards, the Foucauldian model applies very well to life in the new province. Yet, as I explored in Chapter 7, a puzzle emerges in the case of competitions designed to heighten citizens' achievement motivation. Riau Islanders will readily set about the task of shaping themselves into young achievers, just as theories of governmentality would predict, only for their faith in that achieving identity to fluctuate dramatically. Equally, Welly, the Chinese beauty contest participant that I discussed in Chapter 8, entered the contest simultaneously believing that she might be able to win it because the provincial definition of Malayness was integrationist and open to everyone, but also that she would not win it because she was Chinese. In such cases, civic participation is in bad faith. Perceptions of the local government and the region undermine the attempts at self-transformation that these Riau Islanders are making. In the former case, it is doubt regarding the region's human resource base that creates the situation of bad faith to arise; in the latter it is the perception of anti-Chinese feelings at the heart of the provincial government, a sentiment no doubt strengthened by the long history of persecution faced by Indonesia's Chinese minorities. Awareness of this bad faith is important because it illuminates the volatility of such civic engagement as well as its affective consequences. While bad faith itself is not an affect, it is by its very nature unstable, and when it evanesces towards good faith or cynicism, affective states of both joy and anguish can be the result.

An understanding of projects administered by techniques of "governmentality" can thus be greatly enriched by paying more attention to the psychological components of self-transformation as citizens engage with policies and the opportunities they make available in complex and fractious ways. Contrary to what dominant models of governmentality might assume, citizens may be only too aware that the tactics and campaigns exhorting them to behave "as they ought" are forms of political action, and that the categories of "self-interest" that motivate them reflect the agendas of those in power. Such political action can be engaged with and evaluated by the citizens both on ideological grounds and in terms of its perceived quality. Under such conditions, governmentality may still give rise to forms of discursive subjectification and self-formation that concord with the dominant discourse, but this has distinctive psychological dynamics that stem from the subject's consciousness that is constituting itself in a mode of being what it is not. Such circumstances are not unique to the Riau Islands, nor to polities that have recently been created. However, the forms of questioning that were evident in the Riau Islands — in which not only the policies but also the capacities of the government were interrogated — seem especially likely in contexts that are newly recovering from marginalisation, underinvestment or "colonial" rule. Attention to dispositions of bad faith thus stands to prove illuminating for the study of citizenship in newly-decentralised contexts elsewhere.

Finally, my engagement with the Sartrean model of "bad faith" exemplifies what I believe will be the most productive way of incorporating an attention to affect into the discipline of anthropology. As this book has repeatedly shown, it is the affectivity of particular situations, places and events that have rendered them turning points for the social and political lives of Riau Islanders. The enduring horror of what they had experienced during the Japanese Occupation led Maznah and Tahir to disparage Penyengat aristocrats as "Bugis"; when the funding was cut for Teddy's debating team, his deep disappointment led him to consider moving elsewhere; the light-heartedness and fun of the *pantun* contest made watching the performances a joy for Nurul but sickening for Adi; the terrifying thought of what neighbourhood indiscretions would be left unpunished by Malays caused non-Malays such as Jamil to intensify their own surveillance of their *kampung* and staunchly oppose groups such as Malays United. In such ways, affective experience is one of the prime motors of the social and political life in the Riau Islands.

Yet the question of how affect should be theorised remains a point of dispute within the social sciences. Some, such as Kathleen Stewart (2007: 4), caution against the quest for "bottom-line arguments" that would reductively explain all aspects of ordinary life with reference to such categories as "late capitalism" or "neoliberalism".[1] These deterministic approaches, Stewart rightly observes, forget that

---

[1] Examples include Jameson's (1991: 27) assertion that late capitalism has engendered a "peculiar kind of euphoria", or Ong's (2006) analysis of the Riau Islands, in which she suggests that "neoliberal", market-driven policy decisions in the region have led to "mutations in citizenship" and "the redesigning of national sovereignty".

seemingly insignificant details can prove highly consequential, and that some things happen for reasons that seem, and perhaps are, inexplicable. On the other hand, it seems problematic to suggest that affects are entirely autonomous as claimed by authors such as Brian Massumi (1995). As Clare Hemmings (2005) has cogently argued, some affects — such as the states of fear, disgust and hatred that a white racist might experience upon seeing a black body — cannot be explained without reference to the broader systems of power and meaning within which the encounter takes place.

Affective experience in the Riau Islands cannot be said to have been *determined* by political or economic factors: there are too many unexpected moments where immediate circumstances play a more salient role than the broad condition of having decentralised. We might think, for instance, of the vacillations in the debating team's faith in their own capacities to achieve. And yet there are elements of the political, economic and social arena that all stack the odds in favour of particular affective consequences: the proximity of aspira-tional Singapore, the influx of migrants that the Riau Islands' loca-tion draws, the ideological environment that leads to historical and contemporary processes being misrecognised or misunderstood, and the public prominence given to multiple competing formulations of Malayness and "Riau Islands culture".

The theoretical concepts of "bad faith" and "the uncanny", with all its multiple species, offer a helpful way around the danger of theorising "affect" in a way that is either excessively or insufficiently deterministic. Both concepts take a serious interest in the affective domain. Bad faith highlights how feeling "normal" or "comfortable" within one's actions is in fact highly precarious, and always able to give way to bliss or anguish. Moreover, as Sartre identified in his novel *Nausea* (1963 [1938]), the triggers for such vacillations are frequently located amongst the minutiae of ordinary, everyday life. The uncanny interrogates how people might feel when realities they have striven to suppress resurface and disturb their established ways of being. Both, then, theorise the *dispositions* with which human beings go about their normal lives. These dispositions reflect the predicaments they face — predicaments moulded by factors such as policies, economics and the discourses in circulation within a specific locale. Yet both concepts are based on understanding of affective states as in a constant process of flux: they direct our attention to the range of affects that might be felt rather than predicting the exact course of affective fluctuation. How matters then play out in practice is not a question of social theory, but an enquiry that warrants detailed ethnographic observation. Ultimately, then, they remind us that it is only through a concrete engagement with the complexities of human lives that we can develop a more nuanced understanding of the thought processes, experiences, and agency that animate the Riau Islands, the pursuit and evaluation of regional autonomy, and the ongoing challenges of being a Malay person, and a Malay province, in contemporary Indonesia.

Glossary

adat	traditions; customs; customary law
alam gaib	the "mysterious realm", a largely invisible dimension of reality that overlays the normal reality humans experience on a daily basis
angker	spooky; eerie; uncanny
arisan	a regular social gathering in which in which friends, co-workers, or neighbours gather together and draw lots to win a pot of money to which they have all contributed a small amount. Sometimes described as a "rotating credit association"
bujang dara	a type of beauty contest for young, unmarried men (*bujang*) and women (*dara*)
cerita	story
Confrontation	a state of political and military conflict which ran from 1962–66 as a result of Indonesia's opposition to the creation of Malaysia
dukun	a practitioner who specialises in resolving "mysterious happenings". The word *dukun* often has a stronger association with tradition and rurality than its synonym *paranormal*
Fisabilillah	posthumous title conferring the status of martyr

gaib	mysterious; mystical
Gurindam Duabelas	a work by Raja Ali Haji comprising 12 poems, each of which is a sequence of rhyming couplets
ikatan	association whose membership is restricted, usually on the basis of ethnicity and/or region of origin
ilmu hitam	dark arts
jin	a *makhluk gaib* made of fire and believed to be an Islamic subject
kafir	non-believer (of Islam); heretic
kampung	neighbourhood (can also refer to a village in rural settings)
kegaiban	mysterious happening
Keling	person of South Asian descent
LKS (Lomba Kompetensi Siswa)	Students' Competency Competition, an annual tournament for vocational high school students
makhluk gaib	mysterious creature
marwah	dignity; pride
Melayu Square	an outdoor foodcourt located on Tanjung Pinang's seaboard
n Achievement	the "need for achievement", a psychological drive believed to have a significant bearing on personality and behaviour
orang laut	sea people; sea nomads; sea gypsies — a category of Riau Islander distinguished from others by a nomadic maritime lifestyle and, until recently, animistic belief systems. Some consider *orang laut* to be the "indigenous" people of the Riau Archipelago

Pancasila	Five Principles (of the nation)
Panglima	Commander; Chief
pantun	Malay quatrain with an *abab* rhyme scheme
paranormal	a practitioner who specialises in resolving "mysterious happenings". The word *paranormal* often has a stronger association with modernity and urbanism than its synonym *dukun*
pasar	market; marketplace
pasisir	the highly incorporative cultural logic that characterised the Southeast Asian maritime world prior to colonialism
pemekaran	the proliferation of administrative units during Indonesia's Reform Era
pencak silat	an Indonesian martial art
prestasi	achievement
putra daerah	"son of the region", a locally-born citizen. *Putra daerah* may, but need not, have associations with being from a locally "indigenous" ethnic group
raja	viceroy of the sultanate; also a title given to a viceroy's descendants down the male line
Reformasi	an era in Indonesia's political history stemming from the resignation of President Suharto in May 1998 to the present
Riau Merdeka	"Free Riau" — a Pekanbaru-based political movement demanding the creation of a Federal Republic of Riau. Launched in the late 1990s, it remains active in 2013

RT (*rukun tetangga*)	civil-administrative neighbourhood unit of approximately 40 households
rukun	harmony
shariah	Islamic law
tanah	land
tanah Melayu	Malay land
waria	an individual with a male body but a female soul, who therefore dresses and behaves in a "feminine" way. It is much debated as to whether *waria* represent a type of male, a type of female, or a distinct gender category
zina	illicit sexual practice

Bibliography

Acciaioli, G. (1985) "Culture as Art: From Practice to Spectacle in Indonesia". *Canberra Anthropology* 8(1/2): 124–72.

Alatas, S.H. (1977) *The Myth of the Lazy Native: A Study of the Image of the Malays, Filipinos and Javanese from the 16th to the 20th Century and Its Function in the Ideology of Colonial Capitalism.* London: Frank Cass.

———— (1996) *The New Malay: His Role and Future.* Singapore: Association of Muslim Professionals.

Alexander, J. (1998) "Women Traders in Javanese Marketplaces: Ethnicity, Gender and the Entrepreneurial Spirit". In *Market Cultures: Society and Morality in the New Asian Capitalisms*, ed. R.W. Hefner. Boulder: Westview Press.

Ali Haji (1982 [1885]) *The Precious Gift (Tuhfat Al-Nafis): An Annotated Translation.* Kuala Lumpur: Oxford University Press.

———— (2002 [1847]) *Gurindam Duabelas.* Tanjung Pinang: Dinas Pariwisata Kepulauan Riau & Yayasan Khazanah Melayu.

Andaya, B.W. (1977) "From Rūm to Tokyo: The Search for Anticolonial Allies by the Rulers of Riau, 1899–1914". *Indonesia* 24: 123–56.

———— (1997) "Recreating a Vision: *Daratan* and *Kepulauan* in Historical Context". *Bijdragen tot de taal-, land-, en volkenkunde* 153(4): 483–508.

Andaya, B.W. and L. Andaya (1982) *A History of Malaysia.* Basingstoke: Macmillan Press.

———— (2001) *A History of Malaysia. Second Edition.* Honolulu: University of Hawai'i Press.

Andaya, L.Y. (2008) *Leaves of the Same Tree: Trade and Ethnicity in the Straits of Malacca.* Honolulu: University of Hawai'i Press.

Anon. (1957) "Riau Sebagai Daerah Otonom Tingkat I". In private document collection of Aswandi Syahrial.

———— (1958) *Puisi Melayu: Sha'ir, Pantun, Seloka Dan Lain-Lain.* London: Longman, Green & Co.

Apriadi Gunawan (2010) "Autonomy Watch: Most New Regions Perform Poorly". *The Jakarta Post*, 10 May 2010.

Arora, B.D. (1982) "Indians in Indonesia". In *Indians in Southeast Asia*, ed. I.J.B. Singh. New Delhi: Sterling.

Aspinall, E. and G. Fealy (2003) "Introduction". In *Local Power and Politics in Indonesia: Decentralisation and Democratisation*, ed. E. Aspinall and G. Fealy. Singapore: Institute of Southeast Asian Studies.

Bachtiar, H.W. (1993) "Indians in Indonesia: A Component of Indonesian National Integration". In *Indian Communities in Southeast Asia*, ed. K.S. Sandhu and A. Mani. Singapore: Institute of Southeast Asian Studies & Times Academic Press.

Baidhawy, Z. (2007) "Building Harmony and Peace through Multiculturalist Theology-Based Religious Education: An Alternative for Contemporary Indonesia". *British Journal of Religious Education* 29(1): 15–30.

Bakan, M.B. (1999) *Music of Death and New Creation: Experiences in the World of Balinese Gamelan Beleganjur*. Chicago and London: University of Chicago Press.

Banks, D. (1983) *Malay Kinship*. Philadelphia: Institute for the Study of Human Resources.

Bardhan, P. (2002) "Decentralization of Governance and Development". *The Journal of Economic Perspectives* 16(4): 185–205.

Barnard, T.P. (2001) "Texts, Raja Ismail and Violence: Siak and the Transformation of Malay Identity in the Eighteenth Century". *Journal of Southeast Asian Studies* 32(3): 331–42.

———— (2003) *Multiple Centres of Authority: Society and Environment in Siak and Eastern Sumatra, 1674–1827*. Leiden: KITLV Press.

Barnard, T.P. and H.M.J. Maier (2004) "Melayu, Malay, Maleis: Journeys through the Identity of a Collection". In *Contesting Malayness: Malay Identity across Boundaries*, ed. T.P. Barnard. Singapore: Singapore University Press.

Bassett, D.K. (1989) "British 'Country' Trade and Local Trade Networks in the Thai and Malay States, c.1680–1770". *Modern Asian Studies* 23(4): 625–43.

Batam Pos (2007) "Frankim Belum Minta Maaf". Available at http://www.batampos.co.id/content/view/12208/93/ [accessed 5 August 2008].

Beatty, A. (1999) *Varieties of Javanese Religion: An Anthropological Account*. Cambridge: Cambridge University Press.

———— (2005) "Feeling Your Way in Java: An Essay on Society and Emotion". *Ethnos* 70(1): 53–78.

Belaunde, L.E. (2000) "The Convivial Self and the Fear of Anger Amongst the Airo-Pai of Amazonian Peru". In *The Anthropology of Love and Anger: The Aesthetics of Conviviality in Native Amazonia*, ed. J. Overing and A. Passes. London & New York: Routledge.

Benjamin, G. (2002) "On Being Tribal in the Malay World". In *Tribal Communities in the Malay World: Historical, Cultural and Social Perspectives*, ed. G. Benjamin and C. Chou. Leiden & Singapore: International Institute for Asian Studies & Institute of Southeast Asian Studies.

Bergland, R.L. (2000) *The National Uncanny: Indian Ghosts and American Subjects*. Hanover, NH: University Press of New England.

Bhabha, H.K. (1984) "Of Mimicry and Man: The Ambivalence of Colonial Discourse". *October* 28(1): 125–33.

Blackwood, E. (2008) "Not Your Average Housewife: Minangkabau Women Rice Farmers in West Sumatra". In *Women and Work in Indonesia*, ed. L. Parker and M. Ford. Abingdon & New York: Routledge.

Boellstorff, T. (2002) "Ethnolocality". *The Asia Pacific Journal of Anthropology* 3(1): 24–48.

———— (2004) "Zines and Zones of Desire: Mass Mediated Love, National Romance, and Sexual Citizenship in Gay Indonesia". *Journal of Asian Studies* 63(4): 367–402.

Brenner, S. (1996) "Reconstructing Self and Society: Javanese Muslim Women and 'the Veil'". *American Ethnologist* 23(4): 673–97.

Brenner, S.A. (1998) *The Domestication of Desire: Women, Wealth, and Modernity in Java*. Princeton: Princeton University Press.

Brogan, K. (1998) *Cultural Haunting: Ghosts and Ethnicity in Recent American Literature*. Charlottesville: University Press of Virginia.

Brubaker, R. and F. Cooper (2000) "Beyond 'Identity'". *Theory and Society* 29(1): 1–47.

Bubandt, N. (2006) "Sorcery, Corruption, and the Dangers of Democracy in Indonesia". *Journal of the Royal Anthropological Institute* 12(2): 413–31.

Budiman, A. (1979) "Modernization, Development and Dependence: A Critique of the Present Model of Indonesian Development". In *What Is Modern Indonesian Culture? Proceedings of the Conference on Indonesian Studies, July 29th–August 1st 1976, Indonesian Studies Summer Institute, Madison, Wisconsin*, ed. G. Davis. Athens: Ohio University Centre for International Studies.

Bunnell, T. (2002) "*Kampung* Rules: Landscape and the Contested Government of Urban(e) Malayness". *Urban Studies* 39(9): 1685–701.

Bunnell, T., H. Muzaini and J.D. Sidaway (2006) "Global City Frontiers: Singapore's Hinterland and the Contested Socio-Political Geographies of Bintan, Indonesia". *International Journal of Urban and Regional Research* 30(1): 3–22.

Bünte, M. (2007) "Indonesia's Protracted Decentralization: Contested Reforms and Their Unintended Consequences". In *Democratization in Post-Suharto Indonesia*, ed. M. Bünte and A. Ufen. London & New York: Routledge.

Butler, J. (1997) *The Psychic Life of Power: Theories in Subjection*. Stanford: Stanford University Press.

Candra Ibrahim (2008) "Huzrin vs LAM, Tak Lucu!". Available at http://candraibrahim.com/huzrin-vs-lam-tak-lucu [accessed 7 July 2011].

Carsten, J. (1989) "Cooking Money: Gender and the Symbolic Transformation of Means of Exchange in a Malay Fishing Community". In *Money and the Morality of Exchange*, ed. J. Parry and M. Bloch. Cambridge: Cambridge University Press.

Cheah, B.K. (2002) *Malaysia: The Making of a Nation*. Singapore: Institute of Southeast Asian Studies.

———— (2006) "The Left-Wing Movement in Malaya, Singapore and Borneo in the 1960s: 'An Era of Hope or Devil's Decade'?". *Inter-Asia Cultural Studies* 7(4): 634–49.

Chou, C. (2003) *Indonesian Sea Nomads: Money, Magic and Fear of the Orang Suku Laut*. London & New York: RoutledgeCurzon.

Clear, A. (2005) "Politics: From Endurance to Evolution". In *Indonesia: The Great Transition*, ed. J. Bresnan. Lanham: Rowman and Littlefield.

Cohen, C.B. and R. Wilk (1996) "Introduction: Beauty Queens on the Global Stage". In *Beauty Queens on the Global Stage: Gender, Contests and Power*, ed. C.B. Cohen, R. Wilk and B. Stoeltje. New York & London: Routledge.

Cohen, P. (1999) *Strange Encounters: Adolescent Geographies of Risk and the Urban Uncanny*. Dagenham: Centre For New Ethnicities Research, University of East London.

Colombijn, F. (2003) "When There is Nothing to Imagine: Nationalism in Riau". In *Framing Indonesian Realities: Essays in Symbolic Anthropology in Honour of Reimar Schefold*, ed. P.J.M. Nas, G.A. Persoon and R. Jaffe. Leiden: KITLV Press.

Coppel, C.A. (1983) *Indonesian Chinese in Crisis*. Kuala Lumpur: Oxford University Press.

Daillie, F.-R. (1988) *Alam Pantun Melayu: Studies on the Malay Pantun*. Kuala Lumpur: Dewan Bahasa dan Pustaka, Ministry of Education.

Davidson, J.S. (2005) "Decentralization and Regional Violence in the Post-Suharto State". In *Regionalism in Post-Suharto Indonesia*, ed. M. Erb, P. Sulistiyanto and C. Faucher. London & New York: RoutledgeCurzon.

Davidson, J.S. and D. Henley, eds. (2007) *The Revival of Tradition in Indonesian Politics: The Deployment of Adat from Colonialism to Indigenism*. Abingdon & New York: Routledge.

Derks, W. (1997) "Malay Identity Work". *Bijdragen tot de taal-, land-, en volkenkunde* 153(4): 699–716.

Dëtik Kepri (2006) "Duduk Di Melayu Square, Ada Chas Pondok Way!" Week 3, February 2006: 4.

Dhoraisingam, S.S. (2006) *Peranakan Indians of Singapore and Melaka: Indian Babas and Nonyas — Chitty Melaka*. Singapore: Institute of Southeast Asian Studies.

Dick, H. (2002) "Formation of the Nation-State 1930s–1966". In *The Emergence of a National Economy: An Economic History of Indonesia,*

1800–2000, ed. H. Dick, V.J.H. Houben, J.T. Lindblad and K.W. Thee. Crows Nest & Honolulu: Allen & Unwin and University of Hawai'i Press.

———— (2004) "The Indonesian Economy in the 1950s: Multiple Exchange Rates, Business Networks and Centre-Region Relations". In *Indonesia in Transition: Rethinking 'Civil Society', 'Region' and 'Crisis'*, ed. H. Samuel and H. Schulte Nordholt. Yogyakarta: Pustaka Pelajar.

Djamour, J. (1959) *Malay Kinship and Marriage in Singapore*. London: The Athlone Press.

Douglas, M. (1970) "Introduction: Thirty Years after Witchcraft, Oracles, and Magic". In *Witchcraft Confessions and Accusations*, ed. M. Douglas. London & New York: Routledge.

Eco, U. (1986) *Travels in Hyper-Reality: Essays*. San Diego: Harcourt Brace Jovanovich.

Edensor, T. (2005) "The Ghosts of Industrial Ruins: Ordering and Dis-ordering Memory in Excessive Space". *Environment and Planning D: Society and Space* 23(6): 829–49.

Emmons, C.F. (1982) *Chinese Ghosts and ESP: A Study of Paranormal Beliefs and Experiences*. Metuchen & London: The Scarecrow Press.

Endicott, K.M. (1970) *An Analysis of Malay Magic*. Kuala Lumpur: Oxford University Press.

Erb, M., R. Beni and W. Anggal (2005) "Creating Cultural Identity in an Era of Regional Autonomy: Reinventing Manggarai?". In *Regionalism in Post-Suharto Indonesia*, ed. M. Erb, P. Sulistiyanto and C. Faucher. London & New York: RoutledgeCurzon.

Erb, M., P. Sulistiyanto and C. Faucher, eds. (2005) *Regionalism in Post-Suharto Indonesia*. London & New York: RoutledgeCurzon.

Evers, H.-D. and R. Korff (2000) *Southeast Asian Urbanism: The Meaning and Power of Social Space. Second Edition.* Hamburg: Lit Verlag.

Fakhrunnas, M.A.J. (2004) "Riouw Anno 2204". In *Pertemuan Dalam Pipa: Cerita Dari Riau*, ed. Abel Tasman, Gde Agung Lontar, Fakhrunnas M.A.J., Marhalim Zaini, Olyrinson, Murparsaulian and Hang Kafrawi. Jogjakarta: Logung Pustaka & Akar Indonesia.

Faucher, C. (2002) "Magical Discourse, Moral Boundaries, and the Mapping of Interrelations in the Riau Archipelago". *Asian Journal of Social Science* 30(1): 158–76.

———— (2004) "As the Wind Blows and Dew Came Down: Ghost Stories and Collective Memory in Singapore". In *Beyond Description: Singapore Space Historicity*, ed. R. Bishop, J. Phillips and W.-W. Yeo. London & New York: Routledge.

———— (2005) "Regional Autonomy, Malayness and Power Hierarchy in the Riau Archipelago". In *Regionalism in Post-Suharto Indonesia*, ed. M. Erb, P. Sulistiyanto and C. Faucher. London & New York: RoutledgeCurzon.

_____ (2006) "Popular Discourse on Identity Politics and Decentralisation in Tanjung Pinang Public Schools". *Asia Pacific Viewpoint* 47(2): 273–85.

_____ (2007) "Contesting Boundaries in the Riau Archipelago". In *Renegotiating Boundaries: Local Politics in Post-Suharto Indonesia*, ed. H. Schulte Nordholt and G. van Klinken. Leiden: KITLV Press.

Fauconnier, H. (1990 [1930]) *The Soul of Malaya*. Singapore: Oxford University Press.

Flavell, J.H. (1999) "Cognitive Development: Children's Knowledge About the Mind". *Annual Review of Psychology* 50: 21–45.

Florida, N.K. (1995) *Writing the Past, Inscribing the Future: History as Prophecy in Colonial Java*. Durham: Duke University Press.

Ford, M. (2003) "Who Are the *Orang Riau*? Negotiating Identity across Geographic and Ethnic Divides". In *Local Power and Politics in Indonesia: Decentralisation and Democratisation*, ed. E. Aspinall and G. Fealy. Singapore: Institute of Southeast Asian Studies.

Ford, M. and L. Lyons (2006) "The Borders Within: Mobility and Enclosure in the Riau Islands". *Asia Pacific Viewpoint* 47(2): 257–71.

_____ (2008) "Making the Best of What You've Got: Sex Work and Class Mobility in the Riau Islands". In *Women and Work in Indonesia*, ed. L. Parker and M. Ford. London & New York: Routledge.

Foucault, M. (1991) "Governmentality". In *The Foucault Effect: Studies in Governmentality*, ed. G. Burchell, C. Gordon and P. Miller. London: Harvester Wheatsheaf.

Frank, K. (2006) "Agency". *Anthropological Theory* 6(3): 281–302.

Fredrick, C. (1992) *The Legend of Lancang Kuning, Riau*. Jakarta: Directorate General of Tourism.

Freud, S. ([1919] 2003) *The Uncanny*. Harmondsworth: Penguin.

Gade, A.M. (2002) "Taste, Talent, and the Problem of Internalization: A Qur'anic Study in Religious Musicality from Southeast Asia". *History of Religions* 41(4): 328–68.

Galizia, M. (1989) "State and Ethnic Identity among the Rejang in Southwest Sumatera". *Prisma* 46: 57–69.

Gatot Winoto, Suarman and Nurhamidahwati (1995) *Pembinaan Disiplin di Lingkungan Masyarakat Kota Daerah Riau*. Tanjung Pinang: Proyek Pengkajian dan Pembinaan Nilai-Nilai Budaya Riau.

Geertz, C. (1960) *The Religion of Java*. Glencoe: Free Press.

_____ (1962) "The Rotating Credit Association: A 'Middle Rung' in Development". *Economic Development and Cultural Change* 10(3): 241–63.

_____ (1963) *Peddlers and Princes: Social Change and Economic Modernisation in Two Indonesian Towns*. Chicago & London: University of Chicago Press.

Gelder, K. and J.M. Jacobs (1998) *Uncanny Australia: Sacredness and Identity in a Postcolonial Nation*. Carlton: Melbourne University Press.

Geschiere, P. (1998) "Globalization and the Power of Indeterminate Meaning: Witchcraft and Spirit Cults in Africa and East Asia". *Development and Change* 29(4): 811–37.

Gil, D. (1993) "'Il Pleut Doucement sur la Ville': The Rhythm of a Metaphor". *Poetics Today* 14(1): 49–82.

Goddard, C. (1997) "Cultural Values and 'Cultural Scripts' of Malay (Bahasa Melayu)". *Journal of Pragmatics* 27(2): 183–201.

Guinness, P. (1986) *Harmony and Hierarchy in a Javanese Kampung.* Singapore: Oxford University Press.

———— (1994) "Local Society and Culture". In *Indonesia's New Order: The Dynamics of Socio-Economic Transformation*, ed. H. Hill. St Leonard's: Allen & Unwin.

———— (2009) *Kampung, State and Islam in Urban Java.* Singapore: NUS Press.

Gurr, T.R. (2000) "Ethnic Warfare on the Wane". *Foreign Affairs* 79(3): 52–64.

Hadiz, V.R. (2010) *Localising Power in Post-Authoritarian Indonesia.* Stanford: Stanford University Press.

Hage, G. (1996) "Nationalist Anxiety or the Fear of Losing Your Other". *The Australian Journal of Anthropology* 7(2): 121–40.

Halimah Mohd Said and Zainab Abdul Majid (2004) *Images of the Jawi Peranakan of Penang: Assimilation of the Jawi Peranakan Community into the Malay Society.* Tanjong Malim: Universiti Pendidikan Sultan Idris.

Hamilton, A.W. (1959) *Malay Pantuns.* Singapore: Eastern Universities Press.

Hara, F. (2004) "'Death Railway': (Burma-Siam Railway)". In *Southeast Asia: A Historical Encyclopedia, from Angkor Wat to East Timor, Volume 1*, ed. K.G. Ooi. Santa Barbara: ABC-CLIO.

Hartono, A.J. (2005) *Aliran dan Paham Sesat di Indonesia.* Jakarta: Pustaka Al-Kautsar.

Harvey, S.S. (2008) "Mapping Spectral Tropicality in *The Maid* and *Return to Pontianak*". *Singapore Journal of Tropical Geography* 29(1): 24–33.

Hasan Junus (2002) *Karena Emas di Bunga Lautan dan Sekumpulan Esei-Esei Sejarah.* Pekanbaru: Kerjasama Kota Tanjungpinang dengan Unri Press.

———— (n.d.) "Bai Roti". In private document collection of Aswandi Syarhial.

Hatley, B. (1982) "National Ritual, Neighbourhood Performance: Celebrating *Tujuhbelasan*". *Indonesia* 34: 55–64.

———— (2008) *Javanese Performances on an Indonesian Stage: Contesting Culture, Embracing Change.* Singapore: NUS Press.

Hefner, R.W. (2010) "Islam and Spiritual Capital: An Indonesian Case Study". In *The Hidden Form of Capital: Spiritual Influences in Societal Progress*, ed. P.L. Berger and G. Redding. London & New York: Anthem Press.

————, ed. (1998) *Market Cultures: Society and Morality in the New Asian Capitalisms.* Boulder: Westview Press.

Hemmings, C. (2005) "Invoking Affect: Cultural Theory and the Ontological Turn". *Cultural Studies* 19(5): 548–67.

Henderson, A.K. (2008) *Romanticism and the Painful Pleasures of Modern Life.* Cambridge: Cambridge University Press.

Ho, E. (2002) "Before Parochialisation: Diasporic Arabs Cast in Creole Waters". In *Transcending Borders: Arabs, Politics, Trade and Islam in Southeast Asia,* ed. H. de Jonge and N. Kaptein. Leiden: KITLV Press.

Hollan, D.W. (1992) "Cross-Cultural Differences in the Self". *Journal of Anthropological Research* 48(4): 283–300.

Holstein, J.A. and J.F. Gubrium (1995) *The Active Interview.* Thousand Oaks & London: SAGE.

Hooker, M.B. (2008) *Indonesian Syariah: Defining a National School of Islamic Law.* Singapore: Institute of Southeast Asian Studies.

Hooker, V.M. (2000) *Writing a New Society: Social Change through the Novel in Malay.* St Leonards & Honolulu: ASAA in association with Allen & Unwin and University of Hawai'i Press.

Hoskins, J., ed. (1996) *Headhunting and the Social Imagination in Southeast Asia.* Stanford: Stanford University Press.

Howell, S. (1988) "To Be Angry is Not Human, to Be Fearful is". In *Societies at Peace: Anthropological Perspectives,* ed. S. Howell and R. Willis. London: Blackwell.

Huff, W.G. (1994) *The Economic Growth of Singapore: Trade and Development in the Twentieth Century.* Cambridge: Cambridge University Press.

Indra, D.S. (2006) "Kata Pengantar" to T. Suseno, *Mari Berpantun.* Tanjung Pinang: Komunitas Sastra kerja sama dengan Dinas Pariwisata, Seni dan Budaya, Provinsi Kepulauan Riau.

Isjoni Ishaq (2002a) "Antara Stereotif dan Jati Diri Orang Melayu". In *Orang Melayu: Sejarah, Sistem, Norma dan Nilai Adat,* ed. Isjoni Ishaq. Pekanbaru: Unri Press.

———— (2002b) "Saatnya Orang Melayu Bangkit". In *Orang Melayu: Sejarah, Sistem, Norma dan Nilai Adat,* ed. Isjoni Ishaq. Pekanbaru: Unri Press.

Jameson, F. (1991) *Postmodernism, or, the Cultural Logic of Late Capitalism.* Durham & London: Duke University Press.

Jones, S. (2010) "The Normalisation of Local Politics? Watching the Presidential Elections in Morotai, North Maluku". In *Problems of Democratisation in Indonesia: Elections, Institutions and Society,* ed. E. Aspinall and M. Mietzner. Singapore: Institute of Southeast Asian Studies.

Jurnal LKS SMK (2006) "Siapa Pantas Jadi *Jawara*?", 16 June: 4.

Kahn, J.S. (2006) *Other Malays: Nationalism and Cosmopolitanism in the Modern Malay World.* Singapore: ASAA in association with Singapore University Press and NIAS Press.

Karim, W.J. (1990) "Prelude to Madness: The Language of Emotion in Courtship and Early Marriage". In *Emotions of Culture: A Malay Perspective*, ed. W.J. Karim. Singapore: Oxford University Press.

Kathirithamby-Wells, J. (1993) "Restraints on the Development of Merchant Capitalism in Southeast Asia before c.1800". In *Southeast Asia in the Early Modern Era: Trade, Power, and Belief*, ed. A. Reid. Ithaca & London: Cornell University Press.

Kato, T. (1989) "Different Fields, Similar Locusts: *Adat* Communities and the Village Law of 1979 in Indonesia". *Indonesia* 47: 89–114.

Katz, C. (2005) "Lost and Found: The Imagined Geographies of American Studies". *Prospects* 30: 17–25.

Kawash, S. (1999) "Terrorists and Vampires: Fanon's Spectral Violence of Decolonization". In *Frantz Fanon: Critical Perspectives*, ed. A.C. Alessandri. London & New York: Routledge.

Keeler, W. (1987) *Javanese Shadow Plays, Javanese Selves*. Princeton: Princeton University Press.

Kimura, E. (2010) "Proliferating Provinces: Territorial Politics in Post-Suharto Indonesia". *South East Asia Research* 18(3): 415–49.

———— (2013) *Political Change and Territoriality in Indonesia: Provincial Proliferation*. Abingdon and New York: Routledge.

van Klinken, G. (2007a) *Communal Violence and Democratization in Indonesia: Small Town Wars*. London & New York: Routledge.

———— (2007b) "Return of the Sultans: The Communitarian Turn in Local Politics". In *The Revival of Tradition in Indonesian Politics: The Deployment of Adat from Colonialism to Indigenism*, ed. J.S. Davidson and D. Henley. Abingdon & New York: Routledge.

Koentjaraningrat (1969) *Rintangan-Rintangan Mental dalam Pembangunan Ekonomi di Indonesia*. Jakarta: Bhratara.

———— (1974) *Kebudayaan, Mentalitet, dan Pembangunan*. Jakarta: Gramedia.

Koh, K.W. (2007) "Moving People and a Prelude to Colonialism: The Kingdom of Johor 1784–1818". PhD dissertation, University of Hawai'i at Manoa.

Kompas (2008) "Mengasah Kecerdasan dengan Berpantun", 6 May. Available at http://www1.kompas.com/printnews/xml/2008/05/06/00571564/ mengasah.kecerdasan.dengan.berpantun [accessed 5 August 2008].

———— (2010) "Inilah Penjaga Tuah Budaya Melayu", 21 June. Available at http://www1.kompas.com/printnews/xml/2010/06/21/16071563/inilah. penjaga.tuah.budaya.melayu [accessed 24 May 2011].

Komunitas (2005) "Frankim: Walikota Itu Keturunan Cina, Tapi 'Bodoh'". Week 1, December: 1.

Koning, J., M. Nolten, J. Rodenburg and R. Saptari, eds. (2000) *Women and Households in Indonesia: Cultural Notions and Social Practices*. Richmond: Curzon Press.

Laderman, C. (1991) *Taming the Wind of Desire: Psychology, Medicine, and Aesthetics in Malay Shamanistic Performance*. Berkeley: University of California Press.

Leach, J. (2003) *Creative Land: Place and Procreation on the Rai Coast of Papua New Guinea*. Oxford & New York: Berghahn.

Leslie, A.M. (1987) "Pretense and Representation: The Origins Of 'Theory of Mind'". *Psychological Review* 94(4): 412–26.

Li, T. (1989) *Malays in Singapore: Culture, Economy and Ideology*. Singapore: Oxford University Press.

Li, T.M. (2007) "Governmentality". *Anthropologica* 49: 275–94.

Liaw Y.-F. (1976) *Undang-Undang Melaka: The Laws of Melaka*. The Hague: Martinus Nijhoff.

Lindquist, J. (2009) *The Anxieties of Mobility: Migration and Tourism in the Indonesian Borderlands*. Honolulu: University of Hawai'i Press.

Loh, K.S. (2013) *Squatters into Citizens: The 1961 Bukit Ho Swee Fire and the Making of Modern Singapore*. Singapore: NUS Press.

Lombard, D. (1986) "Réflexions sur le concept de 'Pasisir' et sur son utilité pour l'étude des littératures". In *Cultural Contact and Textual Interpretation*, ed. C.D. Grijns and S.O. Robson. Dordrecht & Cinnaminson: Foris.

Long, N. (2009) "Fruits of the Orchard: Land, Space and State in Kepulauan Riau". *SOJOURN: Journal of Social Issues in Southeast Asia* 24(1): 60–88.

———— (2011) "Bordering on Immoral: Piracy, Education and the Ethics of Cross-Border Co-Operation in the Indonesia-Malaysia-Singapore Growth Triangle". *Anthropological Theory* 11(4): 441–64.

Long, N.J. and H.L. Moore (2013) "Introduction: Achievement and Its Social Life". In *The Social Life of Achievement*, ed. N.J. Long and H.L. Moore. Oxford: Berghahn.

Lyons, L. and M. Ford (2007) "Where Internal and International Migration Intersect: Mobility and the Formation of Multi-Ethnic Communities in the Riau Islands Transit Zone". *International Journal on Multicultural Societies* 9(2): 236–63.

Mack, J.S. (2004) "Inhabiting the Imaginary: Factory Women at Home on Batam Island, Indonesia". *Singapore Journal of Tropical Geography* 25(2): 156–79.

Mackie, J.A.C. (1974) *Konfrontasi: The Indonesia-Malaysia Dispute 1963–1966*. Kuala Lumpur: Oxford University Press.

———— (1976) "Anti-Chinese Outbreaks in Indonesia, 1959–68". In *The Chinese in Indonesia: Five Essays*, ed. J.A.C. Mackie. Melbourne: Nelson in association with The Australian Institute of International Affairs.

Mahathir bin Mohamad (1970) *The Malay Dilemma*. Singapore: Asia Pacific Press.

———— (1986) *The Challenge*. Pataling Jaya: Pelanduk.

Maier, H.M.J. (2011) "*Melayu* and Malay — A Story of Appropriate Be-
    havior". In *Melayu: The Politics, Poetics and Paradoxes of Malayness*, ed.
    M. Mohamad and S.M.K. Aljunied. Singapore: NUS Press.
Massot, G. and L. Kalus (2012) "Between Legend and Reality: The Bukit
    Batu Cemetery of the Island of Bintan, Riau Archipelago". *Archipel* 83:
    25–51.
Massumi, B. (1995) "The Autonomy of Affect". *Cultural Critique* 31: 83–109.
Matheson, V. (1979) "Concepts of Malay Ethos in Indigenous Malay
    Writings". *Journal of Southeast Asian Studies* 10(2): 351–71.
―――― (1986) "Strategies of Survival: The Malay Royal Line of Lingga-
    Riau". *Journal of Southeast Asian Studies* 17(1): 5–38.
―――― (1989) "Pulau Penyengat: Nineteenth Century Islamic Centre of
    Riau". *Archipel* 37: 153–72.
McClelland, D.C. (1961) *The Achieving Society*. Princeton: D. van Nostrand.
McClelland, D.C., J.W. Atkinson, R.A. Clark and E.L. Lowell (1953) *The
    Achievement Motive*. New York: Appleton-Century-Crofts.
Media Guru (2010) "Lomba Kompetensi Siswa SMK Se-Provinsi Kepulauan
    Riau", 13 June. Available at http://www.media-guru.co.cc/2010/06/
    lomba-kompetensi-siswa-smk-se-provinsi.html [accessed 17 May 2011].
Media Kepri (2007) "'Perawan Tua' Bersolek Jadi Kota Waisata dan Budaya",
    8 January: 19.
Meenakshisundaram, S.S. (1994) *Decentralisation in Developing Countries*.
    New Delhi: Concept Publishing Company.
Milner, A.C. (2010) *Race or Civilization: The Localizing of 'the Malays'*. Bangi:
    IKMAS, Universiti Kebangsaan Malaysia.
―――― (1982) *Kerajaan: Malay Political Culture on the Eve of Colonial Rule*.
    Tucson: University of Arizona Press.
―――― (1995) *The Invention of Politics in Colonial Malaya: Contesting Na-
    tionalism and the Expansion of the Public Sphere*. Cambridge: Cambridge
    University Press.
―――― (2008) *The Malays*. Oxford: Wiley-Blackwell.
Minnesota Population Center (2011) *Integrated Public Use Microdata Series,
    International: Version 6.1* [*Machine-Readable Database*]. Minneapolis:
    University of Minnesota. Underlying data provided by BPS (Badan
    Pusat Statistik, Indonesia).
Mitchell, J.C. (1956) *The Kalela Dance: Aspects of Social Relationships among
    Urban African in Northern Rhodesia*. Manchester: Manchester University
    Press.
Mohamad, M. and S.M.K. Aljunied (2011) "Introduction". In *Melayu: The
    Politics, Poetics and Paradoxes of Malayness*, ed. M. Mohamad and S.M.K.
    Aljunied. Singapore: NUS Press.
Muhibbullah Azfa Manik (2005) "Toloong!!". Available at <http://www.bung-
    hatta.info/content.php?article.97> [accessed 1 September 2007].

Murray, A. (1991) *No Money, No Honey: A Study of Street Traders and Prostitutes in Jakarta*. Singapore: Oxford University Press.

Nagata, J. (1974) "What is a Malay? Situational Selection of Ethnicity in a Plural Society". *American Ethnologist* 1(2): 331–50.

———— (1979) *Malaysian Mosaic: Perspectives from a Polyethnic Society*. Vancouver: University of British Columbia Press.

Nandy, A. (1987) *Tradition, Tyranny and Utopias: Essays in the Politics of Awareness*. Delhi: Oxford University Press.

Nas, P.J.M. and W. Boender (2002) "The Indonesian City in Urban Theory". In *The Indonesian Town Revisited*, ed. P.J.M. Nas. Singapore & Münster: Institute of Southeast Asian Studies & Lit Verlag.

Nas, P.J.M. and R.J. Sluis (2002) "In Search of Meaning: Urban Orientation Principles in Indonesia". In *The Indonesian Town Revisited*, ed. P.J.M. Nas. Singapore & Münster: Institute of Southeast Asian Studies & Lit Verlag.

Navaro-Yashin, Y. (2002) *Faces of the State: Secularism and Public Life in Turkey*. Princeton: Princeton University Press.

Nazar Machmud (2003) "Membangun Masa Depan Provinsi Maritim Kepulauan Riau". In *Menuju Masyarakat Sejahtera: Tentang Gagasan Pembaharuan Sosial, Politik, Ekonomi, dan Budaya di Kepulauan Riau*, ed. Trisno Aji Putra. Jogjakarta: Taju'ssalatin Press.

Ng, C.K. (1976) *The Chinese in Riau: A Community on an Unstable and Restrictive Frontier*. Singapore: Nanyang University.

Novendra, Dwi Sobuwati, Yussuwadinata and Zakbah (2000) *Peran Serta Ibu Rumah Tangga dalam Pengembangan Kebudayaan Tradisional di Daerah Riau*. Tanjung Pinang: Balai Kajian Sejarah dan Nilai Tradisional.

Novendra, Suarman, Refisrul, Gatot Winoto and Dwi Sobuwati (1996) *Integrasi Nasional di Daerah Riau: Suatu Pendekatan Budaya*. Tanjung Pinang: P2NB Riau.

Nur, Y. (2000) "L'île de Batam à l'ombre de Singapour: Invetissement Singapourien et Dèpendance de Batam". *Archipel* 59: 145–70.

Nurana (1985) *Lancang Kuning dan Cerita Rakyat Lainnya dari Daerah Riau*. Jakarta: Inti Idaya Press.

Ohmae, K. (1994) *The Borderless World: Power and Strategy in the Global Marketplace*. London: HarperCollins.

Ong, A. (1988) "The Production of Possession: Spirits and the Multinational Corporation in Malaysia". *American Ethnologist* 15(1): 28–42.

———— (2000) "Graduated Sovereignty in Southeast Asia". *Theory, Culture and Society* 17(4): 55–75.

———— (2006) *Neoliberalism as Exception: Mutations in Citizenship and Sovereignty*. Durham: Duke University Press.

van Ophuijsen, C.A. (1904) *Het Maleische Volksdicht: Rede*. Leiden: Brill.

Osman, M.T. (1989) *Malay Folk Beliefs: An Integration of Disparate Elements*. Kuala Lumpur: Dewan Bahasa dan Pustaka, Kementerian Pendidikan Malaysia.

Parker, L. (1992) "The Creation of Indonesian Citizens in Balinese Primary Schools". *Review of Indonesian and Malaysian Affairs* 26(1): 42–70.

Peletz, M.G. (1998) "The 'Great Transformation' Among Negeri Sembilan Malays, with Particular Reference to Chinese and Minangkabau". In *Market Cultures: Society and Morality in the New Asian Capitalisms*, ed. R.W. Hefner. Boulder: Westview Press.

Pelras, C. (1996) *The Bugis*. Oxford: Blackwell.

Peters, R. (2012) *Surabaya, 1945–2010: Neighborhood, State and Economy in Indonesia's City of Struggle*. Singapore: NUS Press.

Posmetro Batam (2007a) "Frankim Divonis Percoban, Pengacara Toni Babu Walk Out", 27 July. Available at http://www.posmetrobatam.com/index. php?Itemid=34&id=1840&option=com_content&task=view [accessed 5 August 2008].

———— (2007b) "Gajah Berkelahi, Semutnya Kebingungan", 13 April. Available at http://www.posmetrobatam.com/index.php?option=com_content &task=view&id=101&Itemid=39 [accessed 5 August 2008].

Poulgrain, G. (1998) *The Genesis of Konfrontasi: Malaysia, Brunei, Indonesia, 1945–1965*. Bathurst: Crawford House.

Purdey, J. (2006) *Anti-Chinese Violence in Indonesia, 1996–1999*. Singapore: Singapore University Press.

van der Putten, J. (2001) *His Word Is the Truth: Haji Ibrahim's Letters and Other Writings*. Leiden: CNWS.

———— (2004) "A Malay of Bugis Ancestry: Haji Ibrahim's Strategies of Survival". In *Contesting Malayness: Malay Identity across Boundaries*, ed. T.P. Barnard. Singapore: Singapore University Press.

———— (2011) "Riau: A Malay Heartland at the Borders". In *Melayu: The Politics, Poetics and Paradoxes of Malayness*, ed. M. Mohamad and S.M.K. Aljunied. Singapore: NUS Press.

Quinn, G. (2003) "Coming Apart and Staying Together at the Centre: Debates over Provincial Status in Java and Madura". In *Local Power and Politics in Indonesia: Decentralisation and Democratisation*, ed. E. Aspinall and G. Fealy. Singapore: Institute of Southeast Asian Studies.

Rahim, L.Z. (1998) *The Singapore Dilemma: The Political and Educational Marginality of the Malay Community*. Kuala Lumpur: Oxford University Press.

Rahimsyah, M.B. (2005) *Cinta Tanah Air: Mengenal Budaya Bangsa Indonesia*. Surabaya: CV Pustaka Agung Harapan.

Reid, A. (1988a) "Female Roles in Pre-Colonial Southeast Asia". *Modern Asian Studies* 22(3): 629–45.

———— (1988b) *Southeast Asia in the World of Commerce 1450–1680. Volume One: The Lands Below the Winds.* New Haven & London: Yale University Press.

———— (2004) "Understanding *Melayu* (Malay) as a Source of Diverse Modern Identities". In *Contesting Malayness: Malay Identity across Boundaries,* ed. T.P. Barnard. Singapore: Singapore University Press.

Resink, G.J. (1968) *Indonesia's History between the Myths: Essays in Legal History and Historical Theory.* The Hague: W. van Hoeve.

Riau Wati (2009) *Feminisme dalam Kumpulan Puisi Suryatati A. Manan Walikota Tanjungpinang.* Tanjungpinang: UMRAH Press.

Rickert, T. (2007) *Acts of Enjoyment: Rhetoric, Žižek, and the Return of the Subject.* Pittsburgh: University of Pittsburgh Press.

Ricklefs, M.C. (2007) *Polarizing Javanese Society: Islamic and Other Visions (c. 1830–1930).* Singapore: NUS Press.

Riza Sihbudi, Awani Irewati, N.B. Ikrar, Moch. Nurhasim, Syamsuddin Haris and Tri Ratnawati (2001) *Bara dalam Sekam: Identifikasi Akar Masalah dan Solusi atas Konflik-Konflik Lokal di Aceh, Maluku, Papua dan Riau.* Bandung: LIPI & Mizan Pustaka.

Robby Patria (2008) "Berjuang Untuk Kepri, Lukman Edy 'Dikandang Harimau'". Available at http://robbypatria.blogspot.com/2008/09/berjuang-untuk-kepri-lukman-edy.html> [accessed 11 May 2011].

Robinson, G. (1995) *The Dark Side of Paradise: Political Violence in Bali.* Ithaca: Cornell University Press.

Roth, D. (2007) "Many Governors, No Province; the Struggle for a Province in the Luwu-Tana Toraja Area in South Sulawesi". In *Renegotiating Boundaries: Local Politics in Post-Suharto Indonesia,* ed. H. Schulte Nordholt and G. van Klinken. Leiden: KITLV Press.

Röttger, E.H. (1846) *Berigten Omtrent Indië, Gedurende Een Tienjarig Verbliff Aldaar.* Deventer: Ballot.

Royle, S.A. (1997) "Industrialisation in Indonesia: The Example of Batam Island". *Singapore Journal of Tropical Geography* 18(1): 89–98.

Sakai, M. (2004) "Reviving 'Malayness': Searching for a New Dominant Ethnicity". *Inside Indonesia* 78 (April–June): 17–8.

————, ed. (2002) *Beyond Jakarta: Regional Autonomy and Local Society in Indonesia.* Adelaide: Crawford House.

Sartre, J.-P. (1963 [1938]) *Nausea,* trans. R. Baldick. London: Penguin.

———— (2003 [1943]) *Being and Nothingness: An Essay on Phenomenological Ontology.* London & New York: Routledge.

Sasmita, M. Juramadi Esram, N. Tarigan, Novendra and Yussuwadinata (1996) *Fungsi Keluarga dalam Meningkatkan Kualitas Sumber Daya Manusia di Daerah Riau.* Tanjung Pinang: P2NB Riau.

Sato, S. (2000) *Labour Relations in Japanese Occupied Indonesia.* Amsterdam: International Institute for Asian Studies/International Institute of Social History CLARA Working Paper Series, No. 8.

Schulte Nordholt, H. (1996) *The Spell of Power: A History of Balinese Politics, 1650–1940.* Leiden: KITLV Press.

———— (2003) "Renegotiating Boundaries: Access, Agency and Identity in Post-Suharto Indonesia". *Bijdragen tot de taal-, land-, en volkenkunde* 159(4): 550–89.

Schulte Nordholt, H. and G. van Klinken, eds. (2007) *Renegotiating Boundaries: Local Politics in Post-Suharto Indonesia.* Leiden: KITLV Press.

Scott, D. (1999) *Refashioning Futures: Criticism after Postcoloniality.* Princeton: Princeton University Press.

Scott, J.C. (1985) *Weapons of the Weak: Everyday Forms of Peasant Resistance.* New Haven: Yale University Press.

Sheppard, M. (1982) "Foreword" to K. Sim, *Flowers of the Sun: A Simple Introduction to the Enjoyment of Pantun. Second Edition.* Singapore: Eastern Universities Press.

Siau, M.S. (1953) The Indonesian National Day. In Ikatan Alumni Toan Hoon document collection, Chung Hwa School folio.

Siegel, J.T. (1998) "Early Thoughts on the Violence of May 13 and 14, 1998 in Jakarta". *Indonesia* 66: 75–108.

Silver, L.R. and T. Hall (2001) *The Heroes of Rimau.* Singapore: Cultured Lotus.

Skeat, W.W. (1984 [1900]) *Malay Magic.* Singapore: Oxford University Press.

Sobary, M. (1987) *Between 'Ngoyo' and 'Nrimo': Cultural Values and Economic Behaviour among Javanese Migrants in Tanjung Pinang.* Clayton: Monash Asia Institute.

Srinavasan, T.N. (1994) "Human Development: A New Paradigm or Reinvention of the Wheel?". *The American Economic Review* 84(2): 238–43.

Steenbrink, K. (2008) "The New Decentralisation: 'Blossoming' Ethnic and Religious Conflict in Indonesia". *IIAS Newsletter* 46: 37.

Stewart, K. (2007) *Ordinary Affects.* Durham & London: Duke University Press.

Strassler, K. (2006) "*Reformasi* Though Our Eyes: Children as Witnesses of History in Post-Suharto Indonesia". *Visual Anthropology Review* 22(2): 53–70.

Strathern, M. (2009) "Land: Intangible or Tangible Property?". In *Land Rights*, ed. T. Chesters. Oxford: Oxford University Press.

Suara Karya (2007) "DPD Minta Jaminan Kekebalan Hukum". Available at http://www.suarakarya-online.com/news.html?id=179419 [accessed 22 June 2012].

Sullivan, J. (1992) *Local Government and Community in Java: An Urban Case-Study.* Singapore: Oxford University Press.

Sumanti Ardi (2002) *Amuk Melayu Dalam Tuntutan Provinsi Kepulauan Riau.* Pekanbaru: Unri Press.

Surat Kabar Senior (2006) "Pemerintah Kab. Bintan Dukung Acara 'Bujang dan Dara'". Issue 256b/VI/1521 (May): 5.

Suryadi (2005) "Identity, Media and the Margins: Radio in Pekanbaru, Riau (Indonesia)". *Journal of Southeast Asian Studies* 36(1): 131–51.

Suryatati A Manan (2007) *Melayukah Aku?: Kumpulan Puisi*. Jakarta: CV Alya Jaya Makmur.

Sutton, R.A. (1991) *Traditions of Gamelan Music in Java: Musical Pluralism and Regional Identity*. Cambridge: Cambridge University Press.

Suwardi, M.S. (2002) "Pendidikan Kewirausahaan Sebagai Upaya Pemberdayaan Orang Melayu". In *Orang Melayu: Sejarah, Sistem, Norma Dan Nilai Adat*, ed. Isjoni Ishaq. Pekanbaru: Unri Press.

Suwardi, M.S., M.A. Effendi, M. Daud Kodir and Amir Luthfi (1984) *Sejarah Perlawanan Terhadap Imperialisme dan Kolonialisme di Riau*. Jakarta: Departemen Pendidikan dan Kebudayaan.

Sweeney, A. (1987) *A Full Hearing: Orality and Literacy in the Malay World*. Berkeley: University of California Press.

Tagliacozzo, E. (2005) *Secret Trades, Porous Borders: Smuggling and States Along a Southeast Asian Frontier, 1865–1915*. New Haven: Yale University Press.

Tanjungpinang Pos (2011) "Sosialisasi UUD ke Pelajar", 20 December. Available at http://tanjungpinangpos.co.id/2011/12/sosialisasi-uud-ke-pelajar/ [accessed 20 May 2012].

Tarigan, S.D.S., T. Dibyo Harsono, M. Imran Nuh, Dwi Setiati and Zakbah (1996) *Persepsi Tentang Etos Kerja: Kaitannya Dengan Nilai Budaya Masyarakat Melayu Daerah Riau*. Tanjung Pinang: P2NB Riau.

Thee, K.W. (2002) "The Soeharto Era and After: Stability, Development and Crisis, 1966–2000". In *The Emergence of a National Economy: An Economic History of Indonesia, 1800–2000*, ed. H. Dick, V.J.H. Houben, J.T. Lindblad and K.W. Thee. Crows Nest & Honolulu: Allen & Unwin and University of Hawai'i Press.

Thomas, P.L. (1984) "The Malay Pantun: A Problem of Redundancy". *Indonesia Circle* 33(1): 15–22.

Thompson, J.T. (1847) "A Glance at Rhio". *Journal of the Indian Archipelago and Eastern Asia* 1: 68–74.

Thung, J.L. and Leolita Masnun (2002) "Melayu-Riau: Dari Isu 'Riau Merdeka' Sampai Persoalan Riau Kepulauan". In *Etnisitas Dalam (Re)Konstruksi Identitas Lokal dan Nasional*, ed. Thung Ju Lan, J. Haba, R.P. Abdul and L. Masnun. Jakarta: PMB-LIPI.

Tri Ratnawati (2006) *Potret Pemerintahan Lokal di Indonesia di Masa Perubahan*. Yogyakarta: Pustaka Pelajar kerja sama dengan Pusat Penelitian Politik — LIPI.

Tribun Batam (2005) "Tanjung Api-Api Nang, Persinggahan Para Pelaut (1): Lacak Jejak Sejarah Melayu", 6 January: 24.

———— (2006) "Kuncinya Berdoa Sambil Belajar", 1 July: 1–2.

———— (2007a) "Tatik Siap Ikut Latihan Keronconcong", 8 January: 23–4.

———— (2007b) "Nangis Karena Nilai Ujian Hanya 50", 26 January: 23–4.

Trocki, C. (1979) *Prince of Pirates: The Temenggongs and the Development of Johor and Singapore 1784–1885*. Singapore: Singapore University Press.

Tusiran Suseno (2006) *Mari Berpantun*. Tanjung Pinang: Komunitas Sastra kerja sama dengan Dinas Pariwisata, Seni dan Budaya, Provinsi Kepulauan Riau.

Twang, P.Y. (1998) *The Chinese Business Elite in Indonesia and the Transition to Independence 1940–1950*. Kuala Lumpur: Oxford University Press.

Tyson, A. (2010) *Decentralisation and Adat Revivalism in Indonesia: The Politics of Becoming Indigenous*. London & New York: Routledge.

Vickers, A. (1987) "Hinduism and Islam in Indonesia: Bali and the *Pasisir* World". *Indonesia* 44: 31–58.

———— (1993) "From Bali to Lampung on the *Pasisir*". *Archipel* 45: 55–76.

———— (1997) "'Malay Identity': Modernity, Invented Tradition and Forms of Knowledge". *Review of Indonesian and Malaysian Affairs* 31(1): 173–212.

Vos, R. (1993) *Gentle Janus, Merchant Prince: The VOC and the Tightrope of Diplomacy in the Malay World, 1740–1800*. Leiden: KITLV Press.

Walker, J.H. (2004) "Autonomy, Diversity, and Dissent: Conceptions of Power and Sources of Action in the *Sejarah Melayu* (Raffles MS 18)". *Theory and Society* 33(2): 213–55.

Wee, V. (1985) "Melayu: Hierarchies of Being in Riau". PhD dissertation, Australian National University, Canberra.

———— (1988) "Material Dependence and Symbolic Independence: Constructions of Melayu Ethncity in Island Riau, Indonesia". In *Ethnic Diversity and the Control of Natural Resources in Southeast Asia*, ed. T.A. Rambo, K. Gillogly and K.L. Hutterer. Ann Arbor: University of Michigan, Center for South and Southeast Asian Studies.

———— (2002) *Ethno-Nationalism in Process: Atavism, Ethnicity and Indigenism in Riau*. Hong Kong: City University of Hong Kong Southeast Asia Research Center Working Papers Series, No. 22.

Wessing, R. (2006) "A Community of Spirits: People, Ancestors, and Nature Spirits in Java." *Crossroads: An Interdisciplinary Journal of Southeast Asian Studies* 18(1): 11–111.

Wessing, R. and R.E. Jordaan (1997) "Death at the Building Site: Construction Sacrifice in Southeast Asia". *History of Religions* 3(2): 101–21.

Wilder, W. (1982) *Communication, Social Structure and Development in Rural Malaysia*. London: Athlone Press.

Wilkinson, R.J. (1906) *Malay Beliefs*. London & Leiden: Luzac and Co. & E.J. Brill.

———— (1924) *Malay Literature Part 1: Romance. History. Poetry.* Kuala Lumpur: J.C. Wallace at the FMS Government Press.

Wilkinson, R.J. and R.O. Winstedt (1923) *Pantun Melayu. 2nd Edition.* Singapore: Methodist Publishing House.

Willford, A. (2006) "The 'Already Surmounted' yet 'Secretly Familiar': Malaysian Identity as Symptom". *Cultural Anthropology* 21(1): 31–59.

Winstedt, R. (1951) *The Malay Magician: Being Shaman, Saiva and Sufi.* London: Routledge & Kegan Paul.

Wong, L.K. (1991) "Commercial Growth before the Second World War". In *A History of Singapore*, ed. E.C.T. Chew and E. Lee. Singapore: Oxford University Press.

Yampolsky, P. (1995) "Forces for Change in the Regional Performing Arts of Indonesia". *Bijdragen tot de taal-, land-, en volkenkunde* 151(4): 700–25.

Yong, M.C. (2003) *The Indonesian Revolution and the Singapore Connection, 1945–1949.* Leiden: KITLV Press.

Zaili Asril, Mulyadi, I.J. Taufik, Muslim Kawi, Ramli Lubis and Fakhrunnas M.A.J. (2002) *Tragedi Riau Menegakkan Demokrasi: Peristiwa 2 September 1985.* Pekanbaru: Panitia Peringatan 17 Tahun "Peristiwa 2 September 1985".

Žižek, S. (1994) "Introduction: The Spectre of Ideology". In *Mapping Ideology*, ed. S. Žižek. London: Verso.

———— (2005) "Neighbors and Other Monsters: A Plea for Ethical Violence". In *The Neighbor: Three Inquiries in Political Theology*, ed. S. Žižek, E.L. Santner and K. Reinhard. Chicago & London: University of Chicago Press.

Zurbuchen, M.S. (2005) "Historical Memory in Contemporary Indonesia". In *Beginning to Remember: The Past in the Indonesian Present*, ed. M.S. Zurbuchen. Seattle: University of Washington Press.

About the Author

Nicholas J. Long is Assistant Professor of Anthropology at the London School of Economics and Political Science. His first degree was in Archaeology and Anthropology at the University of Cambridge, where he stayed to complete an MPhil in Social Anthropological Research and a PhD on social, cultural and political change in the Riau Islands. Having worked in Cambridge for four years, initially as a fixed-term lecturer in social anthropology and subsequently as a British Academy Postdoctoral Fellow and Junior Research Fellow at St Catharine's College, Nick joined the LSE in 2012. He has also held visiting positions at the University of Sydney, Aarhus University and STISIPOL Raja Haji.

Nick's previous publications include *Southeast Asian Perspectives on Power* (co-edited with Liana Chua, Joanna Cook and Lee Wilson, and published by Routledge in 2012), *Sociality: New Directions* (co-edited with Henrietta L. Moore, and published by Berghahn in 2013), and *The Social Life of Achievement* (co-edited with Henrietta L. Moore, and scheduled for release by Berghahn in November 2013), as well as numerous scholarly articles. He is currently working on two major research projects. The first of these is investigating how and why Riau Islanders' attitudes to democracy have changed over time, while the second is examining emergent techniques for "motivating" and improving the "human resource quality" of Riau Islands youth with a view to developing more sophisticated understandings of motivated agency in the social sciences.

He can be contacted by email at N.J.Long@lse.ac.uk, or by post at the Department of Anthropology, Old Building (6th Floor), London School of Economics, Houghton Street, London, WC2A 2AE, United Kingdom.

Index

achievement, *see also* competitions;
  under marketplace
  as basis for social hierarchy,
    183, 211, 220–1, 223
  as civic duty, 179, 212
  as object of personal desire, 182
  as object of policy, 179, 222,
    247–8
  associative logic of, 190, 196
  bad faith in, 195–8
  capacities for, 179, 186–7, 196
  differing conceptions of,
    179–80
  disciplinary dimensions of, 209,
    218
  geographies of, 189–94, 196
  pleasures and rewards of, 182–3
  psychology of, 176–9, 182, 185
  recognition of, 262
  relational aspects of, 184–7
  self-replicating character of,
    221–2
active interviewing, 86
adat, 7, 15, 50, 55, 72, 125, 131,
  238, 239
aesthetification
  of cultural forms, 208, 238
affect, 4, 7, 28–9 187, 234, 241,
  244
  autonomy of, 250
  significance of, 5, 7, 23–5, 94,
    175, 182, 205, 207, 245–9

ways of conceptualising, 25–7,
  54, 151, 171, 249–51
ways of investigating, 10, 27–8,
  151, 244, 249–51
affective turn, 4
affirmative action, 23, 54, 60–1,
  98, 113n8
agency, 10, 160, 175, 214, 221
Alatas, Syed Hussain, 21, 104
angker, 149–50, 158, 160–2, 166,
  171, *see also* uncanny
  ideological aspects of, 150–1,
    162–3, 165–6
ang-pai, 111
anthropology, *see also* ethnographic
  methods
  approaches to political
    psychology, 10, 249–51
  approaches to spirit beliefs,
    152–5, 157
  approaches to urbanisation,
    128
  nature of the discipline's
    enquiry, 3–4
  Riau Islanders' conceptions of,
    67
anxiety, 4, 8, 23, 27, 127–8, 146–7,
  166, 195
  castration, 150
arisan, 135–7
aristocrats, *see also* sultanate, Johor-
  Riau-Lingga

after Indonesian Independence
  as Bugis, 70–5, 93–7
  as Malay, 49–50, 69–70,
    72–3, 97
  attempts to restore the
    sultanate, 92–3
  conflict amongst, 74–5
  denial of Indonesian
    sovereignty, 49, 88
  interest in business, 123–4
  memories of Japanese
    Occupation, 88
  monopoly on history-telling,
    65–8, 77, 81–2, 87
  opposition towards, 70–5,
    97
  power under the New
    Order, 49–50, 70
  relations with Hoezrin
    Hood, 50, 53
  support for provincial
    secession, 50
before Indonesian Independence
  achievements of, 50, 68–9
  as Bugis, 71–3, 95–6
  as Malay, 72–3, 95–6
  centrality to personal
    identity, 19, 94
  conflict amongst, 71–2
  introduction of Islam, 81,
    83
  prohibition of wearing
    yellow, 213
  regulation of trade, 31–2,
    44–5, 68, 95, 105
  relations with Chinese,
    32–3
  relations with Dutch, 32,
    44–5
  relations with Japanese, 45,
    88–93, 96, 163
  staging of contests, 180

ethical obligations upon, 94–6,
    105
Javanese, 101
mythical accounts of, 78–9
representation in public culture,
    65, 68–9
skill in the dark arts, 83
Australia, 26, 62, 199
  military forces, 92
authenticity
  of excellence, 195–6, 203
  of regional cultures, 208
  of the self, 9–10, 195–6

backwardness (perceived)
  of Kelings, 111
  of Malays, 98–100, 103, 112–5,
    120, 122–3, 126, 167, 179
  of primary resource
    exploitation, 102
  of small islands, 117
  of Tanjung Pinang, 236
  of the Riau Islands Province,
    126, 173, 186, 204, 243
  of West Sumatra, 194
bad faith, 8–11, 175, 194–8,
    204–5, 223–4, 241, 244,
    247–51
Bandar Riau, 31–2, 68
Barnard, Timothy, 17
Bataks
  conflict with Malays, 145–6
  conflict with Minangkabau, 128
  discrimination towards, 188–9
  migration to Riau Islands, 35,
    62, 110
  perceptions of, 30, 60, 136
  population size, 43
  smuggling activities, 111
Batam
  crime levels, 57

development of, 38–40
ethnic conflict in, 42, 56,
    128–9
human resource quality in,
    189–92
pantun team, 232–6
beauty
    ability to perceive, 227
    conceptions of, 211–4
beauty contests, 182, 210–24
belonging, 3–4, 22–3, 26–7, 54,
    129, 152, 224
    claims by non-Malays and
        migrants, 58, 61–2, 144–5,
        163
    feeling of, 101, 134–5
Bintan Resorts, 2, 38–9, 201
Boellstorff, Tom, 47, 179–80
bridges
    Barelang, 167
    Batam-Bintan, 166–7
    Ramayana, 169
brokers
    for study abroad, 199–200
Brukbaker, Rogers, 28, 246–7
Brunei Darussalam, 21, 102
Buddhism, 157–8, 161
Bugis
    as colonisers, 73
    historical role in Riau Islands,
        71–2, 74
    Malayness of, 70–5, 93–7
    population size, 33n3, 43
bujang dara, see beauty contests
Butler, Judith, 24

capital, 61
    human, 8, 174, 201, 204
    investment, 38
    political, 202
    social, 183

capitalism, 10, 99, 113–5, 118
    colonial, 104
    late, 249
capital city status, 45–6, 51–3, 64,
    74
cemeteries, *see also* graves
    Chinese, 160–1, 163, 165
    Teluk Keriting, 161
Central Sumatra (province), 45
cerita, 75–7, 93
chauvinism
    ethnic, 97, 246
    local, 75, 97, 237
Chewong, 94
Chinese, *see also* Suryatati A Manan
    adoption by Malays, 15
    burial practices, 160–1, 165
    citizenship loyalties, 188
    cosmology, 156–7, 159, 163–5,
        169–70
    discrimination towards, 70,
        109, 222, 248
    dominance in the marketplace,
        100, 110–2, 114
    emulation of, 123–4
    in politics, 14–5
    in Singapore, 202–3
    labour relations, 114, 125–6
    marginalisation in public
        sphere, 70, 161, 163, 165,
        171–2, 222
    population size, 33, 43
    rape of, 92
    relations with the Dutch, 32–3
    role in colonial period, 31–3,
        76, 105–6
Christians, 58, 145–6, 154–5,
    188–9, 222
citizenship, 3–4, 21, 23, 60, 103,
    129, 132, 179, 209, 212,
    223–4, 249
civil service, 60, 103, 117, 119

clothes, 20n8, 35, 192, 231
  aesthetification of, 206, 208
  agency of, 214–5
  palace, 206, 213–5, 228
  retail of, 110, 115–7
coffee shop politics, 119
collaboration
  with the Japanese, 90–2, 95–6,
    163
colonialism, 124, 150
  in maritime Southeast Asia,
    19–21, 225–6
  in Riau Islands
    British, 33
    Bugis, 73–4, 96
    Dutch, 32–4, 44–5, 104–5,
      113
    internal (by Java), 49–50
    internal (by Mainland
      Riau), 7–8, 48, 187–9,
      243, 249
    Singaporean, 2, 203
communal labour, 134, 137
communists, 36–7
competitions, 132–4, 180–4,
    187–96, 207–41, see also beauty
    contests; debating; *pantun*
  adjudication of, 219–21, 237
  success of, 221
competitiveness
  as character trait, 184
  in local economies, 39, 47,
    103, 110, 112, 119–20
  in the global economy, 3, 173,
    176, 181, 184, 187–8,
    196–7, 243
Confrontation, 36, 111
consciousness, 9–10, 24, 150,
    248–9
consumption
  of foreign goods, 35–6
  of literature, 227
Cooper, Frederick, 28, 246–7

cooperatives, 117–8
corruption, 8, 53–4, 182, 221,
    242–3
crime, 40–2, 57, 111, 128, 142–3,
    167, see also war crimes
crisis, see also human resources crisis
  economic, 40, 156
cross-border collaborations, 38,
    201–4
cultural performance, 47–8, 207–41
cultural policy, 47, 208
currency, 35–7, 40
cynicism, 10, 195, 197, 248

Daeng Celak, 32
dark arts, 80–4, 86–7, 155n2
dance, 47, 194, 197, 208, 212
debating, 188–98
decentralisation, 2
  affective and psychological
    consequences, 8–11, 247–50
  approaches to the study of, 3,
    5–11
  relationship to democratisation,
    6
  relationship to ethnic identity,
    7, 22, 27–8, 75, 246
  relationship to resentment, 8
  structural and social
    consequences for Indonesia,
    5–6, 242–3
  structural and social
    consequences for the Riau
    Islands, 4, 243–9
democratisation, 5–6, 51, 242
  and "culture", 210
descent, 15–6, 20, 80, 83
  matrilineal, 72
  patrilineal, 73, 93, 125
determinism, 113, 186–7
  in anthropological theory,
    249–50

development
  differentials in, 37, 46, 190–2,
    198–9, 203
  ideologies of, 102, 168
  indices of, 243
  memories of, 37, 52
  policies for, 38–9, 174,
    179–98, 201–5, 211
  psychological dimensions of,
    176–9
  reliance on human sacrifice,
    168, 170
development-mindedness, 114, 177
diligence, 113, 178–80, 184–5,
    199–200
  relationship to academic
    achievement, 179
discipline, 178, 184–5
discos, 144
discourse,
  theory of, 10
dukun, 156–7
Dutch East India Company
  conflicts with Riau-Lingga
    sultanate, 32, 44, 71–2

Effendy, Tenas, 56–7
elections
  neighbourhood, 141 146
  regional, 12, 47
Endicott, Kirk, 153–4, 157, 164
energy
  negative, 159–60
English language
  associations with modernity,
    221
  quality of, 189–92, 195, 201
  role in beauty contests, 222–3
  teaching of, 202–3
entrepôts, 31–2, 34, 105
entrepreneurship, 176
  Malay, 98–9, 115–26

ethnicity, 55, *see also* ethnolocality;
    Malayness; multiethnicity
  ambiguity of, 14–5
  as basis for group membership,
    42, 128
  as situational, 18, 23, 108
  European concept of, 19
ethnographic methods, 5–6
  advantages of, 7, 23, 27, 151,
    205, 244, 251
  limitations of, 81
ethnolocality, 47, 61
ethnonationalism
  Malay, 50–1, 57, 96, 165
everyday life
  as a domain of study, 4, 250
exemplars
  of achievement, 178
existentialism, 9

factionalism, 75, 97, 208
failure, 10
  on migration circuit, 41n5
fishing, 112–4
food
  for spirits, 160
  retail of, 55, 111, 118–9
  shortages, 89–92
  trade, 31–2, 106
Foucault, Michel, 175, 247–8
FPI, 57, 59
Freud, Sigmund, 25–7, 149–50,
    168

gait
  Malay, 206
Galang, 78–80, 115
gambier, 32
gamelan, 208–9
Geertz, Clifford, 101, 135, 152,
    154–5

gender relations, 116–8, 120–2
gendruwo, 155
ghosts, 150, 156–66, 170–2
globalisation, *see also*
    competitiveness, in a global
    economy
    attitudes towards, 12–3
good faith, 10, 195–6, 224, 248
government, provincial, *see under*
    Riau Islands Province
governmentality, 175, 247–8
graves, *see also* cemeteries
    as sites of pilgrimage, 66, 96
    mass, 159, 162
Growth Triangle, 2, 38–9, 46, 53,
    174–5, 201, 203

Habibie, B.J., 5, 38
hairdressing, 120–2
hairstyles, 228, 232–3
halal bihalal, 11
harmony, 56, 131–7
headhunting, 166–8, 170
headscarf
    Islamic, 133–4, 232–3
hegemony, 10
Hemmings, Clare, 4, 250
heroic epics, 21
higher education, 175
hikayat, *see* heroic epics
Hizbut Tahrir, 57–8
history
    as resource for ideological
        debate, 21, 56, 94, 100–1
    dangers of, 64–5, 75–87, 93, 97
    in public culture, 65–70
    in school syllabus, 65
    role in branding the Riau
        Islands, 30–1, 64, 216–7
    role in provincial politics, 64
    subversion through ghost
        stories, 161–6

home industries, 117–8, 120–2
homeliness, *see also* uncanny
    feelings of, 4, 23, 54, 125–7,
        132, 142, 147, 151–2,
        171–2, 245–6
    relation to theories of the
        uncanny, 25–7, 54, 142,
        151–2, 166, 171–2
homosexuality, 137–40, 179–80
Hood, Hoezrin, 48–51, 53–4
human resources
    creation of, 185–7, 189–90,
        195–6, 198–9, 204
    crisis of, 173–4, 176, 197
    definition of, 176
    origins of the terminology, 174
    quality of, 61–2, 173–205, 207,
        211, 215–8, 221–3, 248
    role in creation of Riau Islands
        Province, 48, 51
    significance for studies of
        decentralisation, 11
humour, 74, 232, 234–41
    ethics of, 236–8
    toilet, 236
    translatability of, 240

identity, *see also* identity politics;
    Malayness
    inheritance of, *see* descent
    theories of, 17–24, 214, 246–7
identity politics, 94
    Australian, 26
    character of, 28
    Malay, 22n9, 74–5
ideology, 10, 26, 150–1, 171–2
ikatan, 42, 53, 128–9, 146
Ilanun, 32
Independence Day
    celebration of, 132–4
Indians, *see also* Kelings
    persecution of, 109–10

Indonesian language, 239–40
Indragiri Hulu
  pantun team, 232–3
industrial parks, 2, 38, 53
Institute of Malay Customs, *see*
  LAM
Islam, *see also* FPI; *halal bihalal*; *jin*;
  Sufism; syncretism; *zina*
  arrival of, 81, 83
  cosmology of, 80, 163–4
  moral geographies of, 139–43,
    152
  proselytisation of, 58–9
  reformist, 58–9, 152, 233
  relationship to Malayness, 15,
    21, 57–9, 72, 104, 125,
    143–4, 165, 232–4
  role in neighbourhood
    integration, 132, 136

Japanese Occupation, 45, 85,
  87–93, 95–6, 131, 159–63,
  171–2
Javanese
  adaptation to life in Riau
    Islands, 55, 136, 238
  entrepreneurialism, 114, 118,
    125
  in Singapore, 17
  population size, 33, 43
  preservation of tradition, 136
  proselytisers, 58–9
  relations with Hoezrin Hood,
    51, 53
  valorisation of "harmony", 131,
    135
jenglot, 155
jin, 80, 83, 149, 152, 154, 156,
  169–70
Johor, *see* sultanate; Sultan Mahmud
  Shah II

kampung
  definitions of, 130
  importance of *kampung rules*,
    140–1
  moral geographies of, 139–40,
    142
Karimun, 89, 146
Kelings, 106–12
  identifications with India, 107,
    110
Koentjaraningrat, 177

labour relations
  between workers and bosses,
    114
  recruitment, 60, 112, 174–5,
    181, 186, 201
LAM, 57, 222
Law No. 22/1999, 5
Law No. 25/1999, 5–6
lazy Malay
  colonial discourse of, 104
  contemporary discourse of,
    13, 61, 112–4, 118, 120,
    122–3
Lingga, 44, 72, 75, 216
LKS, 188–98
Lobam Sea, 166–7
Lombard, Denys, 19
lying, 75–8, 90

Mahathir bin Mohamad, 113
Maier, Hendrik, 17
Mainland Riau, 45, *see also*
  Indragiri Hulu
  as Minangkabau space, 74
  debating team, 188, 196
  demographics of, 48
  economic and political
    problems, 47

history of, 56
public preoccupation with
    Malayness, 22n9, 47–8
makhluk gaib, 79–80, 83, 149–72
    display of, 154, 155n2–3
Malay culture
    as vehicle of resistance, 47–8
    boundaries of, 230–1
    custodianship by aristocrats of
        Bugis descent, 72
    "deep structure" of, 153
    generative agency of, 214–5,
        227
    integrationist vision of, 56,
        209, 217
    "modern", 230–1
    obligations towards, 55, 217
    performances of, 206–7,
        209–15, 228–41
    preservation of, 53, 223, 237–8
Malay language, 199, 230, 239
Malay literature
    scholarly approaches to, 225–6
Malays
    affirmative action towards, 23,
        60–1, 98 113n8
    backwardness of, 13, 61, 99,
        103–5, 112–4, 122–6,
        144–5, 151, 167, 170, 172,
        177–9, 204
    economic marginalisation of,
        50, 98–101, 103–6, 109,
        112, 114, 124–6, 179
    identifying characteristics, 12–3,
        51
    indirect communication style,
        114, 225–8, 231–2, 237,
        240
    involvement in communal
        violence, 42, 56–7, 227
    jealousy amongst, 125
    Keling ancestry of, 108–12

migration within Riau
    Archipelago, 35–6
political culture of, 74–5, 94–5,
    105
political marginalisation of, 48,
    60–1
population size (and perceptions
    thereof), 30, 33, 43, 55,
    57, 62
romantic and melancholic
    character, 225
trading by, 98–9, 103–6, 112,
    114–26
wartime suffering of, 90–2, 95
Malayness
    absorptive character of, 15, 18,
        123
    affectivities of, 23–7, 54, 240
    as a history of ideas, 22, 126,
        241
    as category of political
        opposition, 48
    as resource for tourism industry,
        209, 217
    as strategic and situational, 18,
        108, 110, 112
    Chewong perceptions of, 94
    comic deconstruction of, 232–4,
        238–40
    denial of, 121–3
    embodiment and performance
        of, 212–5, 218, 227–8,
        230–41
    entering of (*masuk Melayu*), 15
    in Brunei, 21
    in colonial period, 20
    indeterminacy of, 14, 16–7,
        99–100
    in Malaysia, 21–2, 60, 113
    in precolonial period, 18–9,
        71–2
    integrationist model of, 55–9,
        132, 136, 209, 211, 223

interactions between multiple
formulations of, 17, 21–2,
25, 210, 232–4, 238, 240,
245–7
multicultural, 23, 59–62, 98–9,
223
of contemporary aristocrats,
70–4, 93–7
of land and space, 54–6,
161–2, 165
of Raja Ali Haji, 69
of Raja Haji Fisabilillah, 95–6
of Riau and Eastern Sumatra,
47–8, 73
of Riau Islands Province, 3, 22,
51, 53–4, 57–9, 64, 170–1,
222, 240, 244
public preoccupation with,
3–4, 11, 22–3, 44, 54, 64,
243–5
public reflexivity towards, 25,
241, 245
pure, 72–3, 87
recombinant, 20–2, 24–5, 54,
57, 59, 207, 241, 245
reification of, 17, 18, 208–9
relation to communication,
225–8, 231–2, 237, 240
relation to descent, 15–6, 20,
72–3, 93, 97, 110, 125
relation to historical sites, 218
relation to Islam, 57–9, 144–6,
232–3
relation to literary studies, 226
relation to modernity, 221, 227
relation to physiognomy, 15,
223
relation to place of birth or
long-term residence, 55, 58
scholarly approaches to, 16–24
under the New Order, 47–50,
73, 117
Malays United, 60–1

Malaysia
citizenship in, 21–2, 60
identity work in, 18, 108
kampung in, 130
language use in, 216, 239
Malayness in, 21–2, 113
relations with Indonesia, 36–8,
49
Maluku, 42, 186
marketplace, 140
associations with success,
100–3, 118–9
ethnic "control" of, 33, 74,
98–126
negative connotations, 116–8,
120–1, 140
planning of, 14, 111
significance in urban landscape,
101–2, 122
martial arts, *see pencak silat*
marwah, 44–6, 104
McClelland, David, 176–8
Megawati Sukarnoputri, 51
Melanesia, 176–7, 179
Melayu Square, 159–60, 168
meritocracy, 221, 223
migrants, *see also* Bataks; Bugis;
Chinese; Javanese; Kelings;
Minangkabau
adoption of Malay dispositions,
55, 144–5, 209
attitudes towards the Riau
Islands, 42, 55, 61–2, 117,
216–7
disappointments of, 40–1,
discrimination towards, 61
knowledge of local history, 64,
67, 70, 163
membership of ethnic
associations, 128–9
susceptibility to hauntings, 160,
164–5

suspicion of, 83, 141–3
vulnerability of, 83, 142
migration, *see also* Malays,
    economic marginalisation of;
    Malays, political marginalisation
    of; Riau Islands Province,
    demographics of
    economic, 35–7, 39
    educational, 198–200
    effects on tourism, 40
    effects on urban life, 40–2,
        61–2, 105, 127, 141–2,
    ideologies and ethics of, 55, 112
    in colonial period, 33–4
    political, 36–7
mimicry, 124
Minangkabau
    as Malay, 17
    conflict with Bataks, 128
    conflict with Bugis, 73–4
    dominance in the marketplace,
        100–1, 105, 110–2, 114
    migration ideology, 55, 112,
        125
    migration to Riau Islands, 35,
        110
    perceptions of, 60, 116
    population size, 43
    smuggling activities, 111
modernisation theory, 176–7
modernity
    as a category of social
        explanation, 170
    ideologies of, 21, 102, 150
monstrosity, 93–6, 95n8
morality
    of Malays, 57–8,
    of neighbourhood life, 138–45
    of political relations, 84, 95–6
    of telling history, 75–81
    sexual, 121, 138–44, 212
motivation, 104–5,113, 133–4,
    176, 178–9, 184–5, 189, 202

MTQ, *see* Qur'an, recitation of
multicosmology, 157, 163–4, 170
multiethnicity, 3, 130, 135–6,
    217–8, 223, 238, *see also*
    kampung; RT
    national "problem" of, 42, 208
mysterious mentors, 87

Nagata, Judith, 18, 23, 108
Napoleonic Wars, 33
national fragmentation
    fear of, 6, 47, 51–2, 129–30,
        210
need for Achievement, 176–8
neighbourhoods
    as sites of shared citizenship,
        129–30, 132–7
    differing conceptions of, 130–2
    importance of surveillance
        and visibility, 121, 127–8,
        137–45
    political leadership, 131, 145–6
    secluded atmosphere, 119
    walking through, 134
neighbours
    labour cooperatives, 117–8
    unknown nature of, 41–2, 127,
        141–3
neoliberalism, 249
New Order
    disappearances under, 82
    ideologies of domestic life, 117
    nostalgia for, 204
    policies, 38, 47, 177, 208
    resistance against, 47–8, 156
novelists, 21
number
    different understandings of, 220

orang laut, 17, 57–8, 78–80, 83–4
Osman, Mohd Taib, 153–4

Paku, 44–6
pan-Malay unity,
   ideology of, 20
pantun, 224–41
   as technology of self-discipline,
      227
   colonial studies of, 225–6
   competitive performance,
      227–41
   Malaysian, 239
   relation to Malayness, 225–41
   strategic dimension of, 228,
      230–4
   structure of, 224, 226, 234–5
paranormal, 160–1, 165, 169
pasisir culture, 19–22, 56, 72
pemekaran, 6–8, 51–2
pencak silat, 190–1
Penyengat, *see also* aristocrats
   as centre of Islamic learning,
      58–9, 69
   as seat of indigenous
      viceroyship, 44–5, 72
   as source of oral traditions,
      65–8, 78
   as tourist attraction, 216–7
personhood, 55, 184–5
poetry, 11–6, 47, 69, 194, *see also*
   pantun
poisoning, 63, 82–3, 86
political economy
   as theoretical approach, 4, 174
pontianak, 156
possession, 79–80, 149, 156–7
prestasi, 179, *see also* achievement
   entry into popular vocabulary
prostitution
   associations with marketplace,
      120–1
   attitudes towards, 2, 41
   colonial, 33
   regulation of, 2, 209
   relation to tourism, 2, 40, 216

psychology
   in anthropological analysis, 10,
      25, 97, 248
   in Indonesian policy, 176–7,
      185
   psychoanalytic, 10, 26, 150,
      162
putra daerah, 22n9, 62

Qur'an
   recitation of, 178, 181, 187
   stance on mysterious creatures,
      169

race
   as basis for social hierarchy,
      222–3
   concept of, 19–21, 73
Raja Ali Haji, 50, 69, 71–2, 75
Raja Haji Fisabilillah, 44, 68–9,
   95–6
Raja Hamzah Yunus, 77, 90
Raja Kecik, 71, 74, 83
Raja Muhammad Yunus, 88, 90–3,
   95
Raffles, Thomas Stamford, 34
Reformasi, 4–6, 22, 42, 48, 61
regional autonomy, *see*
   decentralisation
regional creation, 184, 187, 189–90,
   195, 198–9, 204
regional cultures
   codification of, 208–9, 215,
      224–7
   enactment of, 212–5
   subversion through
      performance, 240
Reid, Anthony, 21, 104, 180
resistance, 10, 47–8, 105
Riau
   etymology of, 68

Riau Islands Province
  as response to internal
    colonialism, 7–8, 47–8, 98,
    167, 196–7, 243
  construction projects, 52–3, 170
  creation of, 2–3, 6, 7–8, 48–52
  debating team, 192–8
  demographics of, 30, 31–43,
    174
  ethnonationalism in, 23, 50–1,
    57, 70, 96, 98, 102–3,
    165, 170, 188, 241, 244
  government of, 2, 22, 66–7,
    173, 183, 194–5, 197–8,
    201–2, 204, 218, 247–9
  initial hopes and fears, 52–4,
    173, 242–4
  interest in cultural performance,
    56, 209, 224–6
  interest in human resource
    quality and achievement,
    102–3, 173, 180–1, 183–4,
    187, 190, 194–5, 197–8,
    201–2 243
  Islam in, 58
  outside expectations of, 187,
    193
  self-presentation, 31, 222–3
  tourism strategy, 216–7
Riau-Lingga sultanate, *see* sultanate
Riau Merdeka, 48, 51–2, 177–8
Riau Province, *see also* Mainland
  Riau
  1958–2004, 45–8, 173, 204
  2004–present, 188, 196
Romanticism, 225
RT (*rukun tetangga*), 131–8, 140–1,
  143, 145–6
rukun, *see* harmony

sacrifice
  construction, 159, 166–71

Sartre, Jean-Paul, 8–10, 196,
  249–50
schools, *see also* LKS
  curriculum, 65, 179, 224–5
  extra-curricular, 145, 200
  facilities, 185–6
  historical development of, 35
  human resources, 185–6, 193,
    201
  Singaporean, 199–200
  social relations within, 183
  vocational, 180–1, 188, 195,
semangat, 153–4
Singapore
  accusations of arrogance, 201,
    203
  ambivalence towards, 204
  as paradigmatic of modernity,
    102, 174, 190, 203
  colonial behaviour, 2
  culture of schools and
    workplaces, 123, 199–200
  diversification of economy,
    37
  evacuees from, 84–5
  founding of, 34
  horror films in, 150
  Indonesian collaboration with,
    38, 201–4
  Indonesian competition with,
    38
  influence on Riau Archipelago's
    economy, 34–40
  Malays in, 17, 21, 118n9
  migration to, 61, 198–200
  resentment of, 204
  trade with, 36–7, 110–1,
    121–2
Singlish, 203
skin colour, 211, 237
smuggling, 35–6, 89, 111
sorcery, 82–4, 86

sovereignty
  enactment of, 95–6
  national, 51, 249n1
  parallel claims to, 26, 32
Special Economic Zone, 201–2
spookiness, *see angker*
Stewart, Katheleen, 249–50
stories, *see cerita*
Sufism, 59
Suharto, *see also* New Order
  interest in Riau Islands, 38
  nostalgia for, 204
  treatment of enemies, 82
suicide, 94, 159, 163
sultanate, Johor-Riau-Lingga, 31–4,
  71
  as making history-telling
    possible, 81
  attempts to restore, 21, 49–50,
    88, 92–3
  claims to enduring relevance
    of, 49
  colonial partition of, 34, 49
  contemporary reimaginings of,
    47, 65, 213–4, 228, 232,
    240
  diarchic character of, 44, 72,
    74–5
  liquidation, 45
  political culture of, 94–5
Sultan Mahmud, 32
Sultan Mahmud Shah II, 71
Surabaya, 127–8
surveillance,
  of neighbourhoods, 121, 127,
    139–43
Suryatati Abdul Manan, 11–6, 24,
  224–5
Suwardi, M.S., 87–8, 179
Sweeney, Amin, 216, 225
swimming pools, 158–61
syariah values, 139

Tanjung Pinang, *see also* capital
    city status; marketplace;
    neighbourhoods
  as a Malay town, 30–1, 165, 209
  as a migrant town, 61
  as a seat of rule, 44–6
  debating team, 188–98
  demographics of, 30–7, 39–43,
    105–12
  etymology of, 76
  founding of, 31–3, 68, 105
  harbour, 2, 30–1
  haunted locations, 148–9,
    158–61
  in late colonial period, 34
  in post-independence years,
    35–6
  pantun team, 224, 230, 235–7
  role in regional creation, 196
  under Japanese Occupation,
    88, 91
  under Reformasi, 40–4
  under the New Order, 36–9
  Raja Kecik, 71, 74, 83
Tanjung Unggat, 169
Thailand-Burma railway, 91
tourism, 166, 215–8
  Department of, 66–7, 183,
    210, 215, 217–8
  economic significance of, 2,
    40–1, 120, 209
  relationship with human
    resource quality, 203, 211,
    218, 221
  significance of history for, 64,
    66
tourism ambassadors, *see* beauty
    contests
trauma, 92–3, 160, 162–3
Treaty of London (1824), 34, 49
truth
  and consciousness, 9–10
  of historical narrative, 75–6

uncanny, the
  as pleasurable, 27, 166, 207
  psychoanalytic explanations of,
    26, 149–50
  relationship to homeliness,
    25–7, 54, 62, 142, 147,
    149–52, 166, 170–2, 250
  relationship to ideology, 150–1,
    171, 162, 166
  species of, 26, 151, 166, 168,
    171–2, 250–1
  value for the study of
    decentralisation, 25, 27, 54,
    250–1
urban space, 127, *see also*
  marketplace; neighbourhoods
  Sumatran versus Javanese
    models of, 101–2
  transformations of, 41, 52–3

vampires, 148–50, 155n2
Vickers, Adrian, 18–20
victimhood, 84, 142
violence
  anti-communist, 36
  communal, 42, 56, 128
  endemic, 57

monstrosity of, 93–4, 96
of language, 24
of neighbourhood relations, 127
relationship to historical
  narrative, 84, 87, 162

Wan Seri Beni, 96
war crimes, 88
waria, 120–2, 140
weddings, 55, 91n6
Wee, Vivienne, 17, 79n2–3, 88–90,
  99
West, the
  perceptions of, 81, 132,
    139–40, 186, 222
work ethic, 99, 103–4, 179

Yogyakarta
  cultural performance in, 208–9
  neighbourhood life in, 130,
    132, 144n3

zina, 139–43
Žižek, Slavoj, 26, 127, 142, 150–1,
  158, 171